Woman to Woman

Photograph of Mary Waldron. Reproduced with the kind permission of Ron Waldron.

Woman to Woman

Female Negotiations
During the Long Eighteenth Century

Edited by
Carolyn D. Williams, Angela Escott, and Louise Duckling

DELAWARE

Newark: University of Delaware Press

Associated University Presses
2010 Eastpark Boulevard
Cranbury, NJ 08512

The paper used in this publication meets the requirements of the American National Standard for Permanence of Paper for Printed Library Materials Z39.48-1984.

Library of Congress Cataloging-in-Publication Data

Woman to woman : female negotiations during the long eighteenth century / edited by Carolyn D. Williams, Angela Escott and Louise Duckling.
    p.   cm.
    Includes bibliographical references and index.
    ISBN 978-0-87413-088-1 (alk. paper)
    1. Feminism and literature—England—History—18th century.   2. Women and the military—England—History—18th century.   3. Women and literature—England—History—18th century.   4. English literature—18th century—History and criticism.   I. Williams, Carolyn D., 1947–   II. Escott, Angela, 1949–
II. Duckling, Louise, 1971–   IV. Waldron, Mary.
PR448.W65W66   2010
820.9'3522—dc22   2009037665

PRINTED IN THE UNITED STATES OF AMERICA

In memory of Mary Waldron

Contents

Foreword

Isobel Grundy

It is right that a book on women working together should begin with a tribute to Mary Waldron, a fine scholar and wonderful friend. Its topics—relations (sometimes fraught and difficult) between women, the operations of class and gender as oppressive or exclusionary forces in the long eighteenth century, current scholarship on woman writers—were all illuminated by her own incisive thinking. Besides, the authors were friends of Mary's: they had often turned to her for information, for scholarly or critical opinions, and for emotional and personal support. When I think of educational or academic mentoring, not as something that institutions wish to encourage but as something personal, a way of living, I think of Mary.

My first memories of Mary begin more than twenty years ago. Her husband, Ron, had for years been a respected colleague at London University before Mary came to my door to ask me about supervising her thesis, which she had undertaken as an external student. Mary had a successful teaching career behind her, as a school Head of English. Even in retirement she tutored children who were not attending school, and taught for the Workers' Educational Association. She already possessed the necessary skills; her choice of research topic had been influenced by the discovery of unpublished letters. She certainly did not need me to teach her how to identify a genuinely interesting issue, use archives, organize work, or persevere until it was done. Fascinated by the celebrated quarrel between Hannah More (1745–1833) and Ann Yearsley (1752–1806), she initially intended to write about the quarrel itself, before closer acquaintance with Yearsley's poetry, character, and striving made her decide that a critical biography of this underestimated and misunderstood figure must be her focus.

This literary quarrel is the kind of incident to make a feminist blush. Although the story is now well-known to eighteenth-century scholars in general and to Mary's friends in particular, it must be

9

briefly retold here.[1] Yearsley, just past thirty, was a woman with a husband and small children, who owned a few cows and supported the family by selling milk in the streets of Bristol, but who had fallen on desperately hard times. She also wrote poetry. More wrote poetry too, and had recently abandoned her meteoric career as a London playwright to concentrate on nondramatic writing, having decided that the theater was not really the place for a Christian woman. More set out, with perfect goodwill, to be a Lady Bountiful. She enlisted the aid of the leading Bluestocking Elizabeth Montagu (1718–1800), rounded up subscribers for a book of Yearsley's poems, and naturally expected that she and her committee would manage the money thus raised, for the good of a grateful Yearsley and her family. She had reckoned without Yearsley's insistence on keeping control of her own life, not excluding her money. Their predestined collision course was not unlike that of Lord Chesterfield (1694–1773) and Samuel Johnson (1709–84): indeed, the parallel between Yearsley and Johnson was drawn by Anna Seward (1747–1809) and has been commented on by Mary herself.[2]

Literary history in the 1980s showed no particular partiality toward More. With her condescension, self-righteousness, and propensity for preaching to the poor, she was not an appealing foremother. Yearsley, however, found a champion in Donna Landry, whose brilliant study, published while Mary's research was in progress, depicted her as a laboring-class heroine standing up for her rights. Mary Waldron, however, attentively reading the documents in the case, argued that Yearsley, like More herself, came from the yeomanry or lower-middle class. Yearsley worked with her hands, but she owned her cows. She was no proletarian, and definitely not a woman to be condescended to.[3] Donna Landry developed a generous appreciation for Mary's ability and achievement, praising the "intellectual combativeness" as well as the "grace" of Mary's work, and her refusal "to settle for received wisdom or accept the orthodox view without intense archival research and relentless questioning."[4]

Mary's thesis focused "on the way in which the poetry reflects the intricate and shifting mood of the times—how the language now takes up the tone of the Augustan poet-as-teacher, now that of the individual consciousness."[5] The work which had been her dissertation was published in 1996. The book, however, was simply a mountain peak in the range of Mary's contributions to our understanding of Yearsley. It could not offer enough space for everything she wanted to say about the poetry, so she developed her ideas in an essay.[6] She had also begun publishing a stream of articles on Yearsley's life and the issues it involved. Her subsequent research concerned Yearsley's relations with her later patrons Wilmer Gossip (d. 1790) and especially the young Eliza Dawson (1770–1857, later the diarist and letter-writer Eliza Fletcher), who had a taste for literature from an early age and was prepared to admire as well as assist Yearsley.[7]

Mary's scholarly activities were remarkable in quality, quantity, and range. While poking around archives in Bristol, she sent me invaluable information, impossible to obtain elsewhere, about the obscure single-volume poet Mary Bryan (fl. 1815), who, like Yearsley herself, is hugely interesting as a female romantic. Returning to Hannah More, Mary edited her one novel, *Coelebs in Search of a Wife* (1808).[8] At a conference of the British Society for Eighteenth-Century Studies in Oxford, she gave a paper with a particularly memorable title, "'Werterism' in Britain: The Market Value of Suffering Isolation," delightfully probing the unholy alliance of the personal and the commercial.[9] Her book on Jane Austen, which I have greatly enjoyed using, related that unique figure to contemporary novelists. Another major achievement was Mary's groundbreaking edition of *Adam Bede* (1859) by George Eliot (1819–80).[10] She became a visiting fellow in the Literature Department at the University of Essex: her academic career bloomed late but richly.

Being a friend of Mary's involved a lot of fun, much of it emanating from the Women's Studies Group 1558–1837, founded by Yvonne Noble. Mary soon became the membership secretary: as Lois Chaber has said, she was "central to the group's spirit and functioning, its oldest but most dynamic member."[11] Linda Bree, the treasurer, acknowledged Mary's role as "the mainstay throughout": we enjoyed, thanks to them, a "steady sequence of meetings" of intense interest to their small, committed audiences.[12] Mary could always find the energy for organizing, and the sweet reasonableness for dealing with crises.

A great networker, Mary first put me in touch with Angela Escott, who asked me to write this piece, because she accurately suspected that Angela could help me out with some information about another of Hannah More's quarrels: this time, with Hannah Cowley. Another important link was forged when Marie Mulvey-Roberts asked Mary for information about sundry, extremely obscure Gothic novelists. Marie was one of the many who, she later told me, regularly turned to Mary for help and advice, and valued her "great knowledge, wisdom, calm reassurance at every stage."[13] Marie invited her to contribute to her *Handbook to Gothic Literature,* and to serve as guest editor for a special Jane Austen number of *Women's*

Writing, to which she also contributed an article: one of the best issues ever, said Marie.[14] Mary took a practical interest in new enterprises, and even new applications of technology. We engaged in substantial e-mail discussions of the upcoming Cambridge University Press edition of Jane Austen. To the Orlando Project, now an electronic resource available to its subscribers from cyberspace, she contributed splendidly to the entries on Yearsley, More, and George Eliot.[15]

If women writers of the eighteenth century and thereabouts care about their relations with Posterity, some of them initiated very recently, even belatedly, then many of them have cause to be grateful to our friend Mary Waldron. Hannah More, Jane Austen, and George Eliot were doing all right before her informed and sensible, sharply perceptive and down-to-earth voice was added to the continuing richness of the conversations swirling around them. But Mary Bryan, Eliza Fletcher, and assorted Gothic writers far from the center of such conversations have now reappeared on the printed page and in the thoughts of readers. Mary's researches, like the chapters in this volume, including her own study of Jane Austen's views on child rearing, also shed light on the lives of women who may never have published, or even written a line, but whose achievements, sufferings, and dealings with other women now receive the attention they deserve. She struck this balance initially with her interest in Ann Yearsley, equally remarkable for her social predicament, and for the originality, intensity, and ambition of her poetry.

Mary Waldron's actual friends, both personal and professional, and those who were potentially her friends because of their interest in the lives and writings of the past, will understand something of the satisfaction she derived from her scholarly life, and its value to other people. This book is dedicated to her memory: she would have enjoyed its contents.

NOTES

1. The indispensable source for this story is of course Mary Waldron, *Lactilla, Milkwoman of Clifton: The Life and Writings of Ann Yearsley, 1753–1806* (Athens: University of Georgia Press, 1996).

2. See J. M. S. Tompkins, *The Polite Marriage. Also The Didactic Lyre; The Bristol Milkwoman; The Scotch Parents; Clio in Motley, and Mary Hays, Philosophess: Eighteenth-Century Essays* (Cambridge: Cambridge University Press, 1938), 67–68. See also Waldron, *Lactilla*, 76–77, and Mary Waldron, "Mentors Old and New: Samuel Johnson and Hannah More," *New Rambler 1995–1996* Issue D, no. 11 (1996): 29–37.

3. In fact, Landry wrote of Yearsley under the heading "working-class writer, bourgeois subject?," so her ideas were already moving toward the direction that

Mary was to pursue further. Donna Landry, *The Muses of Resistance: Labouring-Class Women's Poetry in Britain, 1739–1798* (Cambridge: Cambridge University Press, 1990), 120.

4. Landry, quoted in memorial service to celebrate Mary Waldron's life.

5. Waldron, *Lactilla,* 271.

6. Mary Waldron, "'This Muse-born Wonder': The Occluded Voice of Ann Yearsley, Milkwoman and Poet of Clifton," in *Women's Poetry in the Enlightenment: The Making of a Canon, 1730–1820,* ed. Isobel Armstrong and Virginia Blain (Houndmills, Hampshire: Macmillan, 1999), 113–26.

7. Mary Waldron, "Ann Yearsley and the Clifton Records," ed. Paul J. Korshin, *Age of Johnson: A Scholarly Annual* 3 (1990): 301–29. Mary Waldron, "'By No Means Milk and Water Matters': The Contribution to English Poetry of Ann Yearsley, Milkwoman of Clifton, 1753–1806." *Studies on Voltaire and the Eighteenth Century* 304 (1992): 801–4. Mary Waldron, "Ann Yearsley: The Bristol Manuscript Revisited," *Women's Writing* 3, no. 1 (1996): 35–45. Mary Waldron, "A Different Kind of Patronage: Ann Yearsley's Later Friends," ed. Paul J. Korshin and Jack Lynch, *Age of Johnson: A Scholarly Annual* 13 (2002): 283–335.

8. Mary Waldron, "The Frailties of Fanny: *Mansfield Park* and the Evangelical Movement," *Eighteenth-Century Fiction* 6, no. 3 (1994): 259–82. Mary Waldron, "Men of Sense and Silly Wives: The Confusions of Mr. Knightley," *Studies in the Novel* 28, no. 2 (1996): 141–57. Mary Waldron, "Marriage Prospects: The Austen Treatment" in *Re-Drawing Austen: Picturesque Travels in Austenland,* ed. Beatrice Battaglia and Diego Saglia (Naples: Liguori, 2004), 427–35. Mary Waldron, *Jane Austen and the Fiction of her Time* (Cambridge: Cambridge University Press, 1999). Hannah More, *Coelebs in Search of a Wife,* ed. Mary Waldron (Bristol: Thoemmes, 1995).

9. Oxford, UK, January 3, 2001.

10. George Eliot, *Adam Bede,* ed. Mary Waldron (Peterborough, ON: Broadview, 2005).

11. Quoted in memorial service program.

12. Linda Bree, e-mail to Isobel Grundy, August 27, 2006.

13. Marie Mulvey-Roberts, e-mail to Isobel Grundy, August 27, 2006.

14. Marie Mulvey-Roberts, *The Handbook to Gothic Literature* (Basingstoke: Macmillan, 1998). Mary was a highly valued and efficient reviews editor for *Women's Writing* and was also a member of the editorial committee.

15. Susan Brown, Patricia Clements, and Isobel Grundy, eds., *Orlando: Women's Writing in the British Isles from the Beginnings to the Present Day* (Cambridge University Press Online: 2006).

Acknowledgments

CAROLYN D. WILLIAMS FIRST SUGGESTED THE IDEA FOR THIS BOOK IN THE summer of 2006, following the tragic death of Mary Waldron in March of that year. Mary has been the inspiring figure behind this enterprise, and we hope this volume provides an adequate tribute to her academic integrity, professionalism and generosity. The editors would like to express their gratitude to Ron Waldron for his ongoing support during the various phases of this project; in particular, they would like to thank Ron for the wonderful opportunity to publish posthumously Mary Waldron's essay on Jane Austen.

The essays in this collection are drawn from the scholarly community of the *Women's Studies Group 1558–1837* (WSG), and we would like to thank all of the group's members for their keen interest in this venture. We owe a particular debt to the WSG organizing committee—and especially Lois Chaber—for their intellectual energy, encouragement, and kindness. We would also like to thank Donna Landry, Linda Bree, Lois Chaber, and Marie Mulvey-Roberts for allowing their thoughts on Mary Waldron to be included in Isobel Grundy's Foreword.

Throughout the course of this project we have been fortunate to receive the support of our colleagues: credit is due to the academic and administrative staff of the School of English and American Literature at the University of Reading, and the Royal College of Music. We have received invaluable help from the staff of the Bodleian Library, the British Library, and the University of Reading Library. The Albert Sloman Library at the University of Essex, and the Chawton House Library both provided assistance in our quest for illustrations. We are also deeply indebted to Julien Yoseloff and Christine Retz of Associated University Presses and Donald C. Mell and Karen G. Druliner of the University of Delaware Press for crucial guidance at every turn.

Last but not least, special thanks must go to our friends and family, especially John Escott and Philip Marks, for their enthusiasm, patience, and unswerving support.

❧

ACKNOWLEDGMENT OF PERMISSIONS

Illustrations:

The photograph of Mary Waldron is reproduced with the kind permission of Ron Waldron.

John Kip's view of Flaxley Abbey, photographed by Ann Pethers, appears courtesy of Bristol University Special Collections.

The Frontispiece to vol. 2 of Richard Steele, ed., *The Ladies Library,* appears courtesy of the Bodleian Library, University of Oxford.

The engraving of Emma Hamilton, reproduced from A. T. Mahan, *The Life of Nelson,* appears courtesy of the Albert Sloman Library, University of Essex.

❦

Quotations from previously unpublished letters in the Hunter-Baillie volumes are reproduced in Judith Slagle's essay by kind permission of the President and Council of the Royal College of Surgeons of England.

Quotations from manuscript sources are reproduced in Jennie Batchelor's essay by kind permission of the Division of Rare and Manuscript Collections, Cornell University Library, and the Huntington Library, San Marino, California.

The Epistles of the Aberdeen Women's Quaker Meeting are reprinted in Betty Hagglund's essay with the kind permission of the Library of the Religious Society of Friends in Britain.

Woman to Woman

Introduction

Carolyn D. Williams, Angela Escott, and Louise Duckling

MANY EIGHTEENTH-CENTURY WOMEN LIVED OR WORKED TOGETHER IN A rich variety of domestic, economic, and intellectual alliances. Yet texts from this period often express a profoundly misogynistic view of a world in which groups of women left to their own devices would soon break up in a welter of bad organization and vicious rivalry. If they kept together long enough to achieve anything but a brawl, they might occasionally manage to commit sins, crimes, or triviali-ties, but would find it extremely difficult to achieve anything worth-while. In recent years, scholars have started to look beyond such contemptuous representations of chaotic female communities and are beginning to reveal a neglected history of women's cooperative activity. The purpose of this collection is to provide a multidiscipli-nary approach to this under-explored theme, in order to demon-strate the rich diversity and productivity of female relationships.

Our reevaluation of women as successful collaborators and com-panions is enabled, to a large degree, by the recent explosion of in-terest in women's history. There is now a greater recognition of the achievements and opportunities that existed for women within soci-ety as a whole: despite the "restrictive gender paradigms" that un-questionably existed in the period, gender ideologies were not truly rigid and were open to challenge.[1] Besides, it has become increas-ingly clear that gender itself must be understood in terms of its inter-sections with other factors, such as differences in class, wealth, education, religion, and politics. These fresh ideas on the study of women in general have revealed that there is still much to be learned about female sociability in all its forms. The most important factor to consider is the vast range of eighteenth-century evidence, from public and private archives to visual art and "polite" literature: limitations of space and time, and the demands of relevance, can force investigators to omit some resources from their publications, while devoting close attention to others. Another issue that affects this enterprise is the wide variation in the amount of publicity generated by different forms of female association, and in the care with which they were recorded. Susan Frye and Karen Robertson, writing of the period between 1450 and 1700, point out that while "entire libraries are filled with books analysing men's connections" women's relations "have proved not only less visible but also more difficult to reconstruct, often because women did not formally record their activities or seek memorialization in material structures."[2] In the long eighteenth century, this still applies to most women of the lower classes, but the activities of women writers, learned ladies, Bluestockings and other coteries, and women who engaged in public political debate, attracted much attention from their contemporaries, as well as later investigators. The various priorities of recent scholars need also to be taken into account: although valuable research has been dedicated to images and realities of female cooperation, valuable insights may equally be found in studies whose main focus was on women in general, or not directed toward women at all.

A modest but useful example of the diversity of available evidence, and the different ways in which it can be treated, appears in some eighteenth-century literary references to female friendship, and their subsequent critical reception. The chief importance of *The Way of the World* (1700) by William Congreve (1670–1729) for subsequent gender debate lies in the famous "proviso scene" in act 4, scene 1, where the conceivably reformed rake Mirabell and the chaste heroine Millamant negotiate the conditions of their future married life. Among other conditions, Mirabell requires Millamant to "admit no sworn Confident, or Intimate of your own Sex; no she Friend to screen her Affairs under your Countenance, and tempt you to make Trial of a Mutual Secresie."[3] Critics have responded with varying levels of discomfort. In 1972, Philip Roberts, contributing to a book with no stated feminist agenda, is nevertheless reluctant to believe that Congreve wished his audience to condemn female friendship, and adopts that favorite defense of eighteenth-century specialists, the appeal to irony.[4] For George Parfitt, writing in the same volume, these tactics will not work, because Congreve's play shows little evidence of "aware ironic organization."[5] No appeal to irony can palliate the attack on female companionship in an essay by Jonathan Swift (1667–1745), "A Letter to a Very Young Lady on her Marriage" (1728): even if she chooses her friends from ladies of good reputation, their influence will be so pernicious that "your only safe way of conversing with them, is by a firm Resolution to proceed in your Practice and Behaviour directly contrary to whatever they shall say or do."[6] His warnings appear to be all the more vehement, because, in the nature of things, he cannot have firsthand experience of the situation he describes: "a Knot of Ladies, got together by themselves, is a very School of Impertinence and Detraction, and it is well if those be the worst."[7] There are many useful matters which a young bride might have learned from more experienced women, including household hints, cookery, and health care. Swift mentions none of them. Ricardo Quintana, in his classic defense of Swift's sanity, *The Mind and Art of Jonathan Swift* (1936), finds no cause here to suspect that Swift's attitude to women may be in any way unreasonable: "a genuine soundness and health shows forth in his detestation of sentimentality. Nor is he an anti-feminist."[8] Quintana's assumption that this passage needs no further comment is not shared by later scholars. Louise Barnett, writing in 2002, still believes there is a charge of misogyny to answer.[9] A complete contrast, in the emphasis laid on the subject in the original texts, and in the focus and thoroughness of the critical response, appears in Janet Todd's *Women's Friendship in Literature* (1980), whose majestic sweep takes in the novels of Samuel Richardson (1689–1761), Jean Jacques Rousseau (1712–78), Jane Austen (1775–1817), and the Marquis de Sade (1740–1814).[10]

Periodical literature, an increasingly accessible happy hunting ground for feminist research, has so far been unevenly exploited, despite the pioneering work of Kathryn Shevelow.[11] For example, in her groundbreaking study, *Pope to Burney, 1714–1779: Scriblerians to Bluestockings* (2003), Moyra Haslett judiciously cites an essay by Eustace Budgell (1686–1737) for the *Spectator,* no. 217, Thursday, November 8, 1711, as an example of suspicion and hostility toward female assemblies.[12] Budgell begins with a fictitious letter from "Kitty Termagant," describing the "Club of She-Romps," which holds weekly meetings "from ten at Night till four in the Morning"; their late hours are scandalous in themselves, but their behavior makes matters even worse: they are "as rude as you Men can be, for your Lives. As our Play runs high the Room is immediately filled with broken Fans, torn Petticoats, Lappets of Head-dresses, Flounces, Furbelows, Garters, and Working-Aprons."[13] Yet Haslett ignores another *Spectator* paper which provides a subtler, but potentially more widely relevant, account of women's behavior, based on the concept of sociability as the key determinant of female nature. Richard Steele (1672–1729), in no. 158, Friday, August 31, 1711, has created another female correspondent, who defends her sex from the charge that they prefer the company of foolish men to that of men of sense. He makes her explain that this is not from choice, but because they are the only men available: "You cannot imagine but that we love to hear Reason and good Sense better than the ribaldry we are at present entertained with; but we must have Company, and among us very inconsiderable is better than none at all. We are made for the Cements of Society, and came into the World to create Relations among Mankind; and Solitude is an unnatural Being to us."[14] Richard Steele does not speculate on the solidity of the structure that might be created if such tightly adhesive "Cements" were to bond with each other. This assumption that women's sociability was properly expressed only in forming links with men recurs often in the period, and warrants closer scrutiny than it has yet received.

Many examples of cooperation and collaboration between women have emerged from the research of social historians. They have not always been conspicuous: it is only too easy to understand why a book devoted to groups of lower-class working women should have been entitled *The Invisible Woman*.[15] Again, much valuable material has emerged from works that were not exclusively concerned with female cooperation. Olwen Hufton's study of women in early modern Europe from 1500 to 1800 shows that the ability to live together harmoniously could be a matter of life and death for poor single women who lacked the shelter of a family home. Facing a precarious existence, they often had to rely on each other: "One solution might be spinster clustering, grouping together in twos or threes or even more (just as widows sometimes did) to share rental and heating and lighting costs, and to minimise the time spent at market, or queuing for the household's water, or delivering work to manufacturers."[16] The "demographic constant" confirming their desperate need for a support network is the "failure of spinsters to live as long as married women."[17] Such humble forms of cooperation apparently escaped the notice of contemporary observers. So, too, did instances of "single women pursuing a trade in their own right taking on apprentices," who were also female: these had to await the attention of Bridget Hill in *Women, Work and Sexual Politics in Eighteenth-Century England* (1993).[18] The cooperative labors of Mary Read (ca. 1690–1721) and Anne Bonny (ca. 1698–1782) achieved public recognition much sooner: their spectacularly disreputable exploits were sensational in themselves, and fitted neatly into the paradigm of the evil consequences of female friendship. Their piratical career reached its bloody climax aboard *The Revenge* (captain, Jack Rackham) seven years before Swift sharpened his pen to write his letter to a very young lady.[19]

A prime example of ambiguously represented female cooperation, whose image has been transformed by recent interactions between medical historians and literary critics, is the management of pregnancy and childbirth. For most of the period under review it was the collective female activity par excellence: there was a strong tradition that the mother should be supported by other women, including her female friends and relatives, the midwife, and nurses, both wet and dry. According to Adrian Wilson, "The popular ceremony of childbirth both reflected and helped to maintain a *collective culture of women.*"[20] Historians have established that the women were doing a good job: a high percentage of births concluded with mother and child doing well.[21] Yet midwives were so thoroughly maligned, by rival practitioners or by authors of creative literature, that ideas of them as typically ignorant, lower-class crones, prone to procuring, alcoholism, and witchcraft, lasted well into the twentieth century.[22] The other attendants fared little better: the bourgeois satire *The Ten Pleasures of Marriage* (1682) portrays a wife's first pregnancy as a process during which female activity, speech, and thought betray stupidity, malice, and idiotic priorities: the emergence of a healthy baby from this chaos owes less to realistic probability than to narrative necessity. Apart from the extinction of the human race, a further threat to civilization as the early modern bourgeois citizen knows it comes from the sinister possibility that the females thus assembled might take some form of power: before the gossips' feast can take place, there is "a serious Counsel held, as if the Parliament of women were assembled, to consult who should be invited, and who not."[23] Lisa Forman Cody, in an article whose title invokes the concept of the "Public Sphere," notes this as just one instance of the "politicized metaphors" used to express the "customary liberties given to women during the lying-in period."[24]

Cody's choice of theoretical approach marks an important trend: many modern attempts to deal with the complexities of eighteenth-century female sociability have been, wholly or in part, responses to Jürgen Habermas's work on public and private spheres; they have abundantly fulfilled Thomas McCarthy's prediction that it would be used as a "case study" by feminist social theorists who had already "identified institutional divisions between the public and the private as a thread running through the history of the subordination of women."[25] Habermas has contributed substantially to the dramatic renegotiation of traditional representations of eighteenth-century women. Indeed, Leonore Davidoff has described the "separate spheres" model as "one of the most powerful concepts within women's history since its recrudescence in the 1960s."[26] Hannah Barker and Elaine Chalus, in their incisive introduction to *Gender in Eighteenth-Century England* (1997), provide an account of the emergence of this model, the way it has been employed by historians, and the problematic nature of a simplistic and routine application of "separate spheres." Prescriptive texts of the eighteenth century argued that men and women are naturally different and therefore suited to different roles and activities in society, and with "varying degrees of polemic" presented idealized versions of the female: "modest, chaste, pious, and passively domestic," without needing or wishing to form any kind of association outside her nuclear family.[27] Barker and Chalus remind us that these ideals were just ideals: the polemic is prescriptive, not descriptive, and the rhetoric should not be confused with reality.

While the spheres model can provide a useful modern framework to initiate historical reflection, at its most simplistic it has been presented as a reductive series of binary oppositions. Aside from the potential inflexibility of this position, there is a fundamental problem in applying our modern definitions of "public" and "private" to the eighteenth century; we are in danger of reading the past anachronistically. In challenging or undermining the fixed view of separate spheres, and recognizing instead the blurred and permeable boundaries that appear to have existed, scholars are now beginning to draw our attention to the complexity and multiplicity of gender roles in the long eighteenth century. Indeed, as Linda Colley has demonstrated, the increasing concerns that women should remain in the domestic sphere arise precisely because more women are active outside the home: in her estimation, the ubiquitous conduct books serve as a reactionary stand against increasing female participation in political and patriotic activity.[28]

This is where the activities of genteel and aristocratic women take center stage. Historians Kathryn Gleadle and Sarah Richardson have described the energetic and wide-ranging participation of women in public debates and political causes in *The Power of the Petticoat* (2000). One of the central themes connecting the essays in this volume is "the concept of women's sociability": they claim that "women's familial and community relationships played a crucial role in facilitating their participation in public affairs."[29] Female involvement was channeled through correspondence groups, salons, kinship, or local networks. Often these social forums would accommodate both men and women—yet it is clear that the "petticoats" had some influence. An obvious example of women's aptitude for political campaigning can be found in the histories of the female abolitionists. Clare Midgley has shown how women worked alongside men to raise awareness for the Abolition Society's extraparliamentary campaigns in the late 1780s, referencing two exceptional cases of women giving public anti-slavery lectures.[30]

The practice of eloquence and oratory had become highly popular in the years preceding the formation of the Abolition Society in 1787. Donna Andrew has provided evidence that "by 1780 the enthusiasm for public debate seemed to reach a crescendo," highlighting a remark in the *London Courant*, February 22, 1780, that "the passion for public speaking is now become epidemical."[31] The first female debating society, *La Belle Assemblée*, had just opened, to be followed soon afterward by several more. Women had been reluctantly welcomed by older institutions, which had been exclusively male for many years, but not until February 1780 did they become paying customers, contribute, and even open and close debates. For a brief period women were able to discuss political concerns in both mixed and in exclusively female debating societies. The state of the debating societies and the questions that they discussed are a barometer of the swings between political freedom and repression, including attitudes to the situation of women in society. In the years of war hysteria following the French Revolution women were gradually excluded and the debating societies began to close down. While the participation of women in debating societies in 1780 significantly marked their entry into public political life, their association with these societies was also a focus for the pressure on women to remain in the domestic sphere, and for the spread of views about the intellectual inferiority of women. The suspicion, hostility, and contempt expressed in earlier lampoons of female parliaments still persisted.[32]

Feminist scholarship has irrevocably shown that the early modern woman could intellectually engage with more than simply fashion and trivia. The cross-disciplinary collection of essays *Women, Writing and the Public Sphere, 1700—1830* (2001) plays an important role in this respect, questioning "received paradigms of knowledge" concerning women and the theory of public and private gendered spheres.[33] The collection examines the diversity of women's activities and writings, progressing from negative stereotypes of public women ("Misses, Murderesses and Magdalens"), through more positive role models of women as consumers and producers of culture, and finally to women involved in intellectual, philosophical, and political enterprises. While the primary emphasis is on women's engagement with the public sphere, the collection also offers some examples of female cooperation and collaboration. This appears clearly in Mary Jacobus's reappraisal of *Vindication of the Rights of Woman* (1792) by Mary Wollstonecraft (1759–97). She notes the author's allusions to her female precursors, the historian Catharine

Macaulay, née Sawbridge (1731–91), and Anna Laetitia Barbauld, née Aikin (1743–1825), and Hester Chapone, née Mulso (1727–1801), who were celebrated for their poetry and essays; these references reveal a female literary community with a rich sense of tradition and intertexuality.[34] This feminist scholarship, with its exploration of women participating in a remodeled intellectual culture, has provided inspiration for our own collection of essays.

Female collaboration, companionship, and conversation have been explored through the lives and works of many women, particularly members of the Bluestockings, a group of friends of both sexes led by Elizabeth Montagu, née Robinson (1718–1800). The fact that "Bluestockings" rapidly became a term of ridicule for female intellectuals bears witness to the ease with which the presence of women in any gathering might become its most conspicuous—and possibly suspect—feature. Moyra Haslett, however, argues they were simply an extension of a contemporary trend: she highlights the pervasive culture of "conversation," "debate," and "sociability" in eighteenth-century literature, and describes how the "clubbable" nature of literary culture nurtured creativity and a sense of community among literary coteries and Bluestocking circles.[35] One of the most beneficial effects of the Bluestocking phenomenon was its generation of a public awareness of a community or tradition of female writers. Sylvia Harcstark Myers has drawn attention to the fact that the Bluestockings served as role models, bringing to public notice not only the idea that women could study, write, and publish but that they could support each other through friendship.[36] By 1785, the biographer Joseph Towers (1737–99) was so impressed by the potential for this kind of cooperation that he observed, "The English female authors of the present age are sufficiently numerous to form a very agreeable female academy; and I should like to be present at a meeting in which they were all assembled. Mrs. *Montague*, I think, would make a very proper president."[37]

The concept of female communities has also been analyzed in the context of women's literary visions, which generated utopian possibilities for alternative female societies. While these examples of female partnerships provide an opportunity for modern critics to explore female agency and benevolence, they have also revealed how these societies—imaginary and real—can be equally liberating and oppressive. Haslett, in her study of eighteenth-century literary sociability, wisely observes that there is much to be learned from "the *idea* of specifically female communities," as well as historical realities.[38] A remarkably influential imagined female community appeared in the proposal by Mary Astell (1668–1731) that English ladies should pass their time in study and religious contemplation in a "*Monastry*, or if you will (to avoid giving offence to the scrupulous and injudicious, by names which tho innocent in themselves, have been abus'd by superstitious Practices) we will call it a *Religious Retirement*."[39] Astell made repeated efforts to differentiate between her project and a convent, claiming that rather than removing ladies permanently from the world it would "be a Seminary to stock the Kingdom with pious and prudent Ladies."[40] Yet when "a certain great lady" decided to turn the proposal into reality with a donation of ten thousand pounds "towards erecting a sort of college for the education and improvement of the female sex," her good intentions fell foul of sectarian paranoia: Gilbert Burnet (1643–1715), the aggressively Protestant Bishop of Salisbury, remonstrated against the scheme "so powerfully," on the grounds that it would "look like preparing a way for *Popish Orders*" and "be reputed a *Nunnery*," that the scheme was abandoned.[41] Despite its failure to attain reality, Astell's college has a very important place in women's history: Ruth Perry has placed it in the context of earlier pleas for educational female communities, and traced its effect on later women writers.[42]

In *Female Communities*, Rebecca D'Monté and Nicole Pohl have turned their attention to other texts that "negotiate traditional expectations of women even as they revise spaces for female agency and community."[43] *The Convent of Pleasure* (1668) by Margaret Cavendish, née Lucas, Duchess of Newcastle (1623–73), and *Millenium Hall* (1762) by Sarah Scott, née Robinson (1720–95), provide full-scale visions of an imaginary female society. Another significant community of young women appears in *The Governess* (1749) by Sarah Fielding (1710–68). The fictional communities of Cavendish and Scott are "based on principles of inclusion, equality and benevolent economy."[44] One of the strengths of D'Monté and Pohl's book is its exploration of literary utopian visions in the context of actual communal experiments of the time. Sarah Scott, for example, helped to plan (unsuccessfully) a community at Hitcham, Berkshire. In D'Monté and Pohl's estimation the establishment of these social groups in fiction and in reality marked "a clear attempt to blur the boundaries between the public and the private, between market and domestic economy and between prescriptive and essentialist gender paradigms."[45] Yet they point out how Scott's and Cavendish's utopian visions only rewrite the social contract for the upper middle-class or aristocratic woman, while the presence of a "phallic mother" in these texts can "echo and reinforce the absent paternal supremacy."[46] While the collection acknowledges the problematic nature of fictional female societies, there is a strong conclusion that these visions inspired women writers and readers critically to question the contemporary social order.

Sadly, even the seemingly benevolent role of Bluestockings as female patrons could result in unfavorable outcomes or outright failure. This fact is clearly articulated by Moyra Haslett when she states that "groups and circles are not necessarily progressive formations."[47] The most notorious instance of disharmony was the public dispute between the milkwoman-poet Ann Yearsley (1752–1806) and her mentor Hannah More (1745–1833). Mary Waldron investigated this affair with her customary blend of scholarly rigor, wit, and good judgment, and showed from her research into previously neglected archival sources that Yearsley was subsequently able to negotiate for herself a more congenial support network, based on the collaborative efforts of a socially disparate group of men and women.[48] Nevertheless, there was always a danger that, where female collaborations were concerned, problems might receive more publicity than solutions. In 1815, Thomas Rowlandson (1756–1827) captured the satirical mood in his engraving *The Breaking up of the Blue Stocking Club,* where the learned ladies are indulging in all-out mayhem, tearing at each other's hair and sending the tea table flying. Rowlandson's sketch, which would serve as an illustration for Kitty Termagant's "Club of She-Romps," reminds us that even in the nineteenth century women's gatherings could still be viewed as volatile and even dangerous, lacking the stability of any foundation in (presumably masculine) reason.[49]

In their introduction, D'Monté and Pohl comment upon the fact that "the image of a society of women has always titillated and terrified the male imagination."[50] Perhaps this is why so much of the literature of the period—and our subsequent research—has highlighted the satirical and derogatory representations of female groups. The recent work on women, the public sphere, and female communities has provided the foundation for a more thorough exploration of the benign and beneficial qualities of female friendship. This collection will provide evidence of productive and constructive cooperation among women from a wide range of social backgrounds and in a variety of different contexts.

The following essays show how collaboration enabled eighteenth-century women to intervene in military and political affairs, achieve literary success, experience religious fulfillment, and engage in philanthropic projects. Kinship provided a foundation for much communal female activity: some women gained confidence from the intimacy and support of family networks; others derived their challenges and inspirations from rebellion provoked by domestic friction. Other alliances were formed by communities of women brought together by shared religious experience, or shared hardship. Some relationships arose from common involvement in publication and state affairs, while still others were friendships which supported philanthropic work or inspired literary achievement. This study covers women from a very wide range of social backgrounds, including queens, aristocrats and country gentlewomen, daughters of clergymen and laborers, and prostitutes. Despite this broad spectrum of female experience, the essays in this collection can be grouped into three distinct types of alliance. Part 1 focuses on blood ties, analyzing a range of family relationships; part 2 explores female sociability, providing an account of various forms of negotiation and cooperation between female friends and companions; to conclude, part 3 provides fascinating new readings of historic figures and events, highlighting the collaborative activity of extraordinary, adventurous women who knowingly risked their lives in order to achieve their goals.

€

The first group of essays deals with alliances of kinship, exploring various stages of the mother/child relationship and analyzing the collaborative and supportive role of sisters. Mothers as nurturers and educators in the early stages of their children's lives, observed and assisted by grandmothers and aunts, feature in Mary Waldron's essay. In contrast, Jo Goldsworthy and Marie Mulvey-Roberts effectively employ a mother-daughter pairing in order to reveal the complex negotiations that take place between parent and child: their mothers are ambivalent role models to embrace or to rebel against. In her essay on sisterhood, Judith Slagle also employs a pairing technique to explore the personality traits of two leading women writers and their sisters, demonstrating how each author was able to further her artistic enterprises due to the practical and emotional support of her female sibling.

If the management of childbirth and pregnancy by groups of women was ambiguously represented in this period, child rearing and children's education were more positively recognized as a female responsibility.[51] Mary Waldron demonstrates Jane Austen's (1775–1817) commonsense approach to the theme of child rearing, but also shows how, in the negotiation with other texts on child rearing, Austen reacted against her predecessors. Waldron argues that Austen's response to her forerunners—from the authors of conduct books to the novels of Hannah More, Elizabeth Inchbald (1753–1821), Mary Hays (1760–1843), and Mary Brunton (1778–1818)—

constitutes a "quiet revolution," and influenced future writers on the subject, such as George Eliot. From the unorthodox upbringing of Austen's heroine Catherine Morland, to Austen's use of children as a catalyst in the adult relationships between her male and female protagonists, Waldron draws attention to Austen's original and unsentimental approach to the relationships between children and their female and male guardians. Peter Sabor, in his account of the increasing recognition given to Jane Austen's *Juvenilia*, has observed, "In her novels . . . Austen frequently uses children to throw light on her adult characters," and Waldron develops this idea.[52]

Relationships between mothers and daughters are the focus of the second essay in this section. Marie Mulvey-Roberts and Joanna Goldsworthy recount how two daughters, Mary Shelley (1797–1851) and Rosina Bulwer Lytton (1802–82), dealt with the heritage of their famous radical mothers, Mary Wollstonecraft and Anna Wheeler (1785–1848). An exploration of the generational cross-connections between the fiction and nonfiction of these four women highlights the ways in which these daughter novelists negotiated their maternal inheritance. Mary Shelley revered her mother, while Rosina Bulwer Lytton resented hers (and disapproved, too, of her mother's admiration for Mary Wollstonecraft). Shelley's imagined and idealized relationship with her dead mother, and the deaths of her own two young children, had a powerful creative impact on her fictional work. Perhaps unsurprisingly, her novels explore the theme of children separated from their mother, or in the case of *Frankenstein, or the Modern Prometheus* (1818), betray her own awareness that her birth caused her mother's death. In contrast, Bulwer Lytton's creative response to her own maternal inheritance was antagonistic: she reacted strongly against her mother's radicalism, and satirized Wheeler's deification as a "Goddess of Reason" in her novel, *Miriam Sedley, or the Tares and the Wheat: A Tale of Real Life* (1850). One of the central paradoxes revealed within the essay is that despite Shelley's reverence for her mother, she distanced herself from Wollstonecraft's ideas; in contrast Bulwer Lytton, who resented her mother, reflected Wheeler's radical ideas on women and marriage in her own novels.

Mulvey-Roberts and Goldsworthy's pairing strategy draws attention, in particular, to Wheeler and Bulwer Lytton's overlooked importance in the history of women's rights. While parallels are found between the lives and writings of the mothers, Anna Wheeler is shown to be the more radical of the two women, and unjustly neglected. Connections are also revealed between the two creative daughters: both were successful women writers operating within the same literary circles and, intriguingly, the essay speculates as to whether Shelley may have fictionalized aspects of Bulwer Lytton's life in her novel *Lodore*. Yet despite Rosina Bulwer Lytton's contemporary success and influence, her work has been out of print for over a century, and Marie Mulvey-Roberts is committed to reviving interest in this maverick wit.[53] Ultimately, this essay raises the question of how the daughter of an in/famous mother finds her own individuality, and by comparing a well-known philosopher mother and her writer daughter with two lesser-known examples, opens up insights into the privileges and pitfalls of being the female progeny of a "Goddess of Reason."

The final essay in this section focuses on a more harmonious and balanced set of familial relationships. Judith Slagle's essay reveals the importance of female sibling support to the creative activity of two significant women writers of the early nineteenth century. While Wayne Koestenbaum's seminal work, *Double Talk: The Erotics of Male Literary Collaboration* (1989), deals with the phenomenon of male collaboration, he admits that a similar study on collaborating women, or even on supporting sisters, has failed to appear. New archival research has now revealed the role played by Agnes Berry (1764–1852) and Agnes Baillie (1760–1861) in the writing careers of their better-known sisters, Mary Berry (1763–1852) and Joanna Baillie (1762–1851). While collecting the letters of Scottish poet, playwright, and critic Joanna Baillie and writing her biography, Judith Slagle became increasingly aware of the "silent sister" always present in Joanna's background—older sibling Agnes Baillie.[54] Her presence was documented regularly in Baillie's correspondence; she read everything that Joanna wrote, related her readings in history and travel to Joanna, and generally supported her famous sister's creative activity. The same seems to be true of the Berry sisters, Mary and Agnes. Agnes Berry showed creative talent in the area of visual arts, and was a supportive traveling companion in the European tours that inspired her sister. Agnes also acted as "lesser light" in the salons with Mary, while Mary, the more confident sister, took responsibility for directing the foreign tours. Of the Baillie sisters, however, Agnes was the practical partner, the helpmate who took charge of financial affairs, and spared her creative sister the responsibility for household matters, perhaps reminiscent of the relationship between Catherine Bovey (1669–1727) and Mary Pope, described in the following section.

Slagle's essay touches on the psychology of creative and supportive sisters, but it also opens the door for further study of women's collaboration in the eighteenth and nineteenth centuries. Slagle cites the Berry and Baillie examples as only two of a significant number of women writers who were supported by a "community of women" in this period, a "sisterhood" that encompasses both the familial and the non-familial female networks that existed. Slagle highlights the fact that, in the global sense, communities of women have traditionally supported their talented "sisters" and her essay extends its reach into these wider collaborative circles. After all, Mary Berry and Joanna Baillie were friends, commissioning work from one another, and both women were close to sculptor Anne Damer (1748–1828), who is thought to have had a particularly intimate friendship with Mary.

The second group of essays chronicle alliances of friendship between women, portraying the rich diversity and productivity of female companionship. The women discussed here are selected from across class boundaries, and reveal the practical and emotional strengths of female communities in the period—and, in certain instances, the social prejudices that hindered them. Jessica Munns and Penny Richards's essay brings together exciting new archival research to explore the intimate and domestic situation of two gentlewomen living in the same house together. Jennie Batchelor's essay focuses on the other end of the social spectrum, providing important contextualization to the fictional narratives of prostitutes who found themselves united in an institution on a temporary basis. Religion and region bind the third group of women, in Betty Hagglund's account of women Quakers in Aberdeen, which focuses on manuscript evidence from the period. This section concludes with Judith Hawley's fresh insights into the intellectual ties binding the final group of friends, the Bluestockings.

In piecing together the life of the wealthy, childless Dutch widow Catherine Bovey (1669–1727) of Flaxley Abbey and her companion Mary Pope, Jessica Munns and Penny Richards offer an example of "close female friendship in rural retirement." Bovey was the daughter of a wealthy merchant and married into a landowning family, exemplifying the wealthy and pious independent woman, somewhere between noble lady and country gentlewoman. Mining the records of Bovey's Gloucestershire home, which include a valuable series of letters addressed to and from Bovey herself, Munns and Richards reveal how it was possible for a single woman in a lifelong and supportive female relationship to oversee the management of a substantial estate, which included industries, farms, and many houses, as well as undertake significant charitable work. Bovey was known and admired in her day: she was featured in Ballard's *Memoirs of Several Ladies of Great Britain* (1752) and was known to and written about by Richard Steele (1672–1729) and Delarivier Manley (1663 or 1670–1724). She lived a public life in metropolitan and domestic venues, benefiting from and participating in the growth of print culture, and was supported throughout her life by her friend and attendant Mary Pope. Bovey had been widowed at a young age, and her choice not to remarry was regarded as unusual: evidence from correspondence suggests that Mary protected Catherine from importunate suitors, and indicates a division of labor between the two friends. Bovey's naming of Mary Pope, rather than one of her male relatives, as executrix of her will was further confirmation of their close friendship. Indeed, Munns and Richards suggest that Bovey's wealth and position in society meant that she did not have to elope in order to live with a female companion, unlike the later couple Eleanor Butler (1739–1829) and Sarah Ponsonby (1755–1831).

Munns and Richards's study seeks to fill a gap between the categories of noble women, who have featured in the distinguished works of Frances Harris, Amanda Foreman, and Stella Tillyard, and the class of gentry women featured in Amanda Vickery's groundbreaking study of the "gentleman's daughter."[55] This essay therefore concentrates on a member of a substantial merchant family who also held landed estates and was very much involved with literary, philosophical, religious, and musical life in London and the country. Bovey's decision not to remarry, but rather enjoy the support and friendship of her female companion, enabled her to experience freedoms of movement, taste, and executive power, facilitated by her wealth and widowhood. Bovey's strong connection to Anglican charitable concerns and institutions was similarly liberating: the role of the Church of England and Nonconformism in providing spaces and activities for energetic women offers a rich arena for feminist scholarship. Hence, this study raises questions as to how far Catherine Bovey was unique or was, perhaps, representative of a "new" type of merchant-based gentlewoman whose life was neither enmeshed in national politics nor substantially local.

Jennie Batchelor's discussion of female companionship moves the spotlight away from the figure of the benefactress, and considers instead a wholly different social scenario: women brought together by their need for charitable support. Batchelor's essay provides a close reading of *The Histories of Some of the Penitents in the Magdalen-House* (1760), an anonymous novel which describes a community of women united not only by sympathy in their common distress, but by their loss of chastity. *Histories* was once a little-known work, but has recently come to prominence in a small but significant body of scholarship by a number of feminist critics interested in gender and sexuality.[56] It was arguably authored by a woman, possibly Sarah Scott, née Robinson, or Sarah Fielding, and while it was written principally in support of the philanthropic Magdalen House, it contains thinly veiled critiques of the ideology underpinning the running of the institution. The novel also reappraises the common trope of libertine prostitute narratives: the objectification of the prostitute. Batchelor demonstrates how *Histories* challenges the measuring of women's worth by their productive, or reproductive, capacity, rather than their moral status, and, through the women's stories, critiques the disciplinary regime and rigid social stratifications the Magdalen House tries to impose. Prostitution is depicted as a debased form of labor, with the prostitute's virtue remaining intact, while society's virtuous women are blamed for the prostitute's predicament: these are radical departures from anything to be found in Fielding's *The Governess* or Scott's *Millenium Hall*.

However, Batchelor reveals how *Histories* does share common ground with other female-authored, midcentury utopian novels, particularly in its reliance on sentimental community as a solution to the exploitation and dependence of women. Yet Batchelor points out that only in fiction could the prostitute be saved, because even Sarah Scott could not employ a fallen woman in her household. The fictitious *Histories* widened its focus to expose some of the more general obstacles that prevent women from supporting one another: one character is unable to obtain help from her successful sister, because the sister's husband controls the family finances. Batchelor's contextualization of the novel, in light of the moral sense philosophy of the period, provides a fascinating insight into how and why the *Histories'* model of female community is compromised. Ultimately, the novel's sentimentalism, which is the basis of the sympathy between the women, and between reader, author, and female protagonists, undermines the community's credibility, because sentimentalism itself depends upon class hierarchy and division, rather than equality and unity. Batchelor argues, therefore, that the novel's conception of community fails to an extent because of the conflicting need for identification between spectator and sympathetic object, and the consequent gentrification of the Magdalens: a salutary reminder that however important gender may be it can never be the only criterion for distinguishing between one human being and another. Therefore the novel's vision of utopian community fails because of, rather than in spite of, the sentimental ethos upon which it is founded. In this way, the essay is in dialogue with a significant collection of scholarship on both women's utopian writing and on sentimentalism.

The privileging of printed works over manuscript texts and the focusing on "high" literary genres, such as fiction, drama, and poetry, has resulted in the exclusion of a large number of women's texts from serious academic consideration. Margaret Ezell has noted this in her groundbreaking study of women's literary history.[57] Letters such as the ones considered in Betty Hagglund's essay fall into this category of "excluded" writings, and therefore provide a valuable resource for reconstructing real-life female relationships and sociability in the period. In her study of a collection of multiple-authored epistles, Hagglund charts the development of a spiritually and emotionally supportive relationship between groups of women Quakers in Aberdeen and in London, in the early years of the Quaker movement. Although printed Quaker women's writings have received increasing attention over the past fifteen years, the prioritization of print over manuscript in the critical canon has meant that much less attention has been paid to Quaker women's manuscript writings.[58] This has been particularly true of collective or collaborative writings—the only critical study to discuss such texts in any detail is Catie Gill's study of women in the seventeenth-century Quaker community, which looks at four genres of multiauthored texts: prophecy, sufferings narratives, petitions, and deathbed testimonies. Gill does not, however, address the subject of women's collective letter writing and her discussion of Women's Meetings focuses on the debates surrounding the establishment of separate women's business meetings, rather than on other types of communication to and from those meetings.

Hagglund's essay builds on Harold Love's work on authorship and scribal publication in the seventeenth century in which he argues for a redefinition of "publishing" which places circulated manuscripts alongside printed texts as of equal status.[59] Hagglund's work privileges these neglected sources, but is equally fascinating for its decision to foreground the typically unnoticed lives of Scottish Quaker women. Alongside the generic exclusion of manuscript writings, general Quaker histories such as those by Braithwaite, Barbour, and Moore focus almost exclusively on England—the histories of seventeenth-century Welsh and Scottish Quakers remain to be written.[60] George Burnet's *The Story of Quakerism in Scotland, 1650–1950* (1952, reprinted 2007) has virtually no mention of women or women's writings.[61] The recent social history of Quakers in Scotland by Paul Burton covers a later period; although there is a brief (eleven-page) summary of what went before, this does not discuss writings or women in any detail.[62]

Hagglund analyzes four multiauthored epistles sent from the Women's Meeting in Aberdeen to the corresponding group in London. These documents provide an impression of unity and community, and offer a valuable means of exploring women's relationship to the Quaker movement as a whole. The development of separate Women's Meetings provided a cooperative space in which Quaker women could find and provide spiritual and emotional support, as well as developing administrative and practical skills. Hagglund indicates that all the women signatories felt a sense of ownership of the correspondence, even if they had not directly composed the letters, with a clear sense of "corporate" understanding and of the importance of group experience. She deduces that the later-established group in Aberdeen began the correspondence with a sense of being spiritually immature, seeking strength and advice from the more mature group in London. Over time, the correspondence from Aberdeen reflected both a sense of greater equality, with the London Quakers addressed as sisters, and a different sense of the female role in the Quaker Meeting. Hagglund reveals how the Aberdeen Meeting played a significant leadership role in the Quaker movement in its early phases, and the epistles provide a clear sense of a female community developing in confidence, maturity, and experience. The essay thus maps changes in the relationships between the two groups of women over a period of twenty-five years and suggests ways in which women's texts can be used to explore relationships between groups as well as between individuals.

Letter writing for spiritual support was not confined to religious communities. Elizabeth Carter (1717–1806) in particular among the Bluestockings used correspondence and poetry dedicated to friends as a means of strengthening their religious faith. Judith Hawley's essay offers an example of intellectual friendship, showing Elizabeth Carter's close friendships to be the inspiration for her writing. Her poetry was addressed to her many friends, and her friendships were the key to her religious faith. Hawley's close readings expose subtle differences in Carter's dialogue with her friends, through poetry and through correspondence. In the particular examples of Carter's writings to Elizabeth Vesey (1715?–91) and Elizabeth Montagu, Hawley reveals Carter attempting to free these companions from worldly preoccupations and attempting to persuade them to accept the existence of an afterlife, into which the emotional experience of close friendship on earth gave an insight.

This essay contributes to current debates about the significance of the Bluestockings in eighteenth-century culture in general and in women's lives and writings in particular. It builds on perceptive readings of Carter's works by critics such as Carolyn Williams, Norma Clarke, Harriet Guest, Claudia Thomas, and Lisa A. Freeman and is in dialogue with recent reevaluations of the Bluestocking circle such as the essays in the collection edited by Nicole Pohl and Betty Schellenberg.[63] Appropriately for the subject of sociability, the spirit of Hawley's inquiry is to enhance rather than contradict these recent studies. While broadly in agreement with this recent work, she proposes some qualifications. For example, she suggests that the Habermasian public/private divide complicates more than it clarifies the issue of gender. Carter demonstrates that there are relative grades of publicity and that individuals can perform in different roles and occupy overlapping positions. Furthermore, Hawley argues that Carter resolved the tensions between public and private and between that other Enlightenment binary, reason and feeling, through her religious belief. The apparently restrictive conservative religious orthodoxy of Carter and other Bluestockings has seemed a stumbling block for feminist critics. Hawley suggests that Carter's Christian beliefs open up the possibility of both intellectual and spiritual equality and a balance between reason and feeling. In particular, Hawley convincingly argues that Carter's feelings for her friends are a mode of knowledge. The lesson they teach Carter, which she feels compelled to share with her friends, is that the feelings and virtues that are activated by their friendship provide evidence of God and of an afterlife in which they will never be separated.

The essays in the final section deal with adventurous women whose collaborations enabled them to play a significant role on the world stage: affecting international diplomacy, waging war, making crucially important strategic decisions, and founding new colonies. Some are well-attested historic figures; others appear mainly in literary representations of questionable reliability; the most formidable groups, the Amazons, have since been redefined as myths, or as misinterpretations of carelessly observed realities. Yet, true or false, they provoked a variety of responses that provide illuminating insights into contemporary attitudes to gender. Since they did not conform to eighteenth-century perceptions of proper womanhood, these women were often the victims of satirical attacks that left their reputations in tatters. Yet they might also be admired for their courage and intellect, and provide empowering role models for other women.

In the first essay of this group Julie Peakman reassesses the contribution made by Emma Hamilton (1761?–1815) and Maria Carolina, Queen of Naples (1752–1814), to Britain's victory in the Napoleonic wars. The second essay, by Tanis Hinchcliffe, recounts the story of the intrepid women from religious communities in France who were among the legendary founders of Quebec; the Ursulines in particular had the adventurous spirit needed to take the hazardous trip and assume the roles of teachers and nurses in New France. In conclusion, Carolyn Williams documents the diversity of eighteenth-century attitudes to warrior women displayed in narrative and dramatic representations of Boadicea, her daughters, and her Amazonian followers.

Emma Hamilton, the subject of Julie Peakman's essay, has always been a notorious celebrity figure in British history. Hamilton's rise from poverty to riches, and her position as mistress of Horatio Nelson (1758–1805) while wife of Sir William Hamilton (1730–1803), engendered hostile publicity and unpleasant caricatures. Emma was attacked by her contemporaries, and even more recently by biographers, as a drunk, a whore, and an uneducated and pretentious socialite; furthermore she is usually considered in relation to the powerful men she attracted, rather than as an individual in her own right. Peakman's recent biography of Emma Hamilton re-evaluated her legacy and provided a fascinating new insight into her life and her achievements, showing how she grew from a childhood of poverty into an educated and influential woman.[64] In this new scholarly essay, Peakman builds upon her previous biographical work, bringing a fresh perspective to studies of Emma Hamilton by considering her relationship with a member of her own sex and exploring the theme of female friendship as a means of political advancement.

With close analysis of Emma's personal correspondence, Peakman focuses on Emma's cultivation of her friendship with the Queen of Naples. While initially Emma viewed her friendship with the Queen as an opportunity to further her position at court, she would ultimately exploit her social position, as the wife of the ambassador to the court of Naples, for political purposes and to the benefit of her own country. Furthermore, it is apparent that Maria Carolina of Naples saw Emma as a useful intermediary with the British court. In focusing on this unusual friendship, Peakman shows these two women were able to influence affairs to the mutual benefit of their respective countries, in the early stages of the Napoleonic wars, and reveals how Emma reluctantly developed into a political operator who built on her phenomenal rise in society. Yet Emma has gone down in history as a fallen woman rather than a diplomat.

Tanis Hinchcliffe's essay deals with a religious subject yet there are surprising connections with Julie Peakman's secular story: both chronicle an important moment in national history and feature brave and influential women. Hinchcliffe describes the courageous, religious French women who traveled to Canada, "La Nouvelle France," to help to convert the vast indigenous population and to make a particularly feminine contribution to the vision of a utopian society, by nursing and teaching. Hinchcliffe relates the hardships of life across the Atlantic Ocean. These were intrepid women who were prepared to undertake the risks of the voyage, and face the difficulties of the new world, in order to achieve their aspiration of a utopian society, modeled after France.

Hinchcliffe outlines the background to these female religious communities, showing that the religious life in sixteenth- and seventeenth-century France offered an alternative space for aristocratic women where a life of learning was possible. Some of the women wanted to work in the community as teachers and carers, but the church authorities were loath to allow this, and the rule of the cloister was used as a deterrent. However, a religious order of women who were permitted to teach and nurse in the community were the Ursulines, first established in Italy. Combined with the desire for service of a practical nature went a mysticism inspired, in the case of the Ursulines, by the Spanish Carmelite nun Teresa d'Avila (1515–82). In early seventeenth-century France, spiritual women held meetings at their homes, in the manner of the later salons. The church authorities discouraged activity outside the cloister, and even deterred communication between convents, so that the type of correspondence practiced by the Quaker women in Britain was not encouraged. However, poor social conditions within France in the seventeenth century were eventually responsible for a relenting by church authorities because of the need for welfare work of the kind performed by religious women. They formed groups, called themselves a "congregation," and managed to maintain autonomy. Hinchcliffe investigates the stories of two religious women, Marie Guyart (1599–1672) and Marguerite Bourgeoys (1620–1700), who resisted family opposition and emotional ties with their children to go to Canada with the purpose of educating girls and women, or setting up religious communities.

That many of the women involved in the founding of New France were members of religious orders or congregations is noted not just by those with an interest in hagiography, but also the historians Natalie Zemon Davis and Elizabeth Rapley.[65] However, Hinchcliffe's essay is important for its exploration of the internal contradictions in the church's attitudes to women, which constricted their freedom while at the same time enabling them to act in the world in a manner denied to secular women, particularly middle-class women. This was especially true of the religious who went to New France in the seventeenth century, and who used the piety nurtured in women at the time as the rationale for their daring journey as unattached females. In Canada the physical conditions and the historical moment conspired to allow these women more autonomy than they would have experienced in France, so that despite the constraints, as we see them, of the religious life, Hinchcliffe's examples of Marie Guyart and Marguerite Bourgeoys, as well as Canadian-born Marguerite d'Youville (1701–71), were able to initiate social institutions which remained for a long time embedded in the life of New France. Hinchcliffe concludes by reminding us that the heroic efforts of the religious women in New France have secured for them a place as "founding mothers" of the French culture within Canada; yet it is only by working together in unity that these women were able to overcome the church's prejudices toward their chosen life.

In the final essay in this group, Carolyn Williams focuses on another notorious female figure. Boadicea (d.ca.62) was a king's widow who, together with her daughters, led his people against the Romans and their British allies in Britain. Some later writers gave her an army of ferocious Amazons. These depictions were used to attack the notion that women could successfully work together and to reinforce negative images of transgressive and unruly women. Old maids, gambling women, and female writers were associated at times with these warrior women, to the detriment of all parties. Yet Boadicea and her followers were also represented in a favorable light: Williams shows that women found inspiration in her strength, associating her with Queen Elizabeth I, or even with women writers and intellectuals. To cite Boadicea was to claim knowledge of the classics, a masculine privilege. However, attitudes were not easily divided by gender, and some male writers were prepared to praise the courage of Boadicea and her warrior women, as well as that of other Amazons, though they were ambivalent about their domestic and maternal virtues.

In recent scholarship, Jodi Mikalachki has provided the most thorough critical examination of early modern literature on Boadicea, with a fascinating commentary on the social background to attitudes to Boadicea, including eighteenth-century attitudes to maternal breastfeeding.[66] However, Mikalachki is more concerned with Boadicea's "legacy" than with Boadicea herself. Antonia Fraser's vast overview of Boadicea concentrates on the theme of "warrior queen," but does draw on a selection of material to comment briefly on eighteenth-century responses to this historic figure.[67] Richard Hingley and Christina Unwin in their *Boudica: Iron Age Warrior Queen* and Vanessa Collingridge in her *Boudica* include information about Boadicea in eighteenth-century literature.[68] There has also been considerable scholarly interest in eighteenth-century attitudes toward history and the ancient Britons.[69] Williams, however, brings to the field a wide variety of texts in many genres, providing a complex picture of the figure of the female warrior in eighteenth-century culture, combined with a tight focus on Boadicea in connection with other women. Boadicea's story, with its religious and political implications, makes her a worthy companion to the other adventurous women in this group. Yet Williams reveals how Boadicea's sufferings and exploits provide points of connection with earlier themes in this collection: motherhood, child care, chastity, and female education. The essay provides a fitting conclusion to this book because, above all, Boadicea provides a fascinating example of the complexity and ambiguity of female companionship in the long eighteenth century.

This collection of essays offers new evidence that despite much negative writing and visual imagery to the contrary in the period, women were not only capable of efficient cooperation and sensitive awareness of female literary traditions, but also of working together to improve the situation of women in general. The contributors have mined a wealth of previously untapped archival sources to provide evidence of collaborative relationships and to shed further light on the diversity of women's experience in this period. These revelations include moments when woman to woman negotiations do *not* work, or are seriously compromised by societal constraints. Yet one point is always assured, as Carolyn Williams makes clear in her essay's concluding remarks: whatever the uncertainty regarding any individual woman's potential, the range of possibilities became much wider when two or more began to work together. With this point in mind it is the intention of this collection, featuring the collaborations and negotiations of twelve leading women academics, to widen the range of possibilities for all scholars interested in this timely and important subject.

NOTES

1. Rebecca D'Monté and Nicole Pohl, eds., *Female Communities, 1600–1800: Literary Visions and Cultural Realities* (Basingstoke: Macmillan, 2000), 12. D'Monté and Pohl's book builds upon Nina Auerbach's seminal work, *Communities of Women: An Idea in Fiction* (Cambridge, MA: Harvard University Press, 1978).
2. Susan Frye and Karen Robertson, eds., *Maids and Mistresses, Cousins and*

Queens: Women's Alliances in Early Modern England (Oxford: Oxford University Press, 1999), 3.

3. William Congreve, *The Way of the World*, 2nd ed. (London: Jacob Tonson, 1706), 46.

4. See Philip Roberts, "Mirabell and Restoration Comedy," in *William Congreve,* ed. Brian Morris (London: Ernest Benn; Totowa, NJ: Rowman and Littlefield, 1972), 45.

5. George Parfitt, "The Case against Congreve," ibid., 37. See also Donald A. Bloom, "Dwindling into Wifehood: the Romantic Power of the Witty Heroine in Shakespeare, Dryden, Congreve, and Austen," in *Look Who's Laughing: Gender and Comedy,* ed. Gail Finney (Langhorne, PA: Gordon and Breach, 1994), 67; Robert Markley, *Two-Edg'd Weapons: Style and Ideology in the Comedies of Etherege, Wycherley and Congreve* (Oxford: Clarendon, 1988), 246.

6. Jonathan Swift and Alexander Pope, *Miscellanies in Prose and Verse,* 2nd ed. (Dublin: Sam. Fairbrother, 1728), 2:62.

7. Ibid., 2:63.

8. Ricardo Quintana, *The Mind and Art of Jonathan Swift* (London: Oxford University Press, 1936), 356.

9. Louise Barnett, "Swift, Women, and Women Readers: A Feminist Perspective on Swift's Life," in *Representations of Swift,* ed. Brian A. Connery (Newark: University of Delaware Press; London: Associated University Presses, 2002), 190.

10. See Janet Todd, *Women's Friendship in Literature* (New York: Columbia University Press, 1980).

11. See, e.g., Kathryn Shevelow, *Women and Print Culture: the Construction of Femininity in the Early Periodical* (London: Routledge, 1989).

12. Moyra Haslett, *Pope to Burney, 1714–1779: Scriblerians to Bluestockings* (Basingstoke: Palgrave Macmillan, 2003), 145.

13. Joseph Addison, *The Spectator,* ed. D. F. Bond (Oxford: Clarendon, 1965), 2:345–46.

14. Ibid., 2:119.

15. See Isabelle Baudino, Jacques Carré, and Marie-Cécile Révauger, eds., *The Invisible Woman: Aspects of Women's Work in Eighteenth-Century Britain* (Aldershot: Ashgate, 2005).

16. Olwen Hufton, *The Prospect before Her: A History of Women in Western Europe, 1500–1800* (London: Harper Collins, 1995), 253–54.

17. Ibid., 254.

18. Bridget Hill, *Women, Work and Sexual Politics in Eighteenth-Century England* (London: Routledge, 1993), 96.

19. See Marcus Rediker, "Liberty beneath the Jolly Roger: The Lives of Anne Bonny and Mary Read," in *Iron Men, Wooden Women: Gender and Seafaring in the Atlantic World, 1700–1920,* ed. Margaret Creighton and Lisa Norling (Baltimore: Johns Hopkins University Press, 1996), 1–33.

20. Adrian Wilson, *The Making of Man-Midwifery: Childbirth in England, 1660–1770* (London: UCL Press, 1995), 38.

21. See Lisa Forman Cody, *Birthing the Nation: Sex, Science, and the Conception of Eighteenth-Century Britons* (Oxford: Oxford University Press, 2005), 197.

22. See David Harley, "Historians as demonologists: the myth of the midwife-witch," *Social History of Medicine* 3 (1990): 1–26.

23. See A. Marsh, *The Ten Pleasures of Marriage, Relating all the Delights and Contentments that are Mask'd under the Bands of Matrimony* (London: A. Marsh, 1682), 148. This is a translation of *De Tien Vermakelijheden des Huwelykes* (Amsterdam: Joannes

INTRODUCTION

Kannewet, [1678?]) by "Hippolytus de Vrye" [Hieronymys Sweerts] (1627–96). For later fictitious and satirical accounts of female parliaments see, e.g., George Colman and Bonnell Thornton, *Connoisseur*, no. 49, Thursday, January 2, 1755, and Arthur Murphy, *Gray's-Inn Journal*, no. 83, Saturday, May 18, 1754.

24. Lisa Forman Cody, "The Politics of Reproduction: From Midwives' Alternative Public Sphere to the Public Spectacle of Man Midwifery," *Eighteenth-Century Studies* 32, no. 4 (1999): 481.

25. Thomas McCarthy, introduction to *The Structural Transformation of the Public Sphere: An Inquiry into a Category of Bourgeois Society*, by Jürgen Habermas, trans. Thomas Burger with the assistance of Frederick Lawrence (Cambridge: Polity, 1989), xiii.

26. Leonore Davidoff, "Regarding some 'Old Husbands' Tales': public and private in feminist history," in *Worlds Between: Historical Perspectives on Gender and Class* (Cambridge: Polity, 1995), 227.

27. Hannah Barker and Elaine Chalus, eds., *Gender in Eighteenth-Century England: Roles, Representations and Responsibilities* (London: Longman, 1997), 2.

28. See Linda Colley, "Womanpower," in *Britons: Forging the Nation, 1707–1837* (London: Vintage, 1996), 251–96.

29. Kathryn Gleadle and Sarah Richardson, eds., *Women in British Politics, 1760—1860: The Power of the Petticoat* (Basingstoke: Macmillan, 2000), 10.

30. Clare Midgley, *Women Against Slavery: The British Campaigns, 1780—1870* (London: Routledge, 1992), 25.

31. Donna T. Andrew, "Popular Culture and Public Debate: London 1780," *Historical Journal* 39, no. 2 (1996): 407. See also Donna T. Andrew, ed. and comp., *London Debating Societies, 1776–1799* (London: London Record Society, 1994); Mary Thale, "London Debating Societies in the 1790s," *Historical Journal* 32, no. 4 (1989): 57–86, and "Women in London Debating Societies in 1780," *Gender and History* 7, no. 1 (1995): 5–24; Angela Escott, "*The School of Eloquence* and 'Roasted Square Caps': oratory and pedantry as fair theatrical game?," *Women's Writing* 8, no. 1 (2001): 59–79; Betty Rizzo, "Male Oratory and Female Prate: 'Then Hush and Be an Angel Quite,'" *Eighteenth-Century Life* 29, no. 1 (2005): 23–49.

32. See note 23.

33. Elizabeth Eger et al., eds., *Women, Writing and the Public Sphere, 1700–1830* (Cambridge: Cambridge University Press, 2001), 3.

34. See Mary Jacobus, "Intimate connections: scandalous memoirs and epistolary indiscretion," ibid., 274–89. See also Isobel Armstrong and Virginia Blain, eds., *Women's Poetry in the Enlightenment: The Making of a Canon, 1730–1820* (Basingstoke: Macmillan, 1999); Jennie Batchelor and Cora Kaplan, eds., *British Women's Writing in the Long Eighteenth Century: Authorship, Politics and History* (Basingstoke: Palgrave Macmillan, 2005); Joan Bellamy, Anne Laurence, and Gill Perry, eds., *Women, Scholarship and Criticism: Gender and Knowledge, c. 1790–1900* (Manchester: Manchester University Press, 2000).

35. Haslett, *Pope to Burney*, 28, 7.

36. See Sylvia Harcstark Myers, *The Bluestocking Circle: Women, Friendship, and the Life of the Mind in Eighteenth-Century England* (Oxford: Clarendon, 1990).

37. Joseph Towers, *Dialogues Concerning the Ladies. To Which is Added, An Essay on the Antient Amazons* (London: T.Cadell, 1785), 151–52.

38. Haslett, *Pope to Burney*, 144.

39. Mary Astell, *A Serious Proposal to the Ladies, for the Advancement of their True and Great Interest* (London: R. Wilkins, 1694), 60–61.

40. Ibid., 73.

41. George Ballard, *Memoirs of Several Ladies of Great Britain, who have been Celebrated for their Writings or Skill in the Learned Arts and Sciences* (Oxford: Printed for the Author, 1752), 446.

42. See Ruth Perry, *The Celebrated Mary Astell: An Early English Feminist* (Chicago: The University of Chicago Press, 1986), 99–119.

43. D'Monté and Pohl, *Female Communities*, xv.

44. Ibid., 2.

45. Ibid., 7.

46. Ibid., 6.

47. Haslett, *Pope to Burney*, 28.

48. See Waldron, *Lactilla, Milkwoman of Clifton*, and Waldron, "A Different Kind of Patronage," 283–335.

49. See note 13.

50. D'Monté and Pohl, *Female Communities*, xvii.

51. The gendering of female education, which Mary Waldron touches upon in this analysis of Austen's approach to child rearing, is analyzed in more detail by Brigitte Glaser, who notes the extent to which different female authors during the century accepted or protested against the education which was designed to maintain women in a subordinate role in a patriarchal society. See Brigitte Glaser, "Gendered Childhoods: On the Discursive Formulation of Young Females in the Eighteenth Century," in *Fashioning Childhood in the Eighteenth Century: Age and Identity*, ed. Anja Müller (Aldershot: Ashgate, 2006), 189–98.

52. Peter Sabor, "Fashioning the Child Author: Reading Jane Austen's Juvenilia," in Müller, *Fashioning Childhood*, 199–209.

53. See Marie Mulvey-Roberts, ed., with the assistance of Steve Carpenter, *The Collected Letters of Rosina Bulwer Lytton*, 3 vols. (London: Pickering and Chatto, 2008).

54. See Judith Bailey Slagle, ed., *The Collected Letters of Joanna Baillie*, 2 vols. (Madison, WI: Fairleigh Dickinson University Press, 1999); and Judith Bailey Slagle, *Joanna Baillie: A Literary Life* (Madison, WI: Fairleigh Dickinson University Press, 2002).

55. Frances Harris, *A Passion for Government: the Life of Sarah Duchess of Marlborough* (Oxford: Oxford University Press, 1991); Amanda Foreman, *Georgiana, Duchess of Devonshire* (London: Harper Collins, 1998); Stella Tillyard, *Aristocrats: Caroline, Emily, Louisa, and Sarah Lennox, 1740–1842* (London: Chatto and Windus, 1994); Amanda Vickery, *The Gentleman's Daughter; Women's Lives in Georgian England* (New Haven: Yale University Press, 1998).

56. See Markman Ellis, *The Politics of Sensibility: Race, Gender and Commerce* (Cambridge: Cambridge University Press, 1996), 177–89; Vivien Jones, "Placing Jemima: Women Writers of the 1790s and the Eighteenth-Century Prostitution Narrative," *Women's Writing* no. 2 (1997): 201–20; and Laura J. Rosenthal, *Infamous Commerce: Prostitution in Eighteenth-Century Literature and Culture* (Ithaca: Cornell University Press, 2006), 117–19.

57. Margaret Ezell, *Writing Women's Literary History* (Baltimore: Johns Hopkins University Press, 1993), 132–33.

58. See ibid., chapter 5; Rosemary Foxton, *"Hear the Word of the Lord": A Critical and Bibliographical Study of Quaker Women's Writing, 1650–1700* (Melbourne: Bibliographical Society of Australia and New Zealand, 1994); Catie Gill, *Women in the Seventeenth-Century Quaker Community; a Literary Study of Political Identities, 1650–1700* (Aldershot: Ashgate, 2005); Elaine Hobby, *Virtue of Necessity: English Women's Writing, 1649–88* (London: Virago, 1988); Kate Peters, *Print Culture and the Early Quakers* (Cambridge: Cambridge University Press, 2005); Christine Trevett, *Women and Quakerism in the Seventeenth Century* (York: Sessions Book Trust, 1995).

59. Harold Love, *Scribal Publication in Seventeenth-Century England* (Oxford: Clarendon, 1993).

60. William Braithwaite, *The Beginnings of Quakerism* (Cambridge: Cambridge University Press, 1955); Hugh Barbour, *The Quakers in Puritan England* (New Haven: Yale University Press, 1964); Rosemary Moore, *The Light in their Consciences: the Early Quakers in Britain, 1646–1666* (University Park: Pennsylvania State University Press, 2000) (despite its title, this book deals entirely with English Quakers).

61. George B. Burnet and William H. Marwick, *The Story of Quakerism in Scotland, 1650–1950* (1952; repr., Cambridge: Cambridge University Press, 2007).

62. Paul Burton, *A Social History of Quakers in Scotland, 1800–2000* (Lampeter: Edwin Mellen, 2007).

63. See, e.g., Carolyn D. Williams, "Poetry, Pudding and Epictetus: the Consistency of Elizabeth Carter," in *Tradition in Transition: Women Writers, Marginal Texts and the Eighteenth-Century Canon*, ed. Alvaro Ribeiro and James G. Basker (Oxford: Clarendon, 1996), 3–24; Norma Clarke, *Dr Johnson's Women* (London: Hambledon and London, 2000); Harriet Guest, *Small Change: Women, Learning and Patriotism, 1750–1810* (Chicago: University of Chicago Press, 2000); Claudia Thomas, "'Th'Instructive Moral and Important Thought': Elizabeth Carter reads Pope, Johnson and Epictetus," *Age of Johnson* 4 (1991): 137–69; Lisa A. Freeman, "'A Dialogue': Elizabeth Carter's Passion for the Female Mind," in Armstrong and Blain, *Women's Poetry in the Enlightenment*, 50–63; and Nicole Pohl and Betty A. Schellenberg, eds., *Reconsidering the Bluestockings* (San Marino, CA: Huntington Library, 2003).

64. Julie Peakman, *Emma Hamilton* (London: Haus, 2005).

65. See, e.g., Natalie Zemon Davis, "City Women and Religious Change," in *Society and Culture in Early Modern France* (Stanford, CA: Stanford University Press, 1975), 65–95; Natalie Zemon Davis, "New Worlds, Marie de l'Incarnation," in *Women on the Margins, Three Seventeenth-Century Lives* (Cambridge, MA: Harvard University Press, 1995), 63–139; Elizabeth Rapley, *The Dévotes: Women and Church in Seventeenth-Century France* (Montreal: McGill-Queen's University Press, 1990).

66. Jodi Mikalachki, *The Legacy of Boadicea: Gender and Nation in Early Modern England* (London: Routledge, 1998).

67. Antonia Fraser, *The Warrior Queens: Boadicea's Chariot* (London: Phoenix, 2002).

68. Richard Hingley and Christina Unwin, *Boudica: Iron Age Warrior Queen* (London: Hambledon and London, 2005); Vanessa Collingridge, *Boudica* (London: Ebury, 2005).

69. See, e.g., Stuart Piggott, *William Stukeley: An Eighteenth Century Antiquary* (Oxford: Clarendon, 1950); Christine Gerrard, *The Patriot Opposition to Walpole: Politics, Poetry, and National Myth, 1725–1742* (Oxford: Clarendon, 1994); Aidan Lloyd Owen, *The Famous Druids: A Survey of Three Centuries of English Literature on the Druids* (Oxford: Clarendon, 1997). Previous publications by Carolyn D. Williams that have a bearing on ancient Britons in general include: "'In Albion's Ancient Days': George Richards (1767–1837) and the Dilemmas of Patriot Gothic," in *The Early Romantics*, ed. Thomas Woodman (New York: St. Martin's, 1998), 256–72; "*The Way to Things by Words:* John Cleland, the Name of the Father, and Speculative Linguistics," *Year's Work in English Studies* 28 (1998): 250–75. For Carolyn D. Williams's previous writing on Boadicea, see "'This Frantic Woman': Boadicea and English Neoclassical Embarrassment" in *Uses and Abuses of Antiquity*, ed. Maria Wyke and Michael Biddiss (Bern: Peter Lang, 1999), 19–35.

I
Family Alliances

Childhood and Child Rearing in Late Eighteenth and Early Nineteenth-Century Fiction: A Quiet Revolution

Mary Waldron

THERE WAS A SOMEWHAT NEW AND OBSESSIVE PREOCCUPATION WITH childhood and parenting in the eighteenth century. Education, education, education—famous names come to mind: John Locke (1632–1704), Bernard Mandeville (1670–1733), Anthony Ashley Cooper, third Earl of Shaftesbury (1671–1713), Jean-Jacques Rousseau (1712–78), and many more. There was an avalanche of conduct books which by their very structure (often epistolary) began to edge into fiction. Samuel Richardson (1689–1761) began as a publisher of books of advice during the first half of the century. There was a very strong belief that fiction was only justified if it set up clearly recognizable moral standards, especially to young readers. How to reconcile this with truthful representations of recognizable actualities became a major subject of debate.

Later in the century, a new phenomenon emerged, appearing alongside this debate and competing with it: an exaltation of the child as a repository of moral good from whom the adult can actually learn; this finds perhaps its fullest English expression in *Intimations of Immortality* (1807), where William Wordsworth (1770–1850) describes the six-year-old child as "best philosopher" (l.110).[1] This continual flux of ideas plays a very large part in the development of the novel during the period under review.

There is a noticeably wide gap between the earlier, more authoritarian theories of child rearing, as expressed in the conduct books of the period as well as in the traditional utterances of individuals, and the way in which it comes to be treated in fiction. Fanny Burney (1752–1840), for example, affixes a highly conventional dedication to her father to her novel *Evelina* in 1778, addressing him respectfully as "author of my being," thus subscribing to the notion of the father as the surrogate on earth of the creator, one entitled to semi-religious propitiation.[2] Yet the novel itself does not present paternal figures as actively deserving such adulation. Indeed, most novels from Richardson onward deal fairly harshly with parents, especially fathers, who are often inadequate in some way—ranging from the merely distant and uninterested, such as the fathers in Elizabeth Inchbald's *A Simple Story* (1791), Mary Hays's *Memoirs of Emma Courtney* (1796), and Mary Brunton's *Self-Control* (1811), to the manipulative and even brutal, as in the last author's *Discipline* (1814), and, further back, the father whose foolish intransigence caused so much distress in Richardson's *Clarissa Harlowe* (1748). Still, heroes and heroines did not upon the whole confront their parents, however much they might seek to circumvent them; there was a tacit agreement to preserve a certain obliqueness in the presentation of an adult child's opposition to the parent. Authors were cautious about rubbishing parental figures altogether.

At least one novel of the period, though, sets out to fulfill a Johnsonian dictum that fiction should not even hint at a challenge to received moral and religious opinion; in the *Rambler* 4, Saturday, March 31, 1750, he declared that it should steadily inculcate the idea that "virtue is the highest proof of a superior understanding, and the only solid basis of greatness."[3] Hannah More's *Coelebs in Search of a Wife* (1808) deliberately constructs a pattern family in which parental authority succeeds in producing paragons who gracefully demonstrate all the ideals of the conduct books. The novel was astonishingly popular—at least, it sold very well. One does suspect, though, that it was chiefly bought by concerned adults for children, especially girls, who quite probably, like Lydia Languish, consigned it to an obscure corner while they got on with Tobias Smollett's *Adventures of Roderick Random* (1748) or Ann Radcliffe's *Mysteries of Udolpho* (1794).[4]

Most novels deal with family life of one kind or another; the late eighteenth and early nineteenth century specialized in novels, particularly by women, which deal, unlike *Coelebs,* with a certain kind of dysfunctional family. Very often the heroine, neglected by her parents or parent-surrogates, though under their nominal authority, more or less brings herself up: most of the novels mentioned earlier are examples of this. Orphans abound. Charlotte Smith's *Emmeline* (1788) has no adult mentor at all, but nevertheless somehow manages to become refined, intelligent, and knowledgeable without the aid of anything that could really be called education, or even upbringing. It is almost as if the novel is being used as a covert attack on the adequacy of the traditional family to fulfill its expected role. This is probably what such moralists as Hannah More were chiefly concerned about; they were probably right in thinking that this often led to a kind of iconoclastic sensationalism, and very undesirable role models for the young. However, a contemporary of hers found a less didactic, and certainly more lasting, solution to the problems of fiction.

Jane Austen was famously ambivalent toward Evangelicals like More, often criticizing their fiction for offenses against what she called "Nature or Probability."[5] She began writing fiction as early as 1791 or 1792, and from the first she took up a satirical attitude to traditional family life in her carnivalesque treatments in the Juvenilia. In *Love and Freindship, Jack and Alice, Lesley Castle,* and the rest, there is no aspect of family life which is not sent up unmercifully. Nothing appears to be sacred—and yet we know perfectly well that the Austens were a united and loving family. Clearly, the target of her humorous contempt was the untruthful representation, as she saw it, of family life in the fiction of the time. In 1809, just after the publication of More's novel, she went back to her much earlier draft of the unfinished juvenile novel, "Catharine, or the Bower," and made a slight alteration. Where she had originally had a particularly useless parental figure protest that Secker's "Catechism" ought to have been enough to teach the slightly recalcitrant Catharine the proper way to conduct herself, she substitutes *Coelebs* —a pretty sure sign of her contempt for it.[6] But as she turned away from burlesque, her critique of received opinion about family life became more seriously analytical, though often just as amusing.

We usually think of realism in fiction as beginning in mid-nineteenth century or thereabouts. I would like to suggest that, at least in matters to do with family life, it was Austen who took the first steps toward a representation that broke with the conduct books, and uncovered a more recognizable and believable version of childhood and family dynamics, at the same time as taking account of the dominant ideas of her time.

There is a vague sort of consensus that Austen rather disliked children than otherwise. This stems, I think, from certain acerbic remarks about births among their neighbors which appear in letters to Cassandra, and perhaps also from the treatment of children in her first published novel, *Sense and Sensibility* (1811). Certainly Austen makes clear her unease about over-large families; she mentions this a number of times, for example, of her niece Anna Lefroy (1793–1872) when pregnant for the third time in three years: "Poor Animal, she will be worn out before she is thirty.—I am very sorry for her.—Mrs Clement too is in that way again. I am quite tired of so many Children.—Mrs Benn has a 13th."[7] In an earlier letter, she recommends "the simple regimen of separate rooms" for a neighboring, over-fertile couple.[8] However, her concern is clearly about the physical drain of childbirth on the mothers; for children out of the womb and in the world she has very different feelings. Nothing could be more tender and appreciative than her relationships with her innumerable nephews and nieces—and she is prepared to enjoy the company of all children in a good-humored, unsentimental way. Of a ten-year-old visitor she says: "She is now talking away at my side & examining the Treasures of my Writing-desk drawer;—very happy I beleive;—not at all shy of course.—Her name is Catherine & her sister's Caroline. . . . What is become of all the Shyness in the World?—Moral as well as Natural Diseases disappear in the course of time, & new ones take their place."[9] Later in the same letter she adds, "Our little visitor has just left us, & left us highly pleased with her;—she is a nice, natural, openhearted, affectionate girl, with all the ready civility which one sees in the best Children of the present day;—so unlike anything that I was myself at her age, that I am often all astonishment & shame."[10] On a much more serious occasion, the death after the birth of her eleventh child of Elizabeth, wife of Jane's brother Edward (1767–1852) in 1808, we find her entertaining her two young nephews, Edward and George, aged 13 and 12, at Southampton. After a serious discussion of their great loss, she deems it right to distract them and prevent them from brooding: "We do not want amusement; bilbocatch, at which George is indefatigable, spillikins, paper ships, riddles, conundrums, and cards, with watching the flow and ebb of the river, and now and then a stroll out, keep us well employed; and we mean to avail ourselves of our kind papa's consideration, by not returning to Winchester [that is, to boarding school] till quite the evening of Wednesday."[11] This energetic and wholly time-consuming program wasn't all: she organized "*a little water-party,*" during which the boys were encouraged to row "a great part of the way."[12] Jane Austen was an ideal aunt, with what we should now call a "child-centered" approach. But she was clear that adults and children do not always interact in an ideal way, and this frequently comes out in her fiction.

All novelists perforce use their own experience to create a story—often as observers rather than participants; as an aunt, Austen was well placed to analyze the way in which children are sometimes used by adults to further some purpose of their own. On the whole, throughout the six completed novels, in all of which young children figure, however fleetingly, she seems to have been on the side of the children, often seeing any misdemeanors as a reflection of their parents' unwise handling. But the lesson is not straightforwardly didactic—the child is often seen from several points of view and the reader left to make a choice. In *Sense and Sensibility,* for instance, we see the spoiled children of Lady Middleton from the perspective of Elinor, who is at the time feeling overburdened with responsibility for her sister's conduct with Willoughby, and anxiety about the rather lax attitude of her mother; she is also a touch disappointed by what she feels is Edward Ferrars's coolness toward her. Like all dutiful young people she is inclined to be censorious. Both she and Marianne are also at pains not to share in the fulsome adulation which the Steele girls are dishing out to Lady Middleton, the archetypal indulgent mother ("child-centered" in a different way). After several hours of fairly violently unruly behavior on the part of the three children, which Lady Middleton has done nothing to discourage, Lucy Steele remarks to Elinor, "what a charming little family . . . I never saw such fine children in my life.—I declare I quite doat on them already, and indeed I am always distractedly fond of children." Elinor replies, "I should guess so . . . from what I have witnessed this morning."[13]

Lucy, who has submitted to having her possessions thrown about and broken, her hair pulled and so on, sees the point, but continues to affect approval—perhaps to support received opinion, but still to stay in Elinor's good books: "I have a notion . . . you think the little Middletons rather too much indulged; perhaps they may be the outside of enough; but it is so natural in Lady Middleton; and for my part, I love to see children full of life and spirits; I cannot bear them if they are tame and quiet." Elinor replies, "I confess . . . that while I am at Barton Park, I never think of tame and quiet children with any abhorrence."[14]

The whole scene has shown up the parents and other adults as incompetent, and the children, by natural consequence, as exploiters—"With such a reward for her tears, the child was too wise to cease crying"—all seen through the eyes of a rather depressed Elinor, who would rather be anywhere but where she is.[15] The same novel shows the unscrupulous way in which the John Dashwoods, in the hilariously ironical account in chapter 2, make their small son Harry an excuse for overturning the spirit of his grandfather's will, and reducing the intended generous financial support of his stepmother and half sisters to occasional "presents of fish and game."[16] Behind it all there is a theory of child rearing which seeks to demonstrate the self-aggrandizement which often lurks within displays of parental concern.

The other novels give a much more cheerful picture of childhood, but the ironical slant is nearly always present. The first chap-

ter of *Northanger Abbey* (1817), for instance, determinedly sets up the
real against the ideal in the description of the childhood of Catherine Morland, the heroine-in-training:

> She was fond of all boys' plays, and greatly preferred cricket not merely
> to dolls, but to the more heroic enjoyments of infancy, nursing a dor-
> mouse, feeding a canary-bird, or watering a rose-bush. Indeed she had
> no taste for a garden; and if she gathered flowers at all, it was chiefly for
> the pleasure of mischief—at least so it was conjectured from her always
> preferring those which she was forbidden to take. . . . She could never
> learn or understand anything before she was taught [this is a hit at
> Smith's Emmeline], and sometimes not even then.[17]

Mrs. Morland is also strangely unlike the conduct-book parent: "Her
mother wished her to learn music; and Catherine was sure she
would like it . . . so, at eight years old she began. She learnt a year,
and could not bear it;—and Mrs. Morland, who did not insist on her
daughters being accomplished in spite of incapacity or distaste, allowed her to leave off."[18] We are also told that she shirked her other
lessons "whenever she could."[19] "What a strange, unaccountable
character!" muses her creator—but "she had neither a bad heart
nor a bad temper; was seldom stubborn, scarcely ever quarrelsome,
and very kind to the little ones [she is the second of ten], with few
interruptions of tyranny; she was moreover noisy and wild, hated
confinement and cleanliness, and loved nothing so well in the world
as rolling down the green slope at the back of the house."[20] There
had been few, if any, little girls like this in fiction so far.

    Pride and Prejudice (1813) is entirely concerned with the intricac-
ies of family relationships. Here I would single out the struggle
which Elizabeth continually has to maintain: her respect for her
father. In this novel what is often implied in earlier fiction is openly
stated: "she endeavoured to forget what she could not overlook, and
to banish from her thoughts that continual breach of conjugal obligation and decorum which, in exposing his wife to the contempt of
her own children, was so highly reprehensible."[21] These feelings are
"painful," as are those toward her mother and most of her sisters:
Elizabeth is caught between the necessity for family affection and
the taste for currently acceptable polite manners which her father
fails to sustain. These are the concerns of grown-up children, but
Austen does not forbear to include glimpses of the young Gardiners,
the offspring of truly sensible and intelligent parents, who will
doubtless have less to "overlook" as they grow up. In one of these
brief references, Austen again states outright what is usually assumed: "The children, two girls of six and eight years old, and two

younger boys, were to be left under the particular care of their cousin Jane, who was the general favourite, and whose steady sense and sweetness of temper exactly adapted her for attending to them in every way—teaching them, playing with them, and loving them."[22] Teaching and playing would have been no surprise in this context, but the word "loving" is less predictable and therefore significant. It is clear that Austen does not share received contemporary opinion that all women were instinctively loving toward children—some are better at it than others. It is a slight touch and is hardly followed through; much later, in *Adam Bede* (1859) George Eliot was to take the matter further, creating Hetty Sorrel, a child early deprived of unconditional love, who is therefore unable to feel anything for her own child, and leaves her newborn baby to die alone in a wood.[23] Austen is edging into a new attitude to the whole question of parenting.

What had been deemed parental love is very thoroughly explored in *Mansfield Park* (1814). While discussion of this novel currently centers obsessively upon such things as whether anyone can really like Fanny Price, Austen's attitude to the theater and the slave trade, or her leanings toward Evangelicalism, the really dominant theme of the novel—child rearing—is often overlooked or forgotten. Sir Thomas Bertram is theoretically the ideal parent—morally upright himself, he provides a conventionally suitable education for his children and makes sure that they are sufficiently in awe of him. Always sure he is right, he fails to check up on the real effects of his regimen. Their mother takes little notice of them, preferring her dog; their aunt, Mrs. Norris, has her own agenda: she likes power. Three of the children are flattered by her into believing they can do no wrong. Although all three parental figures would have protested that they truly loved the children, none of this amounts to love. The result is that Maria, Julia, and Tom grow up selfish and coldhearted. Edmund escapes the worst. Less indulged and perhaps more intelligent than the rest, he is able to construct a warmer personality and a viable moral purpose in his life, though it proves a little shaky when tested by the advent of Mary Crawford.

Mrs. Norris's love of power is the true reason for Fanny's presence at Mansfield; not only is she instrumental in bringing her there, but she does her best to dominate and humiliate her from the very first. Edmund is her only protector—not a particularly effective one. However, unlike most novel-orphans of the period (Fanny is in this position, though not technically an orphan) she is not locked up, starved, or accused of ingratiating herself with the young heir and banished to Sidmouth. This latter fate had befallen the heroine of

Clarentine (1796), a popular novel by Sarah Burney (1772–1844), Fanny's half sister; Austen knew it well.[24] Fanny is not totally un-happy, supported as she is by her early experience of true family love, not so much in her relationship with her parents as with her brother William, and to a lesser extent with those of the siblings that she can remember after a lapse of eight years. Edmund, through his early and continued kindness and affection, also helps to keep her from depression and despair.

Again in this novel Austen zooms in on actualities which cause the reader to share Fanny's sense of inferiority. In the schoolroom again we now witness the thoughtless cruelty of real children:

> The holiday allowed to the Miss Bertrams [Maria and Julia, aged thir-teen and twelve, while Fanny is ten] the next day on purpose to afford leisure for getting acquainted with, and entertaining their young cousin, produced little union. They could not but hold her cheap on finding that she had but two sashes, and had never learnt French; and when they perceived her to be little struck with the duet they were so good as to play, they could do no more than make her a generous present of some of their least valued toys, and leave her to herself, while they adjourned to whatever might be the favourite holiday sport of the moment, making artificial flowers or wasting gold paper.[25]

Fanny, however, ultimately has the advantage of them, for she is, un-like them, wholly human in her ability to love. Suffering and endur-ance teach her the value of unselfish affection, but she had to experience it first. At Portsmouth she is receptive enough to learn much about herself and others through the noisy and disorganized behavior of her siblings and the incompetence of her mother; again, the focus is close and unmerciful.

Emma (1816) is in many ways recognizable as a reaction to *Mans-field Park* (1814) in that its heroine is just as indulged as the Bertram girls, but is not coldhearted, however self-occupied she may initially be. But the innovation which I would like to dwell on here is some-thing different: the treatment of pregnancy and babies, not only in this novel but also in *Sense and Sensibility*. In the latter the pregnancy of Charlotte Palmer is used rather to point up the vulgarity of its grandmother, Mrs. Jennings, and to facilitate certain turns of the plot, such as the sudden revelation of Lucy's engagement to Edward, which is made by Charlotte's physician; and the flight of the Palmer family from the ailing Marianne, when her disease seems to have developed an alarming "putrid tendency."[26] In *Emma,* pregnancy and the early weeks of life have a more symbolic significance.

Such subjects were of course not unknown in pre-Austen fiction.

Richardson builds the second half of *Pamela* (1741) around the birth and rearing of a child.[27] One of the most entertaining figures in his last novel, *Sir Charles Grandison* (1753–54), is the wittily cynical Charlotte, Lady G.; she becomes a reformed character—that is, more submissive and womanly—and the climactic revelation of her change occurs when her husband discovers her breastfeeding her new baby, whom she refers to as a "Marmouset."[28] She still speaks the language of defiance, but her actions are those of a proper mother. Mary Wollstonecraft (1759–97), in *Maria, or the Wrongs of Woman* (1798), explores the plight of the pregnant woman fleeing from a brutal husband, and later her mental and physical sufferings when the baby is snatched from her while she is still lactating. The function of the theme in the message of these three is tolerably obvious. Austen's use of it is by no means so straightforward and much less polemical. Isabella, Emma's sister, is one of the "poor animals" whose sufferings Austen deplores in her letters; she has had five children in nine years. However, no despondency is felt about this— certainly not by Isabella—and Emma looks forward to family visits as a relief from the undiluted company of her elderly father after the marriage of her beloved governess. She is as attentive and enthusiastic an aunt to her two nephews as her creator in a similar situation: "I shall do all in my power to make them happy" she retorts to their father's instructions not to spoil them and not to "physic" them (that is, give them unnecessary medicines), "and happiness must preclude false indulgence and physic."[29]

Eight-month-old "little Emma" appears quite early in the story while Emma and Mr. Knightley are having one of their habitual disputes, this time about Emma's interference in the courtship of Harriet Smith by Robert Martin.[30] The presence of the child has a decisive effect on the narrative because it subtly shifts the reader's perception of Mr. Knightley's relation to Emma. He has previously looked like the mentor/guardian/substitute father who usually appears in the contemporary novel tradition: for instance, in Charlotte Lennox's *The Female Quixote* (1752), Eaton Stannard Barrett's *The Heroine* (1813), and Mary Brunton's *Discipline*. Now, however, he begins to appear as a possible lover/husband/coparent:

> She hoped they now might become friends again. . . . Concession must be out of the question; but it was time to appear to forget that they had ever quarrelled; and she hoped it might rather assist the restoration of friendship, that when he came into the room she had one of the children with her—the youngest, a nice little girl about eight months old, who was now making her first visit to Hartfield, and very happy to be

danced about in her aunt's arms. It did assist; for though he began with grave looks and short questions, he was soon led on to talk of them all in the usual way, and to take the child out of her arms with all the unceremoniousness of perfect amity.[31]

They still wrangle, for Emma cannot resist the temptation to bring up the dispute anew, but they agree to differ by speaking, as it were, through the child:

"Tell your aunt, little Emma, that she ought to set you a better example than to be renewing old grievances, and that if she were not wrong before, she is now."

"That's true," she cried—"very true. Little Emma, grow up a better woman than your aunt. Be infinitely cleverer and not half so conceited."[32]

There is an intimacy here, and an ordinary humanity in Mr. Knightley which is missing from the usual male mentor, like the "good Doctor" in *The Female Quixote* or Robert Stuart in *The Heroine*, neither of whom can possibly be imagined dandling a baby.[33] Whether or not we believe him to be the ultimate outright victor in his war with Emma, he is infinitely more credible than his predecessors.

There is another baby. Mrs. Weston, previously "Miss Taylor," Emma's chief indulger, is pregnant almost throughout the novel, and toward the end gives birth to a little girl, who will perforce replace Emma as the first in her surrogate mother's heart. Emma's sense of despair and isolation at the supposed mess she has made of her life toward the end of the novel is sharply increased by her expectation of this event. Convinced that she has lost Mr. Knightley to Harriet, through, as she thinks, her own agency, she faces a narrow lot, with no one to call her own but her invalid father: "The child to be born at Randall's must be a tie there even dearer than herself; and Mrs. Weston's heart and time would be occupied by it. They should lose her; and, probably, in great measure, her husband also."[34] As Emma muses on all she thinks she will lose, the reader remembers her initial glee at the thought that she "made the match" for Miss Taylor, and observes her mortification at having inadvertently encouraged Harriet to think of Mr. Knightley as a lover.[35] Of course, she is wrong: the living reality of the so-far hidden baby serves to sharpen the reader's perception of the strange fantasies by which Emma, at least for the time being, insists upon living.

By the time the baby is born, in chapter 53, everything has changed. Most of Emma's problems have been solved. Mrs. Weston is at the center of communications; late in her pregnancy she has been the disseminator of the news which has seemed so devastating to Emma; now Emma knows herself to be loved by Mr. Knightley, and Mrs. Weston has been instrumental in reconciling Emma's father to the marriage. Just at this more hopeful time, as all wounds start to heal, we meet her baby: "Mrs. Weston, with her baby on her knee, . . . was one of the happiest women in the world. If any thing could increase her delight, it was perceiving that the baby would soon have outgrown its first set of caps."[36] From that time on, the child is almost always present; just after Emma has heard the joyful news of Harriet's engagement to Robert Martin, which frees her from her remaining anxiety; and on her first embarrassing meeting with Frank Churchill since the news of his own engagement. While he congratulates himself on the perfections of his new possession, Jane, "the others had been talking of the child."[37] Frank, of course, like many self-occupied people, is not interested in children, and swiftly brings the subject back to himself and his concerns, in sharp contrast with Mr. Knightley. Austen, in this novel, seems to use the child as a sort of touchstone of the adults' maturity and right to rational happiness. We are not far, here, though it is not immediately obvious, from that centrality of the child which is a feature of the poetry of Wordsworth and William Blake (1757–1827). Though Austen would hardly have shared anything so nearly approaching mysticism, her sense of the importance of childhood was not unlike theirs.

It is perhaps in her last novel, *Persuasion* (1818), that Austen most clearly analyzes the muddled approach to child rearing which so often stems from adult conflict and rivalry and which can reduce or even destroy what Austen saw as the proper, mutually civilizing relation between children and adults. From the childless desert of Kellynch Anne Elliot goes to Uppercross Cottage, where things are more lively, but all is not well. Her sister Mary Musgrove is a prime example of the woman totally lacking in the maternal feelings supposed to be natural to the female; she is far more concerned with her own prestige and consequence than she is with her two little boys. They are as a result unruly and difficult to manage. Like many people who need to be the center of attention, Mary has somewhat vague and ill-defined health problems. When Anne arrives she is languishing on a sofa, complaining that she has had to send her children back to their nursery: "They are so unmanageable that they do me more harm than good. Little Charles does not mind a word I say, and Walter is growing quite as bad."[38]

Both Anne's internal monologue, and her conversations with Mary, her husband Charles, and his mother add to the sense of incompetence on Mary's part, but also reflect family conflicts in general:

> As to the management of their children, his theory was much better than his wife's, and his practice not so bad.—"I could manage them very well if it were not for Mary's interference,"—was what Anne often heard him say, and had a good deal of faith in; but when listening in turn to Mary's reproach of "Charles spoils the children so that I cannot get them into any order,"—she never had the smallest temptation to say, "Very true."[39]

Other accusations and counteraccusations follow, to which Anne is obliged to listen.

> [Mary]: I hate sending the children to the Great House, though their grandmamma is always wanting to see them, for she humours and indulges them to such a degree, and gives them so much trash and sweet things, that they are sure to come back sick and cross for the rest of the day.

> [Grandmamma]: Oh! Miss Anne, I cannot help wishing Mrs. Charles had a little of your method with those children: They are quite different creatures with you! . . . Bless me, how troublesome they are sometimes! . . . I believe Mrs. Charles is not quite pleased with my not inviting them oftener; but you know it is very bad to have children with one, that one is obliged to be checking every moment; "don't do this, and don't do that;"—or that one can only keep in tolerable order by more cake than is good for them.[40]

This is a pretty strong indictment of a very recognizable situation, even at a distance of nearly two hundred years. However, this is a novel, not a treatise on child management, and Austen has other uses for the children, particularly the willful two-year-old Walter. Like small Emma Knightley, he serves as a catalyst between two adults who need something real and down-to-earth to bring them back together, something to re-infuse life into their relationship. When Walter climbs on to Anne's back while she is attending to his sick brother, and she cannot shake him off, Captain Wentworth is unable to sustain the coolness and distance with which he has seen fit to treat her—he releases her from her burden in a moment of renewed intimacy which begins the slow reversal of eight years of estrangement. It is typical of Austen's method that she should use a child for this purpose.

Hardly noted during Austen's lifetime, this realistic inclusion and centrality of children in fiction continued and developed (though with intervals of more or less revolting sentimentality). I will not make any claim that Austen influenced later writers—though I will just mention the fact (recorded in her journal) that George Eliot had been rereading *Mansfield Park* just before she embarked on *Adam Bede* (1859).[41] Probably the time was simply ripe for a new look at old problems. I leave my readers to make what they can of it.

NOTES

1. William Wordsworth, *Poetical Works*, ed. Thomas Hutchinson, rev. Ernest de Selincourt (Oxford: Oxford University Press, 1936), 460.

2. Fanny Burney, *Evelina, or, a Young Lady's Entrance into the World. In a Series of Letters*, 2nd ed. (London: T. Lowndes, 1779), 1:[iii].

3. Samuel Johnson, *The Rambler* (London: J. Payne and J. Bouquet, 1752), 1:36.

4. For Lydia Languish and her concealment of sensational reading material, see Richard Brinsley Sheridan, *The Rivals, A Comedy. As it is Acted at the Theatre-Royal in Covent Garden* (Dublin: R. Moncrieffe, 1775), act 1, scene 2, pages 25–26.

5. Jane Austen to Cassandra Austen, October 11, 1813, in Jane Austen, *Jane Austen's Letters*, ed. Deidre Le Faye (Oxford: Oxford University Press, 1997), 234.

6. Jane Austen, *Catharine and Other Writings*, ed. Margaret Anne Doody and Douglas Murray, (Oxford: Oxford University Press, 1993), 222, 271, 357. The work replaced by *Coelebs* is Thomas Secker, *Lectures on the Catechism of the Church of England. With a Discourse on Confirmation*, ed. B. Porteus and C. Stinton, 2 vols. (London: J. and F. Rivington, 1769). Upper-class parents and guardians, impressed by its length and well-intentioned solemnity, might easily be tempted to substitute such a publication for their own moral guidance. Austen's choice, however, would not have pleased Elizabeth Carter and her friend Catherine Talbot, who figure in Judith Hawley's chapter in this book, and who both benefited considerably from the support and advice of Thomas Secker (1693–1768).

7. Austen, *Jane Austen's Letters*, Jane Austen to Fanny Knight, March 23, 1817, 336.

8. Ibid., Jane Austen to Fanny Knight, February 20, 1817, 330.

9. Ibid., Jane Austen to Cassandra Austen, February 8, 1807, 119.

10. Ibid., Jane Austen to Cassandra Austen, February 8, 1807, 120.

11. Ibid., Jane Austen to Cassandra Austen, October 24, 1808, 150.

12. Ibid., Jane Austen to Cassandra Austen, October 24, 1808, 151–52.

13. Jane Austen, *Sense and Sensibility*, ed. Edward Copeland (Cambridge: Cambridge University Press, 2006), 141.

14. Ibid.

15. Ibid., 140.

16. Ibid., 13.

17. Jane Austen, *Northanger Abbey*, ed. Claire Grogan (Peterborough, ON: Broadview, 2002), 37–38.

18. Ibid., 38.

19. Ibid., 38–39.

20. Ibid., 39.

21. Jane Austen, *Pride and Prejudice*, ed. Pat Rogers (Cambridge: Cambridge University Press, 2006), 262–63.

22. Ibid., 266.

23. See the section on "Love" in the introduction to Eliot, *Adam Bede*, 32–37.

24. See Austen, *Jane Austen's Letters*, Jane Austen to Cassandra Austen, February 8, 1807, 120.

25. Jane Austen, *Mansfield Park*, ed. John Wiltshire (Cambridge: Cambridge University Press, 2005), 15–16.

26. Austen, *Sense and Sensibility*, 347.

27. See Samuel Richardson, *Pamela: or, Virtue Rewarded. In a Series of Familiar Letters from a Beautiful Young Damsel to her Parents: and afterwards, in her Exalted Condition, between her, and Persons of Figure and Quality, upon the most Important and Entertaining Subjects in Genteel Life. The Third and Fourth Volumes. Publish'd in Order to Cultivate Principles of Virtue and Religion in the Minds of the Youth of Both Sexes*, 2 vols. (London: C. Rivington and J. Osborn, [1741]).

28. Samuel Richardson, *Sir Charles Grandison*, ed. Jocelyn Harris (Oxford: Oxford University Press, 1972), 403.

29. Jane Austen, *Emma*, ed. Richard Cronin and Dorothy McMillan (Cambridge: Cambridge University Press, 2005), 337.

30. Ibid., 106.

31. Ibid., 105.

32. Ibid., 106.

33. Charlotte Lennox, *The Female Quixote: Or, the Adventures of Arabella* (London: A. Millar, 1752), 2:296.

34. Austen, *Emma*, 460.

35. Ibid., 10; see ibid., 460.

36. Ibid., 511.

37. Ibid., 523; see ibid., 522–23.

38. Jane Austen, *Persuasion*, ed. Janet Todd and Antje Blank (Cambridge: Cambridge University Press, 2006), 40.

39. Ibid., 47.

40. Ibid., 48.

41. See George Eliot, *The Journals of George Eliot*, ed. Margaret Harris and Judith Johnston (Cambridge: Cambridge University Press, 1998), 65.

Revolutionary Mothers and Revolting Daughters: Mary Wollstonecraft and Mary Shelley, Anna Wheeler and Rosina Bulwer Lytton

Joanna Goldsworthy and Marie Mulvey-Roberts

JUDITH CHERNAIK'S PLAY, *THE TWO MARYS* (1997), IS A DIALOGUE BETWEEN a mother and daughter, a conversation that never could have taken place because the mother died soon after giving birth to her child. The mother is the woman once described as "that hyena in petticoats,"[1] Mary Wollstonecraft (1759–97), the daughter Mary Shelley (1797–1851), author of *Frankenstein* (1818). The questions a daughter might imagine putting to her mother are answered in this imaginative reconstruction of the hitherto unspoken: Shelley reveals the anguish of her own life—the deaths of her two young children and that of her husband—and is answered by Wollstonecraft's urging that she use her mind rather than her heart to confront her despair.[2] It is easy to believe that Mary Shelley would have longed to have had a conversation with the idealized mother she never knew and whose death had been brought about by her birth.

Yet it was another woman, the radical activist for women's rights, the "Goddess of Reason" Anna Wheeler (1785–1848), who can be said to be heir to Wollstonecraft's legacy rather than the better-known Mary Shelley; but at the same time it was Wheeler's own daughter, Rosina Bulwer Lytton (1802–82), herself a successful writer moving in the same literary and political circles as Shelley, who mocked and resented Wollstonecraft's influence on Wheeler's thinking. Bulwer Lytton herself became notorious as the "mad wife" of politician and best-selling novelist Edward Bulwer Lytton (1803–73) by publicly challenging not only his behavior toward her but the institution of marriage itself, and if she is remembered at all today it is because of this marital scandal. This paired mother-daughter coupling, the one imagined and idealized, the other jealous and antagonistic, are two sides of the same coin: linked thematically and

63

historically, they illustrate the unchanging nature of the mother-daughter relationship while supporting a claim for Wheeler's and Bulwer Lytton's neglected importance in the history of women's rights, bridging Mary Wollstonecraft and Mary Shelley with Emmeline Pankhurst (1858–1928) and her daughter Christabel (1880–1958).

Shelley and Bulwer Lytton were caught up in the backlash against the female radicalism of the French Revolution. Their revolutionary mothers, however, were daughters of the Enlightenment who produced two of the most radical manifestos for women's rights of the eighteenth and nineteenth centuries: Wollstonecraft's *A Vindication of the Rights of Woman* (1792) on the one hand, and on the other, Wheeler's *Appeal of One Half the Human Race, Women, against the Other Half, Men, to retain them in political, and thence in civil and domestic, slavery* (1825), the attack on male/female relationships which Wheeler coauthored with the Irish socialist William Thompson (1775–1833).

Thompson regarded Wheeler, rather than Mary Shelley, as heir to the legacy of Mary Wollstonecraft. In the "Introductory Letter to Mrs. Wheeler" that prefaces the *Appeal,* he singles her out as the woman who should have: "the honour of raising from the dust that neglected banner which a woman's hand nearly thirty years ago unfolded boldly, in face of the prejudices of thousands of years, and for which a woman's heart bled, and her life was all but the sacrifice."[3] But although Wheeler, in her role as transnational mediator, socialist, and activist for women's rights, was the more radical of the two women, feminists have accorded more attention and iconic status to Wollstonecraft, an imbalance that calls for examination. It is by making cross-comparisons and connections between the two sets of mothers and daughters that Wheeler's and Bulwer Lytton's significance in the history of women's rights can be seen.

Wheeler was restricted to a textual relationship with Wollstonecraft, as was Shelley, who venerated her mother's memory and treasured her books. A letter in 1827 to the Owenite socialist Frances Wright (1795–1852) illustrates the depths of Shelley's attachment: "The memory of my Mother has always been the pride & delight of my life; & the admiration of others for her, has been the cause of most of the happiness . . . I have enjoyed. Her greatness of soul & my father['s] high talents have perpetually reminded me that I ought to degenerate as little as I could from those from whom I derived my being."[4]

Wheeler's daughter, conversely, resented her mother's enthusiasm for Wollstonecraft and her writing. During a childhood spent on the border of Limerick and Tipperary, Bulwer Lytton remembered how:

> my mother would be stretched on one sofa, deep in the perusal of some French or German philosophical work that had reached her translated *viâ* London (and who was unfortunately deeply imbued with the pernicious fallacies of the French revolution, which had then more or less seared their trace through Europe, and [she] was besides strongly tainted by the corresponding poison of Mrs. Wollstonecraft's book).[5]

For both Shelley and Bulwer Lytton the burden of being daughters of female avatars whose visionary rebelliousness contributed so much to the nineteenth-century debate on the rights of women presented them with the dilemma of how to rebel against a rebellious mother—more especially in the case of Shelley whose idealization of her mother hampered overt rebellion. At the same time, both daughters had to live with the public opprobrium accorded to their mothers. Wollstonecraft, a dominant figure among the female radicals of the 1790s in England and France, was after her death not only idolized, but also satirized as, for example, "an addlebrained fanatic addicted to utopian system-mongering,"[6] while Wheeler was described as "not so pleasant, something between Jeremy Bentham and Meg Merrilies, very clever but awfully revolutionary,"[7] by the young Benjamin Disraeli (1804–81). He recollected how "she poured forth all her systems upon my novitiate ear . . . while she advocated the rights of woman."[8] Common ground between their daughters was that each had to negotiate the radical maternal heritage bequeathed them by a famous mother, a heritage revered by Shelley and resented and rejected by Bulwer Lytton.

While Rosina did not embrace her mother's radical beliefs, according to one biographer "the daughter hardened into a permanent replica of her mother, becoming and remaining a feminist as wrong-headed and as tedious as ever had been the Goddess of Reason herself."[9] And was Mary Shelley, by apparently refusing to embrace her mother's "great cause" and for being less strident than Wollstonecraft, reverting to the very femininity that her mother had disparaged? In 1835, in a letter to Maria Gisborne (1770–1836), Shelley demonstrates a retreat into helplessness that runs counter to her mother's dictates in *Vindication*: "I have no ambition—no care for fame . . . I was always a dependant thing—wanting fosterage & support . . . I know that however clever I may be there is in me a vaccilation [*sic*], a weakness, a want of 'eagle winged' resolution

... & renders me what I am—one of broken purposes ... My Mother had more energy of character."[10]

Yet on the surface the contours of Mary Shelley's life seemed to follow those of her mother in transgressing sexual and textual conventions. She eloped with Percy Bysshe Shelley (1792–1822), who was a married man, while Wollstonecraft before her had passionately pursued the artist Henry Fuseli (1741–1825), who also had a wife. Both women had at least one child out of wedlock. Shelley's first novel, *Frankenstein,* which had been inspired by the ghost-story competition in which Shelley and Byron (1788–1824) had participated, was seen as blasphemous and breeding "monstrous conceptions."[11] Her second, a novella called *Matilda* written in 1819, with its atheism and exploration of the incestuous relationship between a father and daughter, had disgusted her father William Godwin (1756–1836). In the absence of her own biological mother, it seems likely that Mary was reacting more against the powerful male figures in her life— Shelley, whom she married in 1816, and Godwin—than actively living out the radical legacy of her mother. But unlike her parents and spouse, Shelley had no burning desire to reform the world and in 1838 wrote: "I have never written a word in disfavour of liberalism but neither have I openly supported it. . . . I have no wish to ally myself to the Radicals—they are full of repulsion to me. Violent without any sense of justice—selfish in the extreme—talking without knowledge—rude, envious & insolent—I wish to have nothing to do with them."[12] Mindful of the expectations of those around her, by acknowledging her reserve she chose her own way of being her mother's daughter.

The way in which some daughters prize themselves away from their mothers is often through marriage. Anna Wheeler met her future husband, Francis Massey Wheeler (1781?-1820), rather inauspiciously, at the races, and married him at the age of fifteen to escape her mother's repressive Anglican household. In the case of Shelley and Bulwer Lytton, the act of getting married was to fly in the face of their mothers' polemical writings against the unequal ties of love and marriage. As it turned out, in response to her disastrous marriage to Edward Bulwer Lytton in 1827, Rosina concurred with the sentiments of her mother's writing by admitting that marriage was "a great social error, a Boeotian mistake,—(if so, it is the very worst of all mistakes, as there is no remedy for it)."[13] At the same time, she quipped in her novel *Behind the Scenes* (1854) that "some persons take both marriage and the small-pox so favourably, that neither leave the slightest trace of disfigurement."[14] But this was not true in her case nor in that of either her mother or Wollstonecraft. Both

Wheeler and Wollstonecraft became disastrously involved with charming philanderers. The father of Wollstonecraft's first child, Fanny, was Gilbert Imlay, who deserted her for an actress. In spite of the recognition Wollstonecraft received in France and England for her radical ideas, Imlay's treatment of her led twice to attempted suicide.

As for Wheeler's husband, he soon abandoned her for bottles of claret and foxhunting. In a letter to the editor of the *Crisis* in 1833 Wheeler speaks from first-hand experience of the husband who need not "change his unjust, cruel and insulting laws for woman, when he can by compulsion, and through woman's power of loving, be pleased, served, and flattered, however deficient he may be in all the finer qualities of heart and mind."[15] By the time she was twenty-seven she had given birth to five children of whom only two survived, Henrietta and Rosina. After twelve years of unhappy marriage she left her husband, taking her two daughters and sister with her, and set sail for Guernsey where she took refuge with her uncle, Sir John Doyle (1756–1834), Lieutenant-Governor of the island, and for the next four years became hostess to his lavish household.

Wheeler's egalitarianism and socialism began to develop when she went to live in Caen in 1816, meeting a community of freethinkers and where she was to become known as the "Goddess of Reason." Bulwer Lytton satirizes this deification in her fictional autobiography in which hot-tempered Aunt Marley, a character based on her mother, boxes her ears and smashes ornaments, her "gentle reproofs," as the author ironically noted, "no doubt part of the system of universal benevolence and general philanthropy."[16] By 1823 Wheeler was in Paris, establishing her own salon where she was to meet the French utopian socialist Charles Fourier (1772–1837). He may have had Wheeler in mind when he coined the term "feminism,"[17] although this term would not come into common use until the end of the nineteenth century. Like Wollstonecraft, Wheeler was more highly regarded in France than she was in England and her close relationships with the French activists for women's rights, such as Flora Tristan (1803–44) and Désirée Veret (1810–ca. 1891), and their regard for her, are evidence of this.[18] Moving to London in 1824 Wheeler became part of the circle surrounding Robert Owen (1771–1858). According to Tristan, writing in her *London Journal* (1840), Wheeler was "the only woman socialist I have encountered in London,"[19] while for Veret Wheeler was "a second mother for me."[20] The world of Wheeler's drunken husband had been left far behind.

Wheeler, as had Wollstonecraft before her, found an intellectual equal who shared her beliefs in a philosopher, also known as William. For Wollstonecraft, the "prophetess of modern feminism,"[21] this was the anarchist William Godwin, whose *Enquiry concerning Political Justice* (1793) was published the year after Wollstonecraft's *Vindication*. For Wheeler, it was the socialist William Thompson, author of *Inquiry into the Principles of the Distribution of Wealth* (1824), whom it is likely she met in 1824 at the home of the Utilitarian radical philosopher Jeremy Bentham (1748–1832)[22] who for Wheeler and Thompson was what Tom Paine (1737–1809)[23] had been for Wollstonecraft and Godwin. But, unlike Wheeler, Wollstonecraft was not wholly opposed to wedlock for she married Godwin. As Janet Todd points out in her biography, "She had never attacked marriage, although accepting Dissenting opinion that it was useful rather than sacred."[24] Godwin's pride in her achievements prompted him to publish *Memoirs of the Author of the Vindication* in unflinchingly intimate detail in 1798, the year after her death, and by this act unwittingly besmirched her reputation. As a result her writings, along with her life, fell into obscurity and it was not until the publication of Wheeler and Thompson's *Appeal* in 1825, with its discussion of *Vindication*, that her legacy was revived.

In a similar failure of imagination, Thompson did not include Wheeler's name on the title page of *Appeal*, an omission that has contributed to her neglect by historians of the women's movement. He did nevertheless acknowledge a "debt of justice" to her:

> To separate your thoughts from mine were now to be impossible, so amalgamated are they with my own . . . Anxious that you should take up the cause of your proscribed sex, and state to the world in writing, in your own name, what you have so often and so well stated in conversation, and under feigned names in such of the periodical publications of the day as would tolerate such a theme, I long hesitated to arrange our common ideas. . . . But leisure and resolution to undertake the drudgery of the task were wanting. A few only therefore of the following pages are the exclusive produce of your mind and pen, and written with your own hand. The remainder are our joint property, I being your interpreter and the scribe of your sentiments.[25]

But although Thompson claimed that it was impossible to separate Wheeler's thoughts from his, she did not always agree with his opinions, more pessimistic than he that women would ever achieve true equality with men, and more critical of women's readiness to be slaves of men.[26] It seems likely that the following passage in *Appeal*, addressed to women, came from Wheeler's pen: "Thus degraded to the level of mere automatons, the passive tools of the pleasures and passions of men, your actions are regulated, like those of automatons, or slaves, by the arbitrary will of masters, to whom, by the necessities of existence uniting yourself, you are compelled to vow uninquiring obedience. O wretched slaves of such wretched masters!"[27]

The rhetoric here, in which wives are compared to slaves, was commonly used by women's rights activists in this period of antislavery propaganda. Elsewhere in *Appeal* the rhetoric harks back to revolutionary France: "Arouse! awake! rescue your sex, your species, from the frightful circumstances that surround and degrade you;—demand your rights."[28] With this clarion call to women Wheeler echoes the revolutionary "Declaration of the Rights of Women" (1791) in which Olympe de Gouges (1748–93) urged women to: "Wake up, the tocsin of reason is being heard . . . discover your rights . . . When will you cease to be blind?"[29] Wollstonecraft herself traveled to Paris in 1792, where *Vindication* had already been published to great acclaim, eager to see at first hand "the most extraordinary event that has ever been recorded."[30] It is interesting, then, to note the marked difference in rhetoric between these three documents, illustrating Wheeler's and Wollstonecraft's radically different views about women's rights.

In *Appeal* Wheeler and Thompson stress the importance of securing equal rights for both sexes in the context of a revolutionary transformation of society. Wollstonecraft's emphasis, on the other hand, is less upon women entering the public domain than on their moral state based upon a revisionist approach to feminine virtue. Thompson compares Wollstonecraft's stance unfavorably with Wheeler's in his introductory letter to the *Appeal:* "Were comprehensiveness of mind, above the narrow views which too often marred Mary Wollstonecraft's pages and narrowed their usefulness, the quality wanting . . . yours was the eye which no prejudice obscured, open to the rays of truth from whatever quarter they might emanate."[31]

The comparison of Wheeler's and Wollstonecraft's "rays of truth" lies in the distinction between the radical reformer of 1825 and the revolutionary reformer of 1792. Wheeler was a socialist feminist who advocated a fundamental restructuring of society and who, unlike her predecessor, was not committed to natural rights. Thompson's criticism of Wollstonecraft was that she advocated changes in society that were insufficiently far-reaching, especially in connection with the redistribution of wealth. In contrast to the radicalism of Wheeler, who was more at home in a French salon than in either Ireland or England, Wollstonecraft can be interpreted as conciliatory, compromising, and apologetic. An example of this difference between the two women is Wheeler's description of married life being "an isolated breeding establishment" within which women are forced to deny their "true sensual pleasures."[32] Wheeler goes further by claiming that the education of woman prepares her to be "the obedient instrument of man's sensual gratification, she is not permitted even to wish for any gratification for herself."[33] In contrast, Wollstonecraft confines herself to topics that are more in keeping with the tone of the *Vindication* as a masculinized public discourse, a tone reflected in its opening chapter.[34]

In spite of the fact that Wollstonecraft is clearly considerably less radical than Wheeler, feminists have given her far more attention. Wollstonecraft, the moderate feminist, appears to have trumped Wheeler, the radical feminist, in three ways. Most importantly she is regarded as the pioneer of the English women's rights movement although Wheeler's demands were more forcefully stated and for a time more widely available—in England at least—through the medium of journals and public speaking. Secondly, women have responded to the biographical information on Wollstonecraft that is widely available. Finally, unlike Wheeler, Wollstonecraft was published under her own name.

A striking parallel can be drawn between Wheeler and Thompson and the author of *On Liberty* (1859), John Stuart Mill (1806–73) and his wife Harriet Taylor (1807–58) who was involved in the writing of *The Subjection of Women* (1869) but who, unlike Wheeler, was given no acknowledgment whatsoever.[35] Ironically it was the Utilitarian James Mill (1773–1836), J. S. Mill's father, who prompted the writing of the *Appeal.* James Mill's essay, "On Government," first published in a supplement to the *Encyclopaedia Britannica* in 1820, argued for the exclusion of women from political representation. He included them in the category of those whose interests were "indisputably included in those of other individuals" and who, in consequence, "may be struck off without inconvenience." After eliminating children on these grounds, he continued, "In this light, also, women may be regarded, the interest of almost all of whom is involved either in that of their fathers or in that of their husbands."[36]

When Thompson died in 1833, Wheeler paid tribute to him, paraphrasing the rhetorical imperative in the *Appeal*—"Women of England . . . awake"[37]—and which bear the hallmarks of her words and thoughts:

> The women of England—(I blush while I unwillingly repeat)—the women of England, in those days of intellectual resurrection, will be the

last in Europe who will feel grateful to their benefactor; but are the first, indeed the only women who affect a slavish and ignorant repugnance to peruse the "Appeal of Women." With [P. B.] Shelley, Mr. Thompson would exclaim, "Shall man be free, while woman is a slave?"[38]

In a letter to Robert Owen, Wheeler first used this quotation from Percy Bysshe Shelley's *The Revolt of Islam* (1817).[39] The rhetorical question carries the sentiments of Wollstonecraft expressed in the *Vindication* and her novel *Maria* (1798). Shelley's intense admiration of Wollstonecraft had been projected onto Mary Shelley in the poem's dedicatory stanza where he sees her clothed in the "radiance undefiled" of her mother's "departing glory."[40] The lineage of the connection between women and slavery had been passed down from Wollstonecraft, through P. B. Shelley to William Thompson. It is unlikely that Thompson would have objected, since he believed that only through political rights could women be truly free and eventually achieve the right to vote.

It is particularly appropriate that Wheeler's great-granddaughter, the suffragette Constance Lytton (1869–1923), was to play such an important role in securing the vote for women aged thirty and over in 1919. It was Constance's grandmother, Rosina Bulwer Lytton, who campaigned so publicly and vociferously against the wrongs of married and separated women mainly through a personal tirade against her husband, Edward Bulwer Lytton. As a result of his violence toward her, the mistresses he kept, and his removal of her children from her, Rosina complained that England, though the best country "for men and horses . . . is the very worst in the whole universe for those peculiar beasts of burden, called wives."[41] For such outspokenness, Edward tried to silence his wife by having her locked up in a lunatic asylum in 1857.

Rosina openly retaliated against her husband's mistreatment of her through her novels and a pamphlet "Lady Bulwer Lytton's Appeal to the Justice and Charity of the English Public" (1857)—the title and polemic evoking the substance of her mother's *Appeal*. For example, Bulwer Lytton declaims: "Oh! women of England, in your happy homes—wives, mothers, and daughters—how would *you* feel, how would *you* act under similar outrages, if such should befall you?"[42] An account of her incarceration, *A Blighted Life*, was published in 1880, but in 1872 she sent the manuscript to Walter Besant (1836–1901) and James Rice (1843–82), the novelists and editors of *Once A Week*, who had renamed it "The Rights of Women." Bulwer Lytton had protested by insisting "I know nothing about the rights of women, but plenty of their bitter wrongs, from being the legal victim of 'one of the most eminent of living' literary scoundrels.''[43] Perhaps she wanted to dissociate herself from the "poison" of Wollstonecraft's *Vindication of the Rights of Woman* which had so infected her mother. But in so doing, she had inadvertently identified herself with Wollstonecraft's novel *Maria, or The Wrongs of Woman* whose heroine, like Rosina, had been put in a lunatic asylum by her husband.

Parallels with Rosina's troubled marriage can be seen in Mary Shelley's novel *Lodore* (1835) which she began writing at around the time she dined with the Bulwer Lyttons in 1832, the year that marked "a definite stage in the squalid tragedy of the Bulwers' married life.''[44] She was initially admiring of Edward Bulwer Lytton, who had originated the silver-fork, or fashionable, novel with his highly successful *Pelham* (1827),[45] which she had emulated herself in *Lodore*. By 1835, however, she was calling him "envious as well as vain" and "vulgar,"[46] by which time news of Bulwer's infidelities, especially with Mrs. Robert Stanhope, had become common knowledge.[47] Shelley expressed solidarity with Rosina by declaring her "worth in beauty & wit all the Mrs. R.S.s in the world.''[48]

How much, if any, of the Bulwer Lyttons' unhappy marriage is fictionalized in *Lodore* can only be speculation, but there are some intriguing parallels.[49] For example, Lodore thought that his wife Cornelia's treatment of her baby girl was "unmotherly":[50] "Lodore idolized his little offspring, and felt hurt and angry when his wife, after it had been in the room a minute or two, on the first approach it made to a squall, ordered it to be taken away.''[51] As fiction's real-life counterpart, Rosina was observed as being unable to bear the sight of her daughter Emily "and kept making faces at her and railing at her all the time she was in the room.''[52] As Rosina's acerbic biographer Michael Sadleir noted: "This conduct in Rosina was the very fault from which she had suffered with her own mother, and showed itself in the same manner.''[53]

The main theme in *Lodore*, perhaps unsurprisingly, is the separation of a mother from a daughter, enabling Shelley to reflect upon the loss of her own mother and the joy of an imagined reunion. Shelley had been separated from her mother, who died of puerperal fever, in 1797, at a time in Wollstonecraft's life when she most wanted to live. Several years earlier, as a result of the unhappy love affairs in her life, Wollstonecraft had tried drowning herself. Her lament "in being inhumanely brought back to life and misery"[54] is echoed by Victor Frankenstein's complaint of being brought from the dead after his fever: "Why did I not die? More miserable than man ever was before, why did I not sink into forgetfulness and rest. . . . But I was doomed to live.''[55]

Another comparison may be made between Wollstonecraft's last letter to Gilbert Imlay before she threw herself into the Thames—"I would encounter a thousand deaths, rather than a night like the last"[56]—and Frankenstein's horror at the prospect of being reunited with his creature. He declares: "This suspense is a thousand times worse than the most horrible event: tell me what new scene of death has been acted?"[57] Since both Wollstonecraft and Frankenstein are in the words of the latter "doomed to live," they try to alleviate their suffering by taking an excessive amount of laudanum to induce what Victor describes as "forgetfulness and rest." The notes at the end of Wollstonecraft's unfinished novel *Maria* are an uncanny prefiguring of *Frankenstein* and may well have inspired her daughter's creation. Shelley's sense of her own birth writing her mother's death warrant underwrites the production of *Frankenstein*. For Mary Wollstonecraft, "the maternal body at the moment when it gave birth to the future Mary Shelley, was soon to be the dying body. In post-parturition, the inability of Wollstonecraft's body to expel the placenta spelled death from puerperal fever."[58] The placental life-blood link between mother and infant that nourishes the fetus, in this case, effectively poisoned the mother, who died of septicemia eleven days after childbirth.

After Wollstonecraft's Maria has swallowed laudanum, she has a vision: "Her murdered child again appeared to her, mourning for the babe of which she was the tomb.—'and could it have a nobler?—Surely it is better to die with me, than to enter on life without a mother's care!—I cannot live!—but could I have deserted my child the moment it was born?'"[59] This is of course precisely what happened to Mary Shelley whose mother "deserted" her shortly after her birth. Maria is "restored to life" almost like Frankenstein's creature who represents the dead being brought to life. On looking at her child, who then utters the word "Mamma!," Maria exclaims: "The conflict is over!—I will live for my child."[60] The tragic irony was, of course, that Wollstonecraft, who died before completing the novel, was herself denied that wish.

At the same time, Wollstonecraft had wanted to live for her child, Mary, in an important sense: Shelley's *Frankenstein, Lodore,* and *Falkner* are all novels about the search for lost or dead mothers, and it is unlikely they would have been written—in this form at any rate—had Wollstonecraft not died at the birth of her daughter. How painful it must have been for Mary Shelley to have read at the beginning of her dead mother's *Thoughts on the Education of Daughters* the words: "I conceive it to be the duty of every rational creature to attend to its offspring."[61] The loss was made all the greater because

74   JOANNA GOLDSWORTHY AND MARIE MULVEY-ROBERTS

Wollstonecraft meant so much to so many people, especially to those who had not even met her, and who, like Percy Bysshe Shelley, idealized her.

By way of contrast, Wollstonecraft's "heir," the socialist-feminist Anna Wheeler, favored her elder daughter, Henrietta, while neglecting and beating the younger child, causing her to run away. Rosina bemoaned: "I soon became that most miserable of created beings, the neglected sister of a favourite and favoured child."⁶² Quarrels between mother and daughter drove them apart for long periods of separation, although they were reconciled in the early years of Rosina's marriage; Wheeler's sensible and sensitive support for her daughter in the period after the breakdown of the Bulwer Lyttons' marriage can be seen in a letter she wrote to her at the time of the publication of Rosina's first novel, *Cheveley* (1839), the first of many thinly disguised attacks on her husband:

> The power of that monster, *Law,* made by men to gratify their own selfish and vindictive passions, leaves a woman so entirely at the mercy of a husband . . . However harmless the shafts of satire may fall on the shameless swell mob . . . it is not expected, and therefore never pardoned, when a woman tears the *mask* from any individual amongst them. Therefore *caution!* caution! for none can tell what wounded self-love may do, aided by power and unchecked by conscientious feeling, to double, treble, the injury you have received.⁶³

Rosina's subsequent publication history, of novels satirizing and criticizing the institution of marriage, shows a wronged wife who refused to bow down to her husband's "selfish and vindictive passions," even if it cost her reputation, her children, and her income.

The generational cross-connections and textual links between these four women raise a number of issues relating to mothers and daughters. But seeing the radicalism of both Wollstonecraft and Wheeler as a template upon which Shelley and Bulwer Lytton inscribed their sense of self is to limit them to a familial gridlock by denying their own individuality. Conversely, by acknowledging their rebellion against their respective mothers, whether consciously or not, we see that they were, in fact, living up to their birthright as the daughters of rebel mothers. Shelley's feelings of lack of self-worth are contradicted by her very real success as a published writer, which brought her financial independence. Bulwer Lytton, for her part, in so tenaciously rejecting the wrongs imposed on her by her husband, fulfilled her mother's stringent appeal to all women.

As Virginia Woolf (1882–1941) was later to point out "we live through our mothers if we are women."[64] The twentieth-century American poet Anne Sexton (1928–74), who unlike Wollstonecraft's Maria did not desist from suicide for the sake of her child, wrote a poem for her daughter. The last line could well have been said by Wheeler to Bulwer Lytton, Wollstonecraft to Shelley, and Victor Frankenstein to his creature: "I made you to find me."[65]

NOTES

The authors would like to acknowledge the kind assistance of Professor Nora Crook for sharing with them her extensive knowledge of Mary Shelley.

1. Horace Walpole to Hannah More, January 26, 1795, in Horace Walpole, *Letters of Horace Walpole*, ed. Mrs. Paget Toynbee (Oxford: Clarendon, 1903–5), 15:337–38.

2. Judith Chernaik, "The Two Marys," *Women's Writing* 6, no. 3 (1999): 451–68. The play was written and performed in 1997 at the National Portrait Gallery, London, for the bicentenary of Mary Wollstonecraft's death.

3. William Thompson and Anna Wheeler, *Appeal of One Half the Human Race, Women, against the Other Half, Men, to retain them in political, and thence in civil and domestic, slavery,* ed. Marie Mulvey-Roberts and Michael Foot (Bristol: Thoemmes, 1994), vii. This is the first and only edition to include Wheeler's name as coauthor.

4. Mary Shelley to Frances Wright, September 12, 1827, in Mary Shelley, *The Letters of Mary Wollstonecraft Shelley*, ed. Betty T. Bennett (Baltimore: Johns Hopkins University Press, 1983), 2:3–4.

5. Louisa Devey, *Life of Rosina, Lady Lytton* (London: Swan Sonnenschein, Lowrey, 1887), 8.

6. Barbara Taylor, *Mary Wollstonecraft and the Feminist Imagination* (Cambridge: Cambridge University Press, 2003), 28.

7. A wild, demented gypsy in Walter Scott's novel *Guy Mannering* (1815) and the subject of a ballad by John Keats written in 1818.

8. Lord Beaconsfield, *Correspondence with his Sister* (1886), 3–4, quoted in Michael Sadleir, *Bulwer and his Wife* (London: Constable, 1931), 152.

9. Michael Sadleir, *Bulwer and his Wife: A Panorama* (London: Constable, 1933), 80–81.

10. Mary Shelley to Maria Gisborne, June 11, 1835, in Shelley, *Letters of Mary Wollstonecraft Shelley*, 2:246.

11. Reviewer of *Edinburgh Magazine and Literary Miscellany: A New Series of "The Scots Magazine"* 2 (March 1818), quoted by Fred Botting, *Gothic* (Routledge: London, 1996), 101.

12. Mary Shelley, journal entry for October 21, 1838, in *The Journals of Mary Shelley*, ed. Paula R. Feldman and Diana Scott-Kilvert (Oxford: Clarendon, 1987), 2:554.

13. Rosina Bulwer Lytton, *Miriam Sedley* (London: Newby, 1851), 2:14.

14. Rosina Bulwer Lytton, *Behind the Scenes: A Novel* (London: Skeet, 1854), 1:31.

15. Anna Wheeler, "Vlasta (Anna Wheeler) to the Editor of *The Crisis*, August 31, 1833," *Crisis* 2, nos. 35 and 36 (1833): 280.

16. Bulwer Lytton, *Miriam Sedley*, 1:271.

17. The term was first used in English in *Daily News*, October 12, 1894, with reference to a "Feminist" group being formed in the French Chamber of Deputies in Paris.

18. Flora Tristan, *Flora Tristan's London Journal 1840,* trans. Dennis Palmer and Giselle Pincetl (Charlestown, MA: Charles River Books, 1980), 160. In the early 1790s, Mary Wollstonecraft had been welcomed into the republican salon of the British radical and religious dissenter Helen Maria Williams who had documented the history of the Revolution in France to the Bourbon Restoration during her time in France. Wollstonecraft too was a witness to events of the French Revolution and wrote her own history, *An Historical and Moral View of the Origin and Progress of the French Revolution and the Effect it Has Produced in Europe* (1795).

19. Tristan, *Flora Tristan's London Journal 1840,* 160.

20. Désirée Veret to Victor Considérant, September 7, 1890 (Paris: Archives Nationales, Fonds Fourier et Considérant AN10 AS 42 d. 8).

21. Miriam Brody, introduction to *A Vindication of the Rights of Woman,* by Mary Wollstonecraft (London: Penguin, 1992), 19.

22. Bentham Papers, vol. 27, accounts, add MSS 33563, fol. 131b, British Library.

23. Godwin and Wollstonecraft had first met at the house of Tom Paine, author of *Rights of Man* (1791).

24. Janet Todd, *Mary Wollstonecraft: A Revolutionary Life* (London: Weidenfeld and Nicolson, 2000), 239.

25. Thompson and Wheeler, *Appeal,* vii.

26. See for instance her lecture in 1829, reprinted in the *British Co-operator,* nos. 1 and 2 (May and June 1830).

27. Thompson and Wheeler, *Appeal,* 193–94.

28. Ibid., 209.

29. Olympe de Gouges, "Declaration of the Rights of Woman and the Female Citizen," in *Women in Revolutionary Paris, 1789–1795: Selected Documents,* ed. and trans. Darline Gay Levy, Harriet Branson Applewhite, and Mary Durham Johnson (Urbana: University of Illinois Press, 1979), 87–96.

30. Mary Wollstonecraft to Joseph Johnson, December 26, 1792, in Mary Wollstonecraft, *Collected Letters of Mary Wollstonecraft,* ed. Ralph Wardle (London: Cornell University Press, 1979), 251, quoted in Taylor, *Mary Wollstonecraft,* 148.

31. Thompson and Wheeler, *Appeal,* xxiii.

32. Ibid., 131.

33. Ibid., 102.

34. "The Rights and Involved Duties of Mankind Considered," in Wollstonecraft, *Vindication,* 91–99.

35. Usually remembered only as the woman who inspired Mill's powerful critique of the subordination of women, Taylor had in fact published her own essay, "The Enfranchisement of Women," in 1851 which differed in points of emphasis with Mill. In *The Subjection of Women* Mill upheld the traditional roles in marriage and sanctions the objectification of women as passive rather than as active agents. Without Taylor's influence, the polemic of Mill's feminist writing would probably have been much more restrained and less radical.

36. James Mill, "On Government," in *Essays on Government, Jurisprudence, Liberty of the Press, and Law of Nations* (London: [J. Innes, 1825]), 21 (each essay is separately paginated). This essay is cited in Thompson and Wheeler, *Appeal,* 9.

37. Thompson and Wheeler, *Appeal,* 187. This tone continues to the end of the treatise on page 213.

38. Anna Wheeler, "Letter by Vlasta," in *Hampden in the Nineteenth Century,* by John Minter Morgan (London: Edward Moxon, 1834), 2:322.

39. The actual line is "Can man be free, if woman be a slave," P. B. Shelley, *The Revolt of Islam* (London: C. & J. Ollier, 1817), canto 2, 43, 1. Years later, much to

the indignation of Shelley's wife, Edward Bulwer Lytton would dismiss his verse as "gaudy verbiage" in his life of Friedrich Schiller appended to his translation of *Poems and Ballads* (London: William Blackwood and Sons, 1844), 1:148.

40. Ibid., 12:5–6.

41. Rosina Bulwer Lytton, *Memoirs of a Muscovite* (London: Newby, 1844), 1:161. Rosina's comments appear to echo, and deliberately invert, the proverbial claim that "England is the paradise of women, the purgatory of men, and the hell of horses." (As cited in John Florio, *Florios Second Frutes* [London: Thomas Woodcock, 1591], 205.)

42. Devey, *Life*, 394.

43. Rosina Bulwer Lytton to Walter Besant and James Rice, December 14, 1872, in Rosina Bulwer Lytton, *The Collected Letters of Rosina Bulwer Lytton*, ed. Marie Mulvey-Roberts, with the assistance of Steve Carpenter (London: Pickering and Chatto, 2008), 3. This manuscript is not identified by name, but it seems likely to be that of *A Blighted Life*, which was eventually published without Bulwer Lytton's knowledge or consent in 1880.

44. Sadleir, *Bulwer and his Wife*, 162.

45. Bulwer's grandson Victor suggests that Rosina might have had a hand in the composition of his novel, *Pelham*. See Earl of Lytton (Victor), *Bulwer Lytton* (London: Home and Van Thal, 1948), 40.

46. Mary Shelley to Maria Gisborne, November 1835 in Shelley, *Letters of Mary Wollstonecraft Shelley*, 2:261.

47. See Mary Shelley to Edward John Trelawny, May 7, 1834, in ibid., 202.

48. Ibid.

49. Mary Shelley started writing *Lodore* in 1831 but discontinued it in 1833 for another project. She completed the novel in 1834 but it did not get published until 1835 because the publisher lost some of the manuscript, with the result that she had to rewrite volume 3. The unhappy marriage of Lodore and his wife, which led to separation, may have been inspired by the Bulwer Lyttons, who separated in 1834 though not officially until 1836.

50. Mary Shelley, *Lodore*, ed. Lisa Vargo (Peterborough, ON: Broadview, 1997), 105.

51. Ibid., 104–5.

52. Sadleir, *Bulwer and his Wife*, 167.

53. Ibid., 167–68.

54. Mary Wollstonecraft to Gilbert Imlay, ca. October 1795 in Mary Wollstonecraft, *The Collected Letters of Mary Wollstonecraft*, ed. Janet Todd (New York: Columbia University Press, 2003), 327.

55. Mary Shelley, *Frankenstein or The Modern Prometheus* (Oxford: Oxford University Press, 1969), 177.

56. Wollstonecraft, *Letters*, 326.

57. Shelley, *Frankenstein*, 180.

58. Marie Mulvey-Roberts, "The Corpse in the Corpus: Frankenstein, Rewriting Wollstonecraft and the Abject," in *Mary Shelley's Fictions*, ed. Michael Eberle-Sinatra (London: Macmillan, 2000), 198–99.

59. Mary Wollstonecraft, *Mary and Maria;* Mary Shelley, *Matilda*, ed. Janet Todd (London: Penguin Classics, 1992), 147.

60. Ibid.

61. Mary Wollstonecraft, *Thoughts on the Education of Daughters*, ed. Janet Todd (Bristol: Thoemmes, 1995), 1.

62. Devey, *Life*, 10.

63. Anna Wheeler to Rosina Bulwer Lytton, February 1, 1839, in Devey, *Life*, 158.

64. Virginia Woolf, *A Room of One's Own* (London: Hogarth, 1929), 76.

65. Anne Sexton, "The Double Image," in *The Selected Poems of Anne Sexton*, ed. Diane Wood Middlebrook and Diana Hume George (London: Virago, 1991), 34.

Sisters—Ambition and Compliance:
The Case of Mary and Agnes Berry and
Joanna and Agnes Baillie

Judith Bailey Slagle

> One thing is clear, siblings growing up in the same family are
> very different. It is rare in a field as complex as the behavioral
> sciences to discover such clear and consistent evidence.
>
> —Dunn and Plomin[1]

THIS ESSAY EXAMINES THE LIVES AND CREATIVE ACTIVITIES OF TWO AMBI-
tious Romantic women writers, Mary Berry (1763–1852) and her
friend Joanna Baillie (1762–1851), and of their supportive sisters,
both named Agnes, who were influential in their sisters' successes
but never sought fame for themselves. Both sets of sisters lived as
companions for over eighty years. Based primarily on archival research of family documents and letters, this study examines the psychological and philosophical inclination of these individuals and
raises the question about how creative collaboration and/or support
from sisters may have affected the publications of Mary Berry and
Joanna Baillie. This type of collaboration also raises questions about
how dominant creative personalities are influenced by the assistant
imaginations of those around them.

It is appropriate to describe Mary Berry and Joanna Baillie as geniuses of their time, particularly in the larger sense of exhibiting
"exceptional intellectual or creative power,"[2] for they read critically,
analyzed the social and political world around them, and produced
significant bodies of work. Psychologist Dean Simonton defines creative geniuses as those "individuals credited with creative ideas or
products that have left large impressions on a particular domain of
intellectual or aesthetic activity," particularly, by leaving for posterity "an impressive body of contributions that are both original and
adaptive."[3] But exactly what makes the brain create? More specifically, what makes one sibling creative and another not, especially in

a shared environment? Simonton attributes this to six Darwinian personality characteristics,[4] the majority of which one can easily apply to the literary, artistic, musical, and scientific geniuses of the world—including Mary Berry and Joanna Baillie. How these creative personalities develop depends on various factors. Two of them, according to Simonton and other psychologists, may be early parental loss and birth order. Berry lost her mother as a child and Baillie her father as an adolescent. Such a traumatic event often results in responses such as bereavement syndrome or achievement and unconventionality.[5] As for birth order, firstborn children have "the first shot at parental attention and resources"; but "the later the child comes in ordinal position, the more intense the pressures to diversify, to be sensitive to novel opportunities, to do what no one else has done."[6] Nevertheless, this theory is difficult to apply to writers Berry and Baillie; for Mary Berry was a firstborn, benefiting from the attention that position brings, and Joanna Baillie the last of three surviving children. Baillie was also the only survivor of twins; and that, along with being the last child, may have also inspired ambition. Psychologist Nancy Segal admits that little research has been carried out on "surviving twins," but some research shows that they often exhibit a significant drive toward individuality.[7] So being a "lone twin" and last child possibly contributed to Baillie's development as a leading woman playwright of the Romantic period.

Examples of sibling differences abound among great writers. The children of the Brontë family, for example, differed considerably: "Branwell passionate, violent, uncontrolled; Maria, who was the model for Helen Burns in *Jane Eyre*, mildness, fortitude, wisdom, and patience personified; Charlotte desperately vulnerable to pain and shyness. . . . The catalogue of notable differences is as long as the list of writers we choose to consider."[8] The earlier century provides us with examples too, including Frances Burney (1752–1840) and her sisters, as well as Jane Austen (1775–1817) and Cassandra (1773–1845), and so forth; and the later century gives us, among others, Virginia Woolf (1882–1941) and her sister Vanessa (1879–1961). There are also similarities as well as differences in creativity among siblings. While sisters may certainly be influenced by their brothers, as Joanna Baillie claims to have been by her brother Dr. Matthew Baillie (1761–1823), it is the condition of "sisterhood" that has supported what Nina Auerbach calls "communities of women" for generations: "This community of women that exists . . . at the margins of the social and natural world attains an almost magical affinity with the sources of transformation and rebirth. . . . Women in literature who evade the aegis of men also evade traditional categories of definition."[9] "Sisterhood," of course, comprises both the familial and the global; and, especially for eighteenth- and nineteenth-century women writers, sisterhood in its larger sense provided the support system necessary for freedom of expression. That freedom, explains Auerbach, "is freedom in the sphere of the soul, not society; freedom is attaining access to the heavens, not the professions."[10]

Freedom of expression for many women, however, proved a direct result of their freedom *from* men and, as a consequence, provided even limited freedom in the professions. The cases of playwrights Mary Berry and Joanna Baillie illustrate how early women writers were supported by a community of women that included their own sisters. While Berry and Baillie were significantly close in age to each other and to their own sisters, studies have shown that "the interval between siblings [does] not affect levels of aggressive, cooperative, or imitative behavior for either same-sex or different-sex sibling pairs."[11] That there are differences in levels of aggressive, or at least ambitious, behavior among the Berry and Baillie sisters, however, is apparent in what they contributed to literature. Ambition links Mary Berry and Joanna Baillie as clearly as *they* link the era of George III (1738–1820) to that of Queen Victoria (1819–1901), and both women demonstrate how creative and determined women were often influenced by their more "silent" sisters.

Playwright Mary Berry was born in 1763 and Agnes Berry in 1764. Their father, Robert Berry (d. 1817), was the "maternal nephew of an old Scotch merchant of the name of Ferguson," Mary explains in her *Notes of Early Life,* and Robert Berry lost his inheritance to his younger brother after his uncle decided to make William Berry his heir.[12] Robert had married Miss Seton, a distant cousin, in 1762; and in 1767 Mrs. Berry died giving birth to a third child who did not survive. The Berry sisters then grew up with their maternal grandmother in Yorkshire and in the care of a governess after their father remarried; as far as education was concerned, "they were left to their own devices."[13]

Mary Berry's journal reveals that around the age of four her mother's death initiated "the first feeling of unkindness and neglect which entered into my young mind, accustomed to nothing but the fondness of everybody about me."[14] Berry remembered little from her very early years but, as Baillie later wrote similarly in her memoirs, she did remember a little about learning to read: "But as I have no remembrance at all of the process nor of existence without the power of reading, I can say nothing of the talents of my teacher. Agnes [like Joanna Baillie] was slower than myself at her book, and

I have some faint idea of tribulation over the spelling-book with her."[15] Unfortunately, their father felt that when they reached the ages of eleven and twelve the expense of a governess could be spared. As he had provided them little religious education, their grandmother made Mary read the Psalms aloud every morning; but, wrote Mary, "as neither explanation nor comment was made upon them, nor was their history followed up in any way, I hated the duty and escaped it when I could."[16] The sisters continued into their teens to be self-taught, reading indiscriminately, much like the Baillie sisters.

When Ferguson at last died at the age of ninety-three, he settled a sum of ten thousand pounds on Robert Berry, who, with an additional annuity from his brother, was finally able to take his two daughters on a tour of the west of England and of the Continent. This is where the Berry sisters' "natural" education really began, and an early journal entry dated May 1783 implies that Mary soon took on her leadership role:

At Florence was our first stop; and here for the first time I began to feel my situation, and how entirely dependent I was on my own resources for my conduct, responsibility, and success. . . . I soon found that I had to lead those who ought to have led me; that I must be a protecting mother, instead of a gay companion, to my sister; and to my father a guide and monitor, instead of finding in him a tutor and protector.[17]

Directing these travels inspired Mary Berry's interest in the European political and social climate, with France on the eve of revolution, which she would later address in *A Comparative View of the Social Life of England and France from the Restoration of Charles II to the French Revolution* (1828–31). Their return brought them to stay in London where they soon met Horace Walpole (1717–97), Joanna Baillie, Anne Damer (1748–1828), and other influential members of London society. Ian Haywood writes that Mary Berry was also well acquainted with William Thackeray (1811–63) in her later years and cites a passage in Thackeray's lecture on *The Four Georges* (delivered in America 1855–56) as a reference to her:

A very few years since, I knew familiarly a lady who had been asked in marriage by Horace Walpole; who had been patted on the head by George I. This lady had knocked at Dr. Johnson's door; had been intimate with Fox, the beautiful Georgina of Devonshire, and that brilliant Whig society of the reign of George III; had known the Duchess of Queensberry, and patroness of Gay and Prior, the admired young beauty of the court of Queen Anne. I often thought as I took my kind old friend's hand, how with it I held on to the old society of wits and men of the world.[18]

Obviously, Thackeray's enthusiasm temporarily overcame his head for figures: neither Mary Berry nor any other woman living a "few years" before he delivered this lecture fulfilled all these conditions. Born in 1763, Mary Berry could never have met George I (1660–1727), or even his son, George II (1683–1760). However, she might well have encountered Catherine Douglas (née Hyde), Duchess of Queensberry (1701–77). Haywood suggests that Thackeray's several references on other occasions to an unidentified older lady comprise a "private celebration of Mary Berry's importance";[19] and we know that the author became a favorite at the Berry's salon at No. 8 Curzon Street in the sisters' later years.[20] But the real favorite of the Berry salon was Horace Walpole. Biographer Virginia Surtees disputes the notion that Walpole was more than a friend and actually proposed marriage to Berry, but in her early years he was certainly her closest male friend and mentor.

Walpole, shy, retiring, and in his early seventies when he met the Berrys socially in 1787, at first resisted an introduction, for "having heard too ample an account of their varied accomplishments he assumed that their pretensions were in like degree. However, finding himself next to Mary at a small gathering the following year, he was delighted to discover the reverse."[21] Walpole found Mary " 'an angel inside and out,' fluent in French, acquainted with Latin, well read, and seemingly endowed with every excellence including that of unaffected modesty." Agnes (1764–1852), he discovered, "measured up to her sister, though gentler and more retiring, allowing the lead to the elder, yet her superior perhaps with her pencil and in the modest skill of her sketches in watercolour."[22] He also found Agnes less animated and noted that Mary talked more, but both "dote[d] on each other."[23] Walpole further compared the sisters in verse to honor their forthcoming visit to see his printing press at Strawberry Hill:

The Press at Strawberry-Hill to Miss Mary and Miss Agnes Berry

> To Mary's Lips has ancient Rome
> Her purest Language taught;
> And from the modern City home
> Agnes its pencil brought.
>
> Rome's ancient Horace sweetly chants
> Such Maids with lyric Fire;

>Albion's old Horace sings nor paints—
>He only can admire.
>
>Still wou'd his Press their Fame record,
>So amiable the Pair is!
>But ah! how vain to think *his* Word
>Can add a Straw to Berrys![24]

The forthright Mary Berry replied immediately:

>Had Rome's famed Horace thus addresst
>His Lydia or his Lyce,
>He had ne'er so soft complain'd their breast
>To him was cold and icy.
>
>But had they sought their joy to explain,
>Or praise their generous bard,
>Perhaps, like me, they had tried in vain,
>And found the task too hard.
>
>(Oct. 14, 1788)[25]

Thus was formed the Berry/Walpole relationship that would eventually result in the sisters' financial independence.[26] Meanwhile, as Virginia Surtees indicates, Mary Berry proved the dominant sister in a more personal arena:

>It was Mary who claimed the larger share of his thought and heart and it seems likely that he might have sought a marital companionship had not his fear of the ridiculous prevented him—a lifelong bachelor in his seventies and a regular martyr to gout would be open to derision for contemplating marriage with a young woman in her early twenties, only recently introduced. But that he loved her, letters testify—though subterfuge and self-ridicule play their part.[27]

Nevertheless, as Mary Berry's relationship with Walpole ended with his death in 1797, her career as a writer was just beginning.

Mary Berry began to publish seriously with her edition of *The Works of Horatio Walpole, Earl of Orford,* in 1798, the same year of Joanna Baillie's first volume of *A Series of Plays: in which it is attempted to delineate the stronger passions of the mind.* Less successfully but similar to Baillie, Berry was also trying her hand at playwriting, with *Fashionable Friends* produced at Strawberry Hill for her friends in 1801—a play for which Baillie wrote the prologue and epilogue—and also acted by friends and family, including Mr. Berry, Mary and Agnes Berry, Mrs. Damer, and Lady Elizabeth Cole (1778–1857). Drury

Lane was not so "friendly," however, when the play debuted in 1802, against Berry's wishes, and was unjustly attacked for its "loose principles."[28] Andrew Elfenbein addresses this phenomenon in "Lesbian Aestheticism on the Eighteenth-Century Stage," asserting that Berry, along with Hannah Cowley (1743–1809) and Henry Seymour Conway (1721–95), sculptor Anne Damer's father, created a link between feminine aestheticism and art in their plays.[29] In fact, he argues that Damer even "catalyzed the appearance of these female aesthetes."[30] Furthermore, Berry, Cowley, and Conway wrote for or about Anne Damer—the aristocratic artist often attacked for her intimate friendships with women—who was a close friend of the Berry *and* Baillie sisters. As Elfenbein explains, "Mary Berry's *Fashionable Friends* shared much with Conway's play. Like *False Appearances,* it starred Anne Damer and was written for a highly exclusive audience; also, like Conway's play, it failed miserably when later produced in a public theatre."[31]

Even the titles of these plays contributed to their notoriety, but these were private theatricals by amateur authors written for a highly exclusive compatible audience.[32] Catherine Burroughs explains that Berry "is especially interesting in the context of [the] study of women's theater theory for having sought outlets for theatrical expression by holding salon-like gatherings in the privacy of her English home."[33] Lady Theresa Lewis (1803–65), editor of Berry's papers, later described these gatherings as follows: "For an unusually lengthened period of years she [Berry] formed a centre round which beauty, rank, wealth, power, fashion, learning, and science were gathered; merit and distinction of every degree were blended by her hospitality in social ease and familiar intercourse, encouraged by her kindness and enlivened by her presence."[34]

Berry continued her salon gatherings for many years, with Agnes Berry as "the lesser light of the salon,"[35] but chose not to continue writing plays after the attack on the public performance of *Fashionable Friends.* She did, however, go on to publish biographical and social works based on her travels, including the aforementioned *Comparative View of the Social Life of England and France from the Restoration of Charles II to the French Revolution* (1828–31), later retitled in her *Works* (1844), which also reprinted her annotated editions of letters (1810) by Mme du Deffand (1697–1780)[36] and *The Life of Rachel, Lady Russell* (1819).[37] In her *View of the Social Life of England and France,* which begins with the restoration of Charles II (1630–85) and ends with the ascent of the Duke of Orleans (1773–1850) to the throne of France in 1830, Berry makes clear her partiality for everything French, as in her attack on Restoration drama:

The Restoration, which gave us back our national theatre, gave us back an audience accustomed to the theatres of France; no wonder, then that "unhappy Dryden" and indeed "all the wits of Charles's days," took, the shortest road to theatrical success by translating or by imitating the dramas of France. . . . Hence, Shakespeare himself lay for a time neglected under a mass of writers, whose names are only known to the unerring judgment of posterity by the satire of Dryden.[38]

While Mary glorified the superiority of French culture in print, sister Agnes focused her talents on a less public venue—painting for pleasure. Horace Walpole made a special place in the parlor for her picture of Cardinal Wolsey (ca. 1473–1530) and wrote to Mary, then traveling with her father and sister in France, on October 12, 1790:

Yesterday morning I had just framed Wolsey, and hung him over the chimney of the little parlour, when the D[ss] of Gloucester came, and could scarce be persuaded it was the work of Agnes; but who else *could* have painted it? Milbourne, who is here drawing from some of my pictures for his prints to Shakespeare, cried out at it as the finest piece of water-colours he ever beheld, before he knew whose work it is.[39]

Nevertheless, Agnes Berry seems to have had little ambition to make a name for herself as an artist, but her few extant letters show an eye for detail and a devotion to her sister. From their home in North Audley Street, Agnes wrote to Mary who was traveling in April 1803; she missed her sister and had been suffering from headaches:

This is the finest weather that ever was, dearest Mary, and I do hope you are enjoying it in all your country excursions. . . . I mean it to be well enough to-night to let me go to the French play, the first of my new subscription. My dinner and my evening yesterday I thought did very tolerably and I bothered my guests and myself as little as I could, and I had plenty of men and plenty of women too. . . . Some sort of enjoyments that have to do with the *feelings* and real *attachments* of the *heart* you will no doubt find and I hope *feel with comfort on your return home,* but are too wise a woman not to *prepare yourself* for the great diminution of general interests that must necessarily attend one's every day life and society, compared to the one you have been leading.[40]

Agnes's support and mutual interest in society certainly influenced her sister's social history, *A Comparative View of the Social Life of England and France;* and the fact that the sisters spent some of their young adult lives in France at the beginning of a major revolution contributed to their interest in society, politics, and everything "French."[41] Agnes Berry's "gentler and more retiring" nature, as

Walpole regarded it, mirrored that of Agnes Baillie, whose expertise as an antiquarian also proved compatible with her sister Joanna's playwriting. But unlike the Berry sisters, the Baillie sisters were extremely nationalistic, and cared little for the Continent, regarding their native Scotland above all else.

While the Berry sisters spent their adolescent years with a grandmother and governess and were eventually supported by Horace Walpole, Joanna and Agnes Baillie grew up in a notable extended family with the advantage of their own sufficient income in their adult lives to allow them to live comfortably as single women. The company of well-educated men in their early lives, especially those in the medical profession, and "writing" women relatives (such as their aunt Anne Home Hunter [1742–1821]) inspired the sisters to read voraciously—from Walter Scott (1771–1832) and Maria Edgeworth (1768–1849) to Thomas Malthus (1766–1834) and William Ellery Channing (1780–1842).

Joanna and Agnes Baillie's father, the Reverend James Baillie (1722–78), had married Dorothea Hunter (1721–1806), sister of the famous Hunter physicians of Glasgow and London, in 1757. Their first child, William (James) Baillie, died as an infant in 1760. Their second child, Agnes (1760–1861), was the lifelong companion of her famous younger sister; and the only surviving son, Matthew Baillie (1761–1823), became a celebrated London physician. Joanna Baillie was born a twin, but her sister died a few hours after their premature delivery on September 11, 1762.[42]

In 1831 Joanna Baillie began a brief autobiography at the request of her friend Mary Berry, not surprising given Berry's penchant for biography. There she recollected events that especially piqued her childhood imagination; and, like Berry, she also revealed her earliest memories of reading:

> The farthest back thing that I can remember is sitting with my Sister on the steps of the s[t]air in Bothwell Manse, repeating after her as loud as I could roar the letters of the Alphabet while she held in her hand a paper on which was marked in large letters the A B C &c. I was then about 3 years old, and this was, I suppose the very beginning of my education. . . . not being able to read but in a very imperfect manner at the age of eight or nine. . . . My Mother took pains to teach me and I was sent to day-school at Hamilton where my Father was then settled as Clergyman, but even the sight of a book was hateful to me. . . . I was an active stirring child, quick in apprehending & learning any thing else.[43]

Younger sister Joanna Baillie showed the same hesitancy to read as younger sister Agnes Berry. It was the two older sisters who encour-

aged and taught their younger sisters, but the parallel in learning
here is only in birth order: Mary Berry, the quick learner, was the
creative writer in her family, while Joanna Baillie, the slower learner,
proved the creative one of the Baillies. Certainly, a creative imagination is not uniquely granted to the first born but is a result of personality traits as well.

Agnes Baillie, like Agnes Berry, was the sister with the lesser ambition; yet, *neither* Agnes was untaught nor introverted. Agnes Baillie
apparently read almost everything that Joanna did, and even more
in the field of history. Agnes was the professed "antiquarian" of the
family but, like Agnes Berry, practiced her craft only as a "polite pursuit." As late as July 1833, Joanna wrote to Mary Berry that Agnes
had been somewhat unwell but that both were "engaged with Miss
Aikin's new work, the Court of Charles the 1st."[44] Agnes read local
newspaper stories aloud to Joanna in the evenings and kept her sister apprised of the newest historical works. In May 1842, when the
Baillies were advanced in years, Joanna wrote to her friend Lady Jane
Davy (1780–1855), wife of Sir Humphry Davy (1778–1829), that
Agnes had lately been occupied with American travel writer John
Lloyd Stephens's *Incidents of travel in Yucatan* (1842–43), while Joanna had been engrossed in Frances Burney D'Arblay's *Diary*
(1842)—Agnes, she wrote, "being by nature more of an antiquarian
than a gossip."[45] In addition, Agnes seems to have had the head for
business matters.

After the Reverend James Baillie died unexpectedly in 1778, having just been appointed head of the divinity school at Glasgow, his
wife Dorothea faced difficult financial times. Here, especially, Agnes
Baillie excelled in handling the family's monetary affairs and in corresponding with Matthew, then studying medicine with his uncles in
London. While Joanna's earliest letters do not survive, a few of
Agnes Baillie's do, and they demonstrate a command of business
matters, with which her younger sister seems to have had little to do.
In April of 1781, Agnes wrote to Matthew from Long Calderwood,
the home that Dr. William Hunter was providing for his widowed
sister:

My Dear Brother
   Your Mother received your last letter but as this is to be a letter of
business we shall first dispatch it before we answer the letter. It is with
regard to John Borlands Bond which as it is heritable security is your
property; Mr Borland has sold the land to a Capt Dikes to whom Borland
must give a proper discharge of all security upon payment of the
money. . . . I shall now copy the directions about the signing which was
sent along with the paper.[46]

This business letter ends with news of people from home and assurance of love from the family, but along with other letters it reveals Agnes Baillie's responsibility for pragmatic family matters. In August 1782, Agnes also negotiated the women's "release" from the desolation of Long Calderwood:

My Dear Brother

I got your last letter yesterday and you see how soon I have answered it; But it is a message from My Mother that makes me in such a hurry, it is to acquaint Dr Hunter that she proposes taking a lodging in Glasgow, for two or three months in spring. For here in winter we are shut out from all society, and live as in a desart [sic]. We have had four long tedious winters of it already, and if it is agreeable to him, for we will do nothing without telling and having his approbation, we would go to town for a month or two in the dead time of the year towards spring. You must tell Dr Hunter soon, because we wait his answer. My Mother forgot to tell you in my last letter, to thank him for the 50, which she received from Mr Hill about a month ago.—Your mother nor us is no way attached to Glasgow but go there because we have most acquaintance for we have few any where, and it is pleasanter than this place [Hamilton].[47]

While Agnes was dealing with financial affairs and a new location for her mother, Dorothea, Joanna was working on her first collection of poems (*Poems: Wherein It is Attempted to Describe Certain Views of Nature and of Rustic Manners, etc.*), to appear in 1790, and probably on an early draft of *Rayner*, deferring the financial affairs to Agnes.[48] In her own supportive way, Agnes Baillie, like Agnes Berry, fulfilled an almost spousal role, taking care of routine business affairs and allowing her sister time to be creative. These differences in expertise might today also be attributed to theories of logical left-brained versus intuitive right-brained individuals.

After several moves, Dorothea, Joanna, and Agnes eventually settled in London to keep house for Matthew until his marriage in 1791, escaping their social and intellectual isolation in Scotland. Their living conditions probably helped make the sisters extremely close. Dunn and Kendrick explain that "the warmth of a close relationship between siblings is a source of strength and love far beyond the early years of childhood," and we know "from the writing of poets and novelists rather than from psychologists" that early relationships are of "immeasurable importance through life."[49] Further, argues Valerie Sanders, "the late eighteenth to the twentieth century produced a succession of literary families whose collaborative relationships generated poems, novels, journals, letters, legends, mysteries, and speculative psychoanalytical responses"; but "the most common configuration of these family groups was the brother-sister pair or trio."[50] In *Double Talk: The Erotics of Male Literary Collaboration,* Wayne Koestenbaum confirms that an entire book could be written on "the history of female (and lesbian) collaboration" as well, focusing on the "woman writer's attempt to absorb the strength of a precursor" or on contemporary collaboration as a "politically fraught act."[51] Koestenbaum agrees that sisterly collaboration is generally more fruitful than male/female collaboration, but he leaves that focus for a future study.

Although Agnes Baillie was Joanna's most constant literary critic in mid-to-later life, brother Matthew Baillie was certainly one of her earliest ones, as she revealed in her autobiographical papers in 1830 about her first attempt at playwriting when she was in her early twenties: "seeing a quantity of white paper lying on the floor . . . it came into my head that one might write something upon it . . . that the <u>something</u> might be a play. . . . and though my Brother did not much like such a bent given to my mind, he bestowed upon it so much hearty & manly praise, that my favorite propensity was fixed for ever."[52] As Dr. Baillie's professional and family life became more and more consuming, however, his wife Sophia Denman Baillie (1771–1845) took over his interest in Joanna's poems and plays, reading every work in its manuscript form. Thus Joanna's "sister" Sophia, as she afterward called her, took her supporting role alongside sibling Agnes.

Dunn and Kendrick argue that the quality of a relationship between siblings is "profoundly affected by the extent to which each child perceives and understands the other's feelings and intentions."[53] As she had been in childhood, Joanna's constant companion in later life was her sister. Although Agnes appears to be less obviously ambitious than her imaginative sister, she had, according to brother Matthew, "a quick ready Understanding, with a good deal of various knowle[d]ge, so as to be much beyond the common level of Women in these respects."[54] And, certainly, Joanna's many references to what Agnes read and did outside the home prove that her sister was equal to her in literary tastes and interests—if not in ambition. There are also many anecdotes about Agnes's acute sense of humor. Through Joanna and in her own right, Agnes met famous writers and thinkers who often dined at the Baillies' house, and she was apparently a closer friend to the famous painter Sir Thomas Lawrence (1769–1830) than Joanna. Agnes's letters, though sparsely scattered through collections of Joanna's, along with Joanna's own accounts, reveal her sister's interest in nonfiction and classical as well as contemporary literature. And Baillie mentions her in almost every one of her hundreds of letters. Matthew Baillie later summed up the situation in these terms: "The Characters of both [Agnes and Joanna] are most highly respectable, and their Society has been more courted than in proportion to their situation in the world."[55]

To the extent that the Berry and Baillie sisters moved in similar social circles and were acquainted with many of the same people, they were also close friends. It was Mary Berry to whom Joanna Baillie sent her first anonymous volume of plays in 1798, and Mary wrote excitedly to her friend Mrs. Cholmeley (d. 1810) in 1799 as follows:

> Do you remember my speaking to you in high terms of a series of plays upon the passions of the human mind, which had been sent to me last winter by the author? I talked to everybody else in the same terms of them at the time, anxiously enquiring for the author; but nobody knew them, nobody cared for them, nobody would listen to me; and at last I unwillingly held my tongue, for fear it should be supposed that I thought highly of them only because they had been sent to me. This winter the first question upon everybody's lips is, "Have you read the series of plays?"[56]

On March 21, 1799, she continued: "I am delighted you like 'Basil,' with whom and with his admirable friend I am in love. Nothing to me can be more affecting than the end of that play."[57] And on October 14, 1801, Baillie sent Mary Berry a "plain and simple Prologue of no pretensions, but such I hope as you will not dislike" for *Fashionable Friends*.[58] The two writers shared a professional and personal relationship that spanned decades. Furthermore, theirs might very well have been what Elfenbein calls a "fashionable friendship," a relationship that created "a problem only for women whose lives had to be dominated by men."[59]

Nevertheless, on Christmas Day 1805 Baillie replied objectively to Berry's letter about a possible pending marriage: "You have said to a certain Gentleman of Yorkshire," wrote Baillie, "that you would marry him to morrow, were it not that the different habits of life you have each acquired are not suited to make you live comfortably together."[60] Marriage for Berry, Baillie understood, would be giving up hard-fought independence, yet she perceived that Berry was avoiding her real apprehensions. Baillie continued:

> Let me ask you as a friend if you have really & seriously consider'd w[h]ether these same habits be actually as weighty an objection as you have represented them. You are not I should think of a very unaccommodating disposition; you have not been accustom'd to have every thing

your own way. . . . Such a man as you would marry to morrow . . . must
have many good qualities, and should not be lightly given up.

Encouraging her friend to consider seriously a decision that would
so change her life, but probably make it more financially secure,
Baillie added a personal conviction: "every single woman, who is to
remain so, has great pride in seeing such a woman as you of her
Sister hood, and cannot possibly see you quitting the ranks but with
considerable regret." Anxious about giving such advice, Baillie then
asked what their mutual friend Anne Damer had said about the matter. It is doubtful that Anne Damer, who was at the time making
some editorial suggestions to Baillie's *The Family Legend,* was any
more encouraging than Baillie, for gossips had once accused her of
being Berry's lover. In fact, when Mary Berry was engaged to General O'Hara (1740–1802) in 1795, to whom she alludes in her journals but never married, Anne Damer wrote on September 1, 1795:

> I could have wished to have known (and one day I shall) more of
> O'Hara's conversation. Had he mentioned me, you would have told me,
> but he may think me a disadvantage to you and imagine that we live
> more constantly together than alas! we do. Or he may suppose (for he
> knows me not) that I endeavour to influence you against marrying think-
> ing it probable that in other circumstances I might see you less, and
> ideas of liberty, or what is called liberty, and that, because I have re-
> mained single myself, I think it a fine thing so to do in general.[61]

Berry did not marry O'Hara, her Yorkshire gentleman nor, like the
Baillie sisters, any other gentleman, though both she and Agnes suffered broken engagements.[62] Burroughs contends, however, that
Mary Berry was unable "to regard her social theater as substantive
and productive" and *did* intend to marry at some time if she could
be assured of a union of "intellectual beings" with common goals—
not likely for a woman in the early nineteenth century.[63] Baillie
would have settled for no less either. Around 1810, with Baillie's
Family Legend being performed in Edinburgh, she was inviting the
Berry sisters and Mrs. Damer to come for a walk upon Hampstead
Heath with her and Agnes.[64]

These talented women led, in many ways, very "modern" lives.
Their independence was not only a result of financial security but of
their aestheticism and personality as well. Each personality revealed
what Christine Downing calls an androgynous "feminine energy"
which is ultimately a "transformative energy."[65] Moreover, according to Jungian psychology, both introversion and extraversion are
present in every personality: "To the extent that the conscious adap-

tation moves toward one, the other operates in a compensatory fashion, as part of and through the unconscious."[66] How well an individual equalizes his/her fear of the outer and inner worlds determines a sort of "normalcy" in society. According to analytical psychology,

> the ideally adapted and contented person, free of problems, can be a rather dull, uninteresting and uncreative type. It does not follow, of course, that neurotic or psychotic traits are in themselves prerequisites of creativity, as is sometimes believed. Creativity is not the result of neurotic or psychotic tendencies, but of an individual's *ability to transcend them,* to direct the tendencies toward chaos into consciously accessible channels by shaping them into some sort of concrete expression of their intrinsic meaning.[67]

Perhaps Mary Berry and Joanna Baillie chose writing as a way to transcend what Elfenbein calls "a world of sober bourgeois moralism."[68] As for their more silent sisters, "some theorists," writes Judith Rich Harris, "have proposed that the differences between siblings result from the effects they have on each other, rather than from the way they are treated by their parents."[69] This may be the most plausible of all the behavioral theories. While we know little about the Berry sisters as children, we do know that Joanna Baillie was a gregarious ten-year-old, playing pranks, acting out parts, and writing verses, for her mother scolded that she should at that age act the part of a young lady and "give up making verses."[70] Mrs. Baillie's artistic child obeyed for only a short while, and Agnes remained the more restrained child. Mary Berry must have been much like her friend Joanna in temperament.

That Mary Berry and Joanna Baillie shared creative interests that made them important writers of the Romantic period is revealed in their correspondence and in their published works. That they were very different from their more silent sisters is also evident in their more personal correspondence. That their success was a result of dominant personality traits, birth order, or parental/sibling loss is not so clear. These potential explanations, however, add to an analysis of how creative genius develops in general and how it may have manifested itself in Mary Berry and Joanna Baillie and in other writing sisters as well. As in life, the Berry and Baillie sisters were even similar in death: Joanna Baillie died on February 23, 1851, followed by her friend Mary Berry in 1852, both writers nearing 90. Agnes Berry died that same year. Agnes Baillie lived until April 27, 1861, when she expired at 101 years of age.

NOTES

1. Judy Dunn and Robert Plomin, *Separate Lives: Why Siblings Are So Different* (New York: Basic Books Division of Harper Collins, 1990), 151.

2. Dean Keith Simonton, *Origins of Genius: Darwinian Perspectives on Creativity* (Oxford: Oxford University Press, 1999), 2.

3. Ibid., 6.

4. Ibid., 90–91. These traits include the following: (1) an array of intellectual, cultural, and aesthetic interests; (2) openness to novel, complex, and ambiguous stimuli in surroundings; (3) capability for "defocused attention," allowing the mind to attend to more than one idea or stimulus at one time; (4) cognitive and behavioral flexibility and ability to "incubate" a project; (5) introversion (Words-worth said that Newton had "a mind forever / Voyaging through strange seas of thought, alone"); and (6) independence, autonomy, unconventionality.

5. Ibid., 115–16.

6. Ibid., 137.

7. Nancy L. Segal, *Entwined Lives: Twins and What They Tell Us About Human Behavior* (New York: Dutton, 1999), 183. A biography by P. O. Whitmer (*The Inner Elvis*, 1996) analyzes Elvis Presley's early loss of his twin brother, Jesse, for example, to explain his survivor guilt and drive toward individuality (174).

8. Dunn and Plomin, *Separate Lives*, 6–7.

9. Auerbach, *Communities of Women*, 10–11.

10. Ibid., 26.

11. Judy Dunn and Carol Kendrick, *Siblings: Love, Envy, and Understanding* (Cambridge, MA: Harvard University Press, 1982), 158.

12. Lewis Melville [pseud.], *The Berry Papers, Being The Correspondence Hitherto Unpublished of Mary and Agnes Berry (1763–1852)* (London: John Lane, 1914), 4. Most of the following biographical information on the Berrys comes from this source.

13. Ibid., 9.

14. Mary Berry, *Extracts of the Journals and Correspondence of Miss Berry, from the year 1783 to 1852*, ed. Lady Theresa Lewis, 3 vols. (London: Longmans, Green, 1865), 1:5.

15. Ibid., 1:6.

16. Ibid., 1:7.

17. Ibid., 1:12.

18. Ian Haywood, "Thackeray, Mary Berry, and *The Four Georges*," *Notes and Queries* 30, no. 4 (1983): 299. Haywood quotes from William Thackeray's *The English Humourists of the Eighteenth Century: The Four Georges, Etc.* (1904), 209.

19. Ibid., 299.

20. The Berrys' friend Kate Perry writes that at one dinner party "Miss Berry astonished us all by saying, she had never read Jane Austen's novels until lately, when someone had lent them to her. But she could not get on with them; they were totally uninteresting to her—long-drawn-out details of very ordinary people. . . . 'Thackeray and Balzac write with great minuteness,' she added, 'but do so with a brilliant pen'" (Melville, *Berry Papers*, 438).

21. Virginia Surtees, ed., *The Grace of Friendship: Horace Walpole and the Misses Berry* (Norwich, Great Britain: Michael Russell, 1995), 2.

22. Ibid.

23. Berry, *Extracts of the Journals*, 1:151.

24. Horace Walpole, *Miscellaneous Antiquities; or, A Collection of Curious Papers: Ei-*

ther republished from SCARCE *Tracts, or now first printed from* ORIGINAL *MSS.* (Strawberry Hill: Printed by Thomas Kirgate, 1772).

25. Surtees, *Grace of Friendship,* 11–12.

26. Walpole died in March 1797, leaving a generous amount to the Berry sisters. "To them he left Little Strawberry House, its grounds and furniture and to each the interest for life of £4,000. In addition to these bequests he left a wooden box marked with an 'O' to Mr Berry, containing his literary papers, published and unpublished, for a new edition of all his works. It was well understood that Mary, in fact, would be the editor. For a year she laboured at her task, scrupulous and persevering, till in 1798 the *Works of Horace Walpole, Earl of Orford,* were published in five volumes. In the next century she edited and published further letters of Walpole as well as works of her own" (ibid., 223). Walpole often fondly called the Berry sisters his "wives."

27. Ibid., 2.

28. See, Virginia Blain, Patricia Clements, and Isobel Grundy, eds., *The Feminist Companion to Literature in English: Women Writers from the Middle Ages to the Present* (London: B. T. Batsford, 1990), 88; and Paul Schlueter and June Schlueter, *An Encyclopedia of British Women Writers* (New York: Garland, 1988), 36–38. Also see Melville, *Berry Papers.*

29. See Andrew Elfenbein, "Lesbian Aestheticism on the Eighteenth-Century Stage," *Eighteenth-Century Life* 25, no. 1 (2001): 1–16.

30. Ibid., 2.

31. Ibid., 10.

32. Ibid.

33. Catherine B. Burroughs, *Closet Stages: Joanna Baillie and the Theater Theory of British Romantic Women Writers* (Philadelphia: University of Pennsylvania Press, 1997), 67.

34. Ibid., 67–68.

35. Melville, *Berry Papers,* 440.

36. Marie de Vichy Chamrond, Marquise du Deffand, was born in 1697 in Burgundy and married the Marquis de Deffand in 1718, from whom she was later separated. Her letters, of significant historical value, were mostly in the possession of Horace Walpole and were edited and annotated by Berry after his death.

37. Rachel Lady Russell's letters were in the hands of the Duke of Devonshire, who gave them to Berry for selection and publication. Schlueter and Schlueter report that Baillie described *Lady Russell* as an "edifying example to the young women of the day, who consider religion too exclusively connected with mystery" (37).

38. Mary Berry, *A Comparative View Of The Social Life Of England And France, From The Restoration Of Charles The Second, To The French Revolution* (London: Longman, Rees, Orme, Brown, and Green, 1828), 202.

39. Berry, *Extracts of the Journals,* 1:229–30.

40. Melville, *Berry Papers,* 262–63.

41. Apparently, when Maria Edgeworth visited the sisters in 1813, she found the Berrys' house and gatherings "without any comparison the most agreeable" she had seen in town and "quite like French society"; but when she returned in 1819, although she still found the sisters dashing and fashionable, they were without the "well bred low French voices—*Moi je dis* in every tone." Quoted in Surtees, *Grace of Friendship,* 229n.

42. In addition to invaluable information in the Hunterian Museum at the University of Glasgow (William Hunter) and the Hunterian Museum at the Royal College of Surgeons (John Hunter), important Hunter/Baillie biographies include the

following: Jessie Dobson, *John Hunter* (Edinburgh: Livingstone, 1969); J. Kobler, *The Reluctant Surgeon: A Biography of John Hunter* (New York: Doubleday, 1960); G. R. Mather, *Two Great Scotsmen, The Brothers William and John Hunter* (Glasgow: James Maclehose and Sons, 1893); G. C. Peachey, *A Memoir of William and John Hunter* (Plymouth: William Brendon and Son, 1924). Throughout this essay, I quote from Joanna Baillie's letters, now published in *The Collected Letters of Joanna Baillie,* ed. Judith Bailey Slagle, 2 vols. (Madison, WI: Fairleigh Dickinson University Press, 1999). Quotes are identified herein as *Letters* and also by library manuscript notation.

43. Royal College of Surgeons of England (RCS), MS0014/3/56c; Baillie, *Letters,* 3.

44. RCS, MS0014/12/59; Baillie, *Letters,* 174. The Baillies' friend Lucy Aikin's *Memoirs of the Court of Charles I* appeared in 1833.

45. Mitchell Library (Glasgow), Cowie Collection, MS 215c; Baillie, *Letters,* 516.

46. RCS, MS0014/3/22. Reproduced by kind permission of the President and Council of the Royal College of Surgeons of England.

47. Ibid., MS0014/3/33. Reproduced by kind permission of the President and Council of the Royal College of Surgeons of England.

48. Baillie relates in her memoirs that before publishing *Poems* in 1790, she had at least two "failed" attempts at drama with *Rayner.* Wellcome Institute for the History of Medicine (WI) MS 5613/68/1–6; and Slagle, *Joanna Baillie,* 60–61. Anonymous *Poems: Wherein It is Attempted to Describe Certain Views of Nature and of Rustic Manners, etc.,* appeared in 1790.

49. Dunn and Kendrick, *Siblings,* 221.

50. Valerie Sanders, *The Brother-Sister Culture in Nineteenth-Century Literature: From Austen to Woolf* (Basingstoke: Palgrave, 2002), 32.

51. Wayne Koestenbaum, *Double Talk: The Erotics of Male Literary Collaboration* (New York: Routledge, 1989), 13. Koestenbaum explains that if his study included partnerships between women, he might include collaborators such as the Brontës and contemporary women writers but does not do so for the sake of brevity.

52. RCS, MS0014/3/56c; Baillie, *Letters,* 8.

53. Dunn and Kendrick, *Siblings,* 100.

54. See both Franco Crainz, *The Life and Works of Matthew Baillie, MD, FRS, L&E, FRCP, etc. (1761–1823)* (Santa Palomba, Italy: PelitiAssociati, 1995); and Slagle, *Life,* 49.

55. See Crainz, *Matthew Baillie;* Slagle, *Life.*

56. Berry, *Extracts of the Journals,* 2:88.

57. Ibid., 2:90.

58. Ibid., 2:117.

59. Elfenbein, "Lesbian Aestheticism," 13.

60. WI MS 5616/64; Baillie, *Letters,* 156–57. The following two quotes are also taken from this manuscript letter.

61. Melville, *Berry Papers,* 140–41.

62. Mary Berry seems to have broken her engagement with Gen. O'Hara over a series of misunderstandings, and her letters indicate that she was still in love with him years later. Agnes Berry was engaged to marry her cousin Col. Robert Ferguson in 1804, but the engagement was broken off, possibly because of his father's opposition (ibid., 286–87).

63. Burroughs, *Closet Stages,* 70.

64. RCS, MS0014/3/70; Baillie, *Letters,* 163–64.

65. Christine Downing, *The Goddess: Mythological Images of the Feminine* (New York: Crossroad, 1988), 11.

66. See Edward C. Whitmont, *The Symbolic Quest: Basic Concepts of Analytical Psychology* (Princeton: Princeton University Press, 1969), 140.

67. Ibid., 293.

68. Elfenbein, "Lesbian Aestheticism," 2.

69. Judith Rich Harris, "Why Can't Birth Order Account for the Differences Between Siblings?," September 3, 2001, http://xchar.home.att.net/tna/birth-order/sibdiff.htm.

70. Slagle, *Life*, 57.

II
Friends and Companions

II
Facts and Suppositions

A Woman of Extraordinary Merit: Catherine Bovey of Flaxley Abbey, Gloucestershire

Jessica Munns and Penny Richards

THIS TERM—"EXTRAORDINARY MERIT"—IS USED BY GEORGE BALLARD (CA. 1706–55) to describe Catherine Bovey[1] (1669–1727) in his *Memoirs of Several Ladies of Great Britain who have been Celebrated for their Writing or Skill in the Learned Languages, Arts, and Sciences* (1752).[2] He is "not positively assured that this worthy gentlewoman was either a linguist or a writer," but includes her because of her "great genius and good judgment improved by reading the finest authors, and the wit and elegance of her conversation which has been so much admired and celebrated by the best judges."[3] At present, Catherine Bovey is relatively unknown; she was, however, admired by contemporaries, such as Sir Richard Steele (1672–1729) and Delarivier Manley (ca. 1670–1724) for her manners, beauty, and style of life. In the years following her death, she was memorialized for her benevolence and virtues, both in Westminster Abbey and in the chapel in Flaxley Abbey, and a late Victorian descendant wrote a laudatory biography.[4] Papers from Flaxley Abbey (her Gloucestershire home), many of which refer to Catherine Bovey, have been deposited at the Gloucestershire Archives.[5] These papers include a number of letters signed "Catherine Bovey," as well as letters addressed to her, and are pasted into a letter-book compiled for the family in 1915. The letters are written in an educated hand and are pleasant and easy to read. Given the paucity of late seventeenth-century letters by men or women, this series of letters represents a very valuable collection. The letters helpfully augment the somewhat formulaic contemporary and later accounts, allowing us to see Catherine Bovey as an energetic and capable estate manager moving easily between provincial and metropolitan life.[6]

Catherine Bovey was the daughter of a wealthy, naturalized Amsterdam merchant living in London, John Riches (1628–1718), and she was the sole heir of his great wealth.[7] The Dutch mercantile colony in London, where Riches and his daughter lived, was greatly

augmented in the late sixteenth century by the persecutions of Protestants, which occurred when the Duke of Alva reasserted Philip II's
rule in the Netherlands in 1576. The Dutch colony in England was
both prosperous and endogamous. Hence, Catherine was married
in 1684 at the age of fifteen to William Bovey (1657–92), her elder
by some thirteen years, who was descended from a family of wealthy
Dutch merchants whose origins in England can be traced back to
1647 at Flaxley Abbey. In 1692, when she was twenty-two, Catherine
Bovey was left widowed and childless by her husband's "rake's progress," though presumably not heartbroken.[8] Some twenty years
later, when Sir Robert Atkyns (1647–1711) wrote *The Ancient and
Present State of Glostershire* (1712), an account of his "Neighbours and
Countrymen," he described Catherine Bovey as "the present Lady
of the Mannor. She hath an handsome House and pleasant Gardens,
and a great Estate."[9] It is notable that Bovey is the only female land-
holder in his account.[10] The estate included furnaces and forges for
iron casting, which registers its connection with the Forest of Dean
industries; indeed, she was the patroness of the church of Flaxley in
the Forest of Dean, a parish "8 miles in *compass*" and comprised "of
Pasture, Arable, and Woods,"[11] along with forty houses with about
two hundred inhabitants.

The Boveys' near neighbors were the Colchesters at Westbury
Court: they were local county gentry and her good friend, John Maynard Colchester (1664–1715), had married in 1690 a woman of very
similar mercantile social origins, Jane daughter of Edward Clarke
who became Lord Mayor of London in 1696.[12] Colchester used his
wife's large dowry to create the Dutch water garden at Westbury between 1696 and 1704. The Dutch artist John Kip (1653–1722) made
engravings of both Westbury and Flaxley; his Westbury engraving
shows canals and Dutch topiary. The tall pavilion, probably designed
by a Dutch architect, was intended to command a view over the
Bovey lands. Like Westbury, the gardens at Flaxley had the compart-
mented design and long canal typical of the distinctive Dutch style.

William Bovey's will left money to his wife specifically for the com-
pletion of garden work, and it is possible that she was involved in the
design of the gardens in both estates.[13] It is relevant to note that in
1688 the Dutch prince, William of Orange (1650–1702), successfully
ousted James II (1633–1701), giving the Dutch interest in England
a considerable boost. In the years that followed, laying out gardens
in the Dutch manner, including water gardens, was both fashionable
and politic (See ill. on p. 103).

Bovey was, however, to be remarked upon by her contemporaries
not so much for her garden innovations as for her decision not to

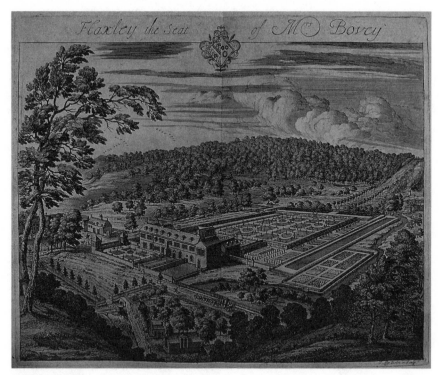

John Kip's view of Flaxley Abbey. Courtesy of Bristol University Special Collections. Photograph by Ann Pethers.

remarry after her husband's death. Instead, she lived as a single woman with her friend and distant relative Mary Pope, who had joined the household during William Bovey's lifetime and lived with her until the end of Catherine Bovey's life. A postscript in Mary Pope's hand to the conclusion of a letter from Catherine from her house in Duke's Street, Westminster, to her estate manager at Flaxley, Joseph Bate, contains instructions to the housekeeper on making primrose oil ointments.[14] As Bovey's letter is filled with instructions regarding large-scale timbering projects in the Forest of Dean, Pope's postscript is suggestive of a division of labor between Catherine Bovey and herself, with Bovey taking the more authoritative and managerial role. The Westminster Abbey monument to Catherine Bovey refers to "Mrs. Pope who lived with her near 40 years in perfect friendship." The Three Choirs Festival Anniversary sermon, preached by the Reverend Peter Senhouse in 1727 and published in Oxford, Gloucester, and London in the following year, was dedicated to Mary Pope.[15] This dedication emphasizes the role of

Catherine Bovey as an active patroness of the Three Choirs Festival and the charitable activities associated with it, but it also confirms Mrs. Pope as the "*long and well-try'd Friend*" of Catherine Bovey.[16] Mrs. Pope's piety and goodness are being expressed in a form that makes her religious faith indistinguishable from her personal regard for Mrs. Bovey:

> And it is not the least Article of her Praise, that she implicitly bequeathed the whole Remainder of her great Substance to pious Uses, by committing it to the Hands of her long and well-try'd Friend Mrs. Pope. You have given the World a convincing Evidence, that you inherit not only the Fortune, but the Spirit of this great and good Woman; by building a beautiful Church at the Place of her Burial, to be as a lasting and most expressive Monument of her, and (I might have Leave to add) your own Piety and Goodness.[17]

It is, therefore, not surprising that, although Catherine Bovey had many male Bovey and Riches relatives alive in her last years, she had named her friend, Mary Pope, as the executrix of her will.

Close female friendship in rural retirement was a well-established trope by the late seventeenth century, particularly celebrated in the poetry of Anne Finch, Countess of Winchilsea (1661–1720), published in 1712. As Lillian Faderman points out, "these Renaissance and seventeenth-century views of romantic friendship were inherited by the eighteenth century. . . . Men of the eighteenth century saw no reason for concern when so many women expressed love and eternal devotion to their women friends."[18] Certainly, Bovey's single state and nearly forty years of friendship and cohabitation with Mary Pope was publicly acknowledged and respected. Nonetheless, an attractive, young, and wealthy widow was generally expected to remarry. However, Bovey's decision to remain single and live with a female companion was conducted in such a way as to be acceptable and not defiant of prevailing norms. Bovey did not have to brave relatives and "elope" like Eleanor Butler (1739–1829) and Sarah Ponsonby (1755–1831) later on in the century. As the heroine of Jane Austen's *Emma* (1816) was to say at a later date (even if she subsequently changed her mind about marrying), no one can laugh at a rich lady who chooses to remain single: "Fortune I do not want; employment I do not want; consequence I do not want . . . It is poverty alone which makes celibacy contemptible to a generous public! A single woman, with a very narrow income, must be a ridiculous, disagreeable, old maid! . . . But a single woman, of good fortune, is always respectable."[19]

Catherine Bovey clearly fell into the happier latter category, and her single life as a widow was depicted by contemporaries and in her funerary memorials as exemplary.

However, Bovey's decision not to remarry, allied with her life of public charitable activity, did make her remarkable to her contemporaries. In the third volume of *The New Atalantis, Memoirs of Europe towards the Close of the Eighth Century* (1710), Delarivier Manley offers an uncharacteristically eulogistic account in her description of Catherine Bovey and a more characteristic condemnation in her description of William Bovey. According to Manley, "their years were as unequal as their Deserts. His Education . . . together with a certain Moroseness of Temper, made him rather a rigid Master, than a tender Consort."[20] Manley had just described Catherine Bovey as "one of those lofty, black, and lasting Beauties, that strikes with reverence, and yet delight; there is no feature in her Face, nor any thing in her Person, Air and Manner, that cou'd be exchang'd for any others, and she not Prove a loser."[21] Manley is equally impressed by her mental and moral qualities: "Then as to her Mind, and Conduct, her Judgment, her Sense, her Stedfastness, her Reading, her Wit, and Conversation, they are admirable . . . Her Sense so solid and perspicuous . . . In short, she knows all that a Man can know, without despising what as a Woman, she shou'd not be ignorant of."[22] Bovey's refusal to remarry, despite her charms of person, mind, and estate, are referred to with approval when Manley comments that at her husband's death Bovey was "very young, very handsome, very rich, but very wise; The three former Qualifications drew Crowds of Adorers, the latter as dexterously dispers'd 'em."[23]

Against Manley's depiction of an unhappy married life, however, one must balance William Bovey's will, which left his wife as his sole executrix and made provision for her life occupancy of Flaxley Abbey. Mary Pope, who had lived with the couple, was also the beneficiary of a bequest in his will. Both Catherine and William Bovey were friends with the most notable nonjurors of the day, in their region, such as Dr. Robert Frampton (1622–1708), the deprived Bishop of Gloucester, and Dr. George Hickes (1642–1715), the deprived Dean of Worcester. It would seem, therefore, that they had at least shared political and religious convictions. Catherine Bovey's "high flying" sympathies may explain Manley's interest and favorable account of her.

There is a tradition that Catherine Bovey's refusal to remarry is referred to by Sir Richard Steele in the Sir Roger de Coverley papers in the *Spectator* (1711). The nineteenth-century chronicler of events and people in the Forest of Dean, the Reverend H. G. Nicholls, draws attention to this tradition.[24] Certainly, Sir Roger's estate is in the neighboring county of Worcestershire, and he is described as remaining a bachelor "by reason he was crossed in love by a perverse beautiful widow of the next country to him" (*Spectator* 2, 1711).[25] Specifically, Sir Roger first met this beauty when presiding as sheriff of the county at a court hearing regarding the widow's dower, which was being contested by one of her husband's relatives (*Spectator* 113, 1711). In 1692 the Bovey inheritance was not without its complications with many Bovey relatives with an interest in the estates. Sir Roger goes on to describe his widow as a "desperate scholar," whose great learning constantly leaves him speechless, and, as we have seen, intelligence, wide reading, and good conversation are characteristics attributed to Catherine Bovey by both Ballard and Manley. Sir Roger also refers to the widow's love of music, and she is said to "sing excellently" (ibid.). Catherine Bovey was later to help found the Three Choirs Festival in 1718, and this involvement may indicate an early love of music and singing, which was an elegant female accomplishment.

Another striking feature of Sir Roger's description of his willful widow is his reference to her as "a reading lady . . . far gone in the pleasures of friendship." In paper 113, there are also references to the widow's confidante, who he feels is overpresent, malicious, and an impediment to his courtship—or the courtship of the widow by other men. While this might be felt to be impolite toward Bovey's friend, Mary Pope, the comments, filtered as they are through Sir Roger's amiable absurdity, can also be read as a kind of backhanded compliment, sketching in as they do the picture of a pair of lively and intelligent ladies who are not above poking fun at a booby country squire.

Whether or not Catherine Bovey was the model for Sir Roger's great love, there is no doubt as to her friendship with Sir Richard Steele. Nicholls asserts that Richard Steele stayed at Flaxley Abbey overnight fairly regularly on the way between London and his house in Carmarthanshire, and that Joseph Addison (1672–1719) also visited.[26] Steele was also a friend—and subsequent enemy—of Delarivier Manley.[27] Their assessments of Bovey's virtues are remarkably similar: perhaps Steele drew on Manley's *Memoirs of Europe,* or their assessments were those generally agreed upon, and also confirmed in conversation with each other. Manley remarks of "Porcia" that "she has desir'd to live unknown, and has confin'd herself to a narrow Part of it [Manley's fictional Eastern Empire] wisely declining all publick Assemblies, she is contented to possess her Soul in Tranquility and Freedom at Home."[28] Steele paid similar tribute to Catherine Bovey's life of retirement when he dedicated volume 2 of *The Ladies Library* (1714) to her:

> Instead of Assemblies and Conversations, Books and Solitude have been your Choice, and you have gone on in the Study of what you should be, rather than attended to the Celebration of what you are. Thus with the Charms of the fairest of your own Sex, and Knowledge not inferior to the more Learned of Ours, a Closet, a Bower, or some Beauteous Scene of rural Nature, has constantly robbed the World of a Lady's Appearance, who was never beheld without Gladness to her Visitants, not ever admired without Pain to Herself.[29]

The first volume of *The Ladies Library* is dedicated to Juliana, Dowager Countess of Burlington (1672–1750), celebrated in his dedication as a wife and, above all, mother. The third volume is dedicated to his own wife, Mary (1678–1718), while the volume dedicated to Bovey stresses the role of the widow. The frontispiece to volume 2 of *The Ladies Library* depicts a lovely lady in widow's weeds, her hand on a book, while in the liminal space of a doorway between the outside world and the widow's interior space, three well-dressed gentlemen look in at her. (See ill. on p. 108).

This image may well represent a portrait of Catherine Bovey, if not literally, figuratively. In the illustration, the widow clearly turns *away* from the world. However, in this section, Steele stresses not merely the obligation of retirement and solitude for the widow but also insists that when the immediate period of mourning is over if the widow "has less of *Martha*'s care of *serving* she is then at Liberty to choose *Mary*'s Part; she has her Time and her Fortune at her own Command, And consequently may much more abound in the Works both of *Piety* and *Charity*."[30] As we shall see, these lines have not only a general application for all widows of some wealth but also seem peculiarly appropriate to Catherine Bovey, whose long widowhood was strongly characterized by consistent acts of benevolence. As Sean Gill has noted, "Richard Steele claimed that Charity Schools were the greatest examples of public spiritedness of which his age could boast, and that their supporters were moved by Christian piety and benevolence as well as by the more prudential social considerations."[31]

Institutions such as the Society for the Reformation of Manners, founded in 1692, and the Society for the Propagation of Christian Knowledge (SPCK), founded in 1698/99, were signs of the times, providing spaces and places quite specifically for female involvement in the works of practical piety. Catherine Bovey was a supporter of both these societies, as was Maynard Colchester. A

VOL: 2.   Lud. Du Guernier inv. et Sculp.

Frontispiece to vol. 2, Richard Steele, ed., *The Ladies Library*, 5th ed., 3 vols. London: J. and R. Tonson, 1739 (Courtesy of the Bodleian Library, University of Oxford, vet.A4 fol. 612/2.)

founding member of the SPCK, he believed strongly in the value of the Christian knowledge imparted by charity schools, maintaining several at his own expense.[32] Bovey and Colchester seem to have shared not only neighborly proximity but a common range of Christian charitable concerns, endowing distinctly similar charities and institutions. A major concern of the SPCK was education, through the medium of charity schools, for girls as well as boys, so that the poor of both sexes might be enabled and encouraged to read the Bible. Catherine Bovey was also a keen sponsor of the charity school movement, supporting a school in Flaxley for thirty children.[33] (Later in the century, 60 percent of the charity schools in the county of Gloucestershire were fully funded.) These activities are acknowledged on the monument to Catherine Bovey in the chapel at Flaxley Abbey, which comments on her generosity

> in frequent distribution to the poor, and especially to the Charity schools round about the countrey; in relieving those in prison, and delivering many out of it; in contributing to the Churches of English Establishment Abroad, as well as aiding several at Home; in clothing and feeding indigent neighbours, and teaching their Children, some of them every Sunday by turns She entertain'd at her House and condescended to examine them her self.[34]

Founding Christian schools and teaching children to know their catechism were generally regarded as valuable services to Christian society, as well as being essential planks in the SPCK program. In addition to local educational charities, the Flaxley and Westminster memorials note that Bovey left £400 to the charity school in the parish of Southwark, as well as £500 to the Grey Coat Hospital school at St. Margaret's Westminster—both of which were SPCK-supported foundations. The same sum of £500 was left to the Blue Coat Hospital school in Westminster. St. Margaret's, it is perhaps worth noting, was a fashionable venue for sermons in the early eighteenth century. For instance, a charity sermon of ca.1710 collected the sum of £163.15s.7d. Bovey also left the very considerable sum of £1,200 to "augment the Living" of Christchurch, Southwark.

Bovey's Flaxley memorial, by recording that she relieved "those in prison" as well as "delivering many out of it," bears witness to her strong sympathy for another major aim of the SPCK in its early years: the release from prison of poor debtors. This was minuted in the annual report of 1706, and money was regularly donated for this purpose, with the numbers released duly noted. Another stated SPCK aim was to provide funds for apprenticing children, mainly boys, and the Flaxley memorial mentions Bovey's bequest of £400 in perpetuity "to put out poor Children Apprentices."

Overseas activities were also kept in view. The SPCK was originally associated with the Society for the Propagation of the Gospel in Foreign Parts, and ultimately absorbed it. A major part of SPCK work in the eighteenth and nineteenth centuries was missionary work in the growing area of the British Empire—their first translation of the Bible into a foreign language being a translation into Tamil in 1712. Again, Bovey's Flaxley memorial records that she bequeathed £500 toward founding a college in the Island of Bermudas. Bovey was a supporter of George Berkeley (1685–1753),[35] whose plan to found Christian colleges overseas was outlined in his 1724 sermon, *Proposal for the Better Supplying of Churches in our Foreign Plantations and Converting the Savage Americans to Christianity by a College to be Erected in the Summer Islands, otherwise called the Isles of Bermuda.*[36] Berkeley moved to America in pursuit of this project in 1728, having been promised £20,000 (which never materialized) by the British government. Bovey's bequest, therefore, was made at the very height of the excitement over the project and at a point when founding a college in the Bermudas still seemed possible. Berkeley, in fact, was not to give up the idea until 1731 when he was informed that the large governmental grant would not be forthcoming.[37] Lady Elizabeth Hastings (1682–1739), the Aspasia of *Tatler* paper 63, also gave £500 to the project, together with Catherine Bovey, Mary Astell (1666–1731), and Elizabeth Elstob (1683–1756), and formed a group of learned ladies associated with Dr. George Hickes. He heaps his praises on Catherine, calling her "*Præstantissima & honestissima matrona*" (a most outstanding and virtuous matron) and "*Angliæ* nostræ *Hypatia Christiana*" (an English Christian Hypatia).[38] It is significant that Hickes proceeds from defining her moral worth to acknowledging a unique combination of piety and intellect: she is not just a local benefactress, but a national treasure.

It is worth noting that these schemes and societies are very much the work of a group of friends who share convictions with regard to charitable Christian work locally, nationally, and in the colonies. Despite her nonjuring sympathies, Catherine Bovey's involvement with these benevolent activities, as well as her careful accounting,[39] makes her an early exemplar of the very type of Whig memorably described by J. H. Plumb in *The First Four Georges:*

> They wanted order, decency, thrift, which they knew well enough were the concomitants of success and prosperity. And they looked for reform from both above and below. They belonged to all the movements which

encouraged it. They became ardent members of the Society for the Reformation of Manners of the Lower Orders; they worked for the repression of wakes, fairs, cockfighting, and bull-baiting; they founded schools; endowed musical festivals; hospitals and orphanages bore their names.[40]

These public-spirited activities were enjoyed by women as much as by men; Ingrid Tague reminds us: "*The Spectator,* for instance, stressed its goal of instructing not just men but women, teaching the latter 'all the becoming Duties of Virginity, Marriage, and Widowhood.'"[41]

Many of the public aspects of Bovey's life have an institutional and charitable character, insofar as her activities were carried out in conjunction with societies and groups associated with the Anglican establishment. Amanda Vickery, writing about women's lives in Georgian England, notes that "the institutionalization of fashionable benevolence constructed altogether new arenas for the expression of female conviviality and officiousness."[42] As we can see, the framework for such fashionable female benevolence and conviviality (perhaps officiousness, as well) was moving into place in the last years of the seventeenth century and was able to provide a pattern of life for Catherine Bovey and her companion Mary Pope. Many other women at this time also found places for public activity in these early-formed societies and within the ample shade of the Anglican establishment. However, it is clear that Bovey was especially well-placed to lead a life of metropolitan and provincial sociability, combined with practical Christian action: the two essential elements were her great wealth and her widowhood. Bovey, as we have seen, divided her life between London, which of course offered many venues for respectable conviviality, and Gloucestershire. Her summers in Flaxley need not be regarded as entirely "rural" and separate from her London interests and friends. In *A Tour Through the Whole Island of Great Britain,* which first appeared in three volumes between 1724–26, Daniel Defoe (ca. 1660–1731) describes the regions around Gloucester as "fertile, rich country," and Gloucester as an "ancient middling city, tolerably built, but not fine."[43] Nevertheless, Gloucester had a bowling green and a walk by the castle used by the local notables and gentry from 1680 onward, and, by the 1720s at least, Gloucester was a relatively lively place. In addition, by the 1720s there were regular balls and assemblies at Tolsey Market House, as well as race meetings, and from 1718 onward there was a scientific society, lectures, and exhibitions, and a musical club whose regular meetings fed into the foundation of the Three Choirs Festival, which was very warmly supported by the local gentry, and, as we have noted, by Catherine Bovey.

Frances Harris's biography of Sarah, Duchess of Marlborough (1660–1744); Amanda Foreman's biography of Georgiana, the fifth Duchess of Devonshire (1757–1806); and Stella Tillyard's study of the Lennox sisters have increased our knowledge about the "great" ladies of the eighteenth century.[44] Equally, Amanda Vickery's *The Gentleman's Daughter* has provided fascinating material on the very outward-reaching lives of women of the relatively modest gentry, who were not merely mistresses of their own households but ran the farms associated with their estates, established and encouraged local industries, and participated in local politics.

Catherine Bovey's status falls between that of the aristocratic lady and the country gentlewoman. As we have shown, she was born into a substantial mercantile family and married into wealth and a landed estate. The study of her life fills a gap between the categories of noble and gentry and raises questions as to how far she was unique or perhaps affords an instance of a "new" type of merchant-based gentlewoman, whose life was neither enmeshed in national politics nor substantially local. Her early widowhood and decision not to remarry was a decision surely made easier by her husband's bequeathing her a life residency at Flaxley Abbey, and by the fact that there was no son to inherit the estates and move her to a dower house on a more limited income. These circumstances enabled Catherine Bovey to live an unusually independent life. However, we suggest that there were also social and cultural conditions in this period that allowed her life to be lived in metropolitan and local public venues as well as the more domestic realms of home and estate management. Developments in print culture made her known to a wider circle than would have been possible a mere sixty years earlier, so that she participated in the larger world of journals, novels, dedications, and literary projects. The growth of institutional charitable organizations similarly gave her a role and a reputation in the world beyond the Forest of Dean.

We can begin to adumbrate the public venues she inhabited and the institutions in which she played a part, and, we believe, in the process, indicate how very early on in the period—late seventeenth and early eighteenth century—wealth and widowhood enabled a gentlewoman to live an active and public life. She exemplifies a female method of engagement with the public and social worlds in which she lived through sociability, benevolence, and patronage. Her varied and strenuous activities were undertaken inside the spheres open to a wealthy woman on her own and able to make significant choices in both the public and private realms. In *Women of Quality*, Ingrid Tague has traced in detail the ways in which didactic male "ideals" could be adapted and exploited to enable women to have a high degree of empowerment and agency within a patriarchal system. In Bovey's case, it is possible to argue that her concerns with religion, education, charity, and benevolence fitted with contemporary ideas of appropriate female behavior. Certainly, during her lifetime she was remarked upon by a wide and varied range of people with approval and admiration. After her death, the Westminster and Flaxley Abbey memorials pay tribute to her neighborly hospitality and consistent generosity to the poor. Family tradition respected her memory to the extent of keeping many of her papers intact when the Flaxley Abbey papers were reviewed and catalogued in the early twentieth century. All this would surely have pleased her.

As the following anecdote suggests, it was her intention to be remembered as a gentlewoman and a benefactor. Nicholls has left this engaging account, derived from oral history sources, of Catherine Bovey's last Christmas. According to this account, Rachel Vergo, her housekeeper of twenty years, gave this description of a Christmas feast for poor children:

> During the Christmas holidays before Mrs. Bovey died she had the thirty children who were taught at her expense to dine at the Abbey upon beef and pudding . . . After dinner Mrs. Bovey had them all into the parlour, where she was sitting dressed in white and silver. She showed them her clothes and her jewels, talked pleasantly and with great good nature to them, and having given to each of them sixpence she dismissed them. When they left her they had a harp and a fiddle playing in the great hall where they danced two hours and went away in good time. When Mrs. Bovey was dressing before dinner she said to Mrs. Vergo, "Rachel, you will be surprised that I put some fine clothes on to-day; but I think that these poor children will remember me the longer for it."[45]

On this note, we leave Catherine Bovey as the head of a largely female household. She is well-dressed and ornamented in jewels, good-natured and generous. Equally she is conscious of her role, status, and duties as she informally explains her actions to her devoted housekeeper. Her "fine clothes" are as much a part of her "self-fashioning" as a Christian gentlewoman as is her generosity to the children with a feast, a harp, and a fiddle.

NOTES

1. The spelling "Bovey" is used in this essay as it is the form used by Catherine Bovey herself: it is also the spelling used in the title of the Dutch engraver John

Kip's image of her Gloucestershire estate, Flaxley Abbey, in 1707, and by Sir Robert Atkyns, who reproduces Kip's spelling in *The Ancient and Present State of Glostershire* (London: Robert Gosling, 1712), 436. The original Dutch form was "Boeve"; see A. R. J. Juřica, "Flaxley," in *Bledisloe Hundred, St. Briavels Hundred, The Forest of Dean,* vol. 5, *A History of the County of Gloucestershire,* ed. N. M. Herbert, in *The Victoria County History of England* (Oxford: Published for the Institute of Historical Research by Oxford University Press, 1996), 142. Later Crawley descendents spelled the name "Boevey," as they linked their family name to the Bovey/Boevey estates, i.e., "Crawley-Boevey."

2. Ballard, *Memoirs of Several Ladies of Great Britain,* 438.

3. Ibid.

4. See Arthur William Crawley-Boevey, *The "Perverse Widow": Being Passages from the Life of Catherina, Wife of William Boevey, Esq., of Flaxley Abbey, in the County of Glouces-ter. With Genealogical Notes on the Family and Others Connected therewith* (London: Longmans, Green, 1898).

5. This paper was first discussed at a session of the Women's Studies Group 1558–1837 in 2002, and subsequently at a humanities seminar, University of Denver (2002), and a Chawton House conference (2003). We are grateful for suggestions and comments made on these occasions. We should like to express our gratitude to Peggy Keeran, Penrose Library, the University of Denver; Carole Wrightson, University of Gloucestershire Learning Centre, and Daniel Singer, English Department, University of Denver. In addition we should like to thank Caroline MacIntosh, University of Gloucestershire Archives. We are extremely grateful for the help and kindness shown to us at the Gloucestershire Archives over a number of years. Last but not least, we should like to record our thanks to Dr. Charles More for many stimulating discussions on Gloucestershire gardens and on Catherine Bovey.

6. See the collection of documents compiled for the Crawley-Boeveys in 1915, (GA) D9282, with reference to "Mrs. Bovey's Memorandum" dealing with leases and boundary disputes.

7. Ballard, *Memoirs of Several Ladies of Great Britain:* "She was heiress to her father, a gentleman of great riches," 439.

8. Nicholas Kingsley, *The Country Houses of Gloucestershire,* 2 vols. (vol. 1 Cheltenham: N. Kingsley, 1989; vol. 2, Chichester: Phillimore, 1992), 2:164.

9. Atkyns, *Ancient and Present State,* A2r, 436.

10. Catherine Bovey is the only woman referred to as holding land in her own right. The few other women featured by Atkyns are referred to in relation to their late husbands.

11. Atkyns, *Ancient and Present State,* 437.

12. See David W. Hayton, Eveline Cruickshanks, and Stuart Handley, *The History of Parliament: The House of Commons, 1690–1715,* 5 vols. (Cambridge: Cambridge University Press for the History of Parliament Trust, 2002), 1:646–47.

13. See Juřica, "Flaxley," 142–43. See also, Irvine Gray, "The Making of Westbury Court Gardens," *Garden History Society* 1 (1968): 15–18; Timothy Mowl, *Historic Gardens of Gloucestershire* (Stroud: Tempus, 2002), 53. They, too, suggest that "Caterina" influenced Westbury Gardens. Both gardens are agreed to be of Dutch design, though there is some discussion about the precise nature of the design, whether also Flemish and French, or purely Dutch.

14. GA Box 22496, D9282, call AC 1982, *Letter Book #* 1433, 42–43.

15. For information about Peter Senhouse, see John Burke, *A Genealogical and Heraldic History of the Commoners of Great Britain and Ireland, Enjoying Territorial Posses-*

sions or High Official Rank: But Uninvested with Heritable Honours, 4 vols. (London: Henry Colburn, 1835–38), 1:216.

16. Peter Senhouse, *The Right Use and Improvement of Sensitive Pleasures, and more particularly of Music: A Sermon Preach'd in the Cathedral Church of Gloucester, at the Anniversary Meeting of the Choirs of Gloucester, Hereford, and Worcester, Sept. 20, 1727* (Gloucester: John Palman, 1728), vii.

17. Ibid.

18. See Lillian Faderman's interesting discussions on female friendships in *Surpassing the Love of Men: Romantic Friendship and Love Between Women from the Renaissance to the Present* (London: Junction Books, 1982), 73.

19. Austen, *Emma,* 90–91. See also, the rather similar comments made by Lady Happy, in Margaret Cavendish's *Convent of Pleasure* (1668), act 1, sc. 2.

20. Delarivier Manley, *Memoirs of Europe towards the Close of the Eighth Century* (London: John Morphew, 1710), 275. Manley refers to Catherine Bovey as "Porcia." Porcia is identified as "Mrs. Bovey of Gloucestershire" in *A Key to the Third Volume of the Atalantis, Call'd Memoirs of Europe* ([[London? [Delarivier Manley] 1712?]), 3. The work was attributed to Manley. This identification was accepted by Ballard, who cites Manley's description of Bovey's moral qualities in his *Memoirs of Several Ladies of Great Britain,* 438–40.

21. Manley, *Memoirs of Europe,* 273–74.

22. Ibid., 274.

23. Ibid., 275.

24. H. G. Nicholls, *The Personalities of the Forest of Dean. Forming an Appendix to "An Historical and Descriptive Account of the Forest of Dean"* (London: John Murray, 1863), 40.

25. See O. M. Myers, ed., *The Coverley Papers from the "Spectator"* (Oxford: Clarendon, 1940).

26. Nicholls, *Personalities of the Forest of Dean,* 40–43.

27. In 1707, a correspondence between Steele and Manley was published in Madame Catherine La Mothe, Countess d'Aulnoy, *Memoirs of the Court of England. In Two Parts. By the Countess of Dunois . . . To which is Added, The Lady's Pacquet of Letters, Taken from her by a French Privateer in her Passage to Holland* (London: B. Bragg, 1707). This was later attributed to Manley; see Delarivier Manley, *The Adventures of Rivella,* ed. Katherine Zelinsky (Peterborough, ON: Broadview, 2002), app. C, 127–28, 249.

28. Manley, *Memoirs of Europe,* 274.

29. Richard Steele, ed., *The Ladies Library. Written by a Lady. Published by Mr. Steele,* 3 vols. (London: W. Mears and J. Brown, 1714), 2:A5R–V.

30. Ibid., 2:222. Interestingly, Stephen Parks has argued that George Berkeley contributed significantly to *The Ladies Library;* see "George Berkeley, Sir Richard Steele, and *The Ladies Library,*" *Scriblerian* 13, no. 1 (1980): 1–2. If Parks is correct in his supposition, this would certainly confirm the links between Berkeley, Steele, and Catherine Bovey.

31. Sean Gill, *Women and the Church of England from the Eighteenth Century to the Present* (London: SPCK, 1994), 48–49. For further information on the aims and work of the SPCK in the eighteenth century, see http://www.spck.org.uk/about_spck/history.php.

32. Nicholls, *Personalities of the Forest of Dean,* 56–57.

33. See Juřica, "Flaxley," 149.

34. This inscription is taken from Crawley-Boevey, *"Perverse Widow,"* 136–39. A similar inscription can be seen on her memorial in Westminster Abbey.

35. Parks, *Scriblerian.*

36. There are a number of articles on this project; for a brief description see Edwin S. Gaustad, "George Berkeley and the New World Community," *Church History* 48, no. 1 (1979): 5–7.

37. Reference to Bovey's involvement with Berkeley and the Bermudas project can also be found in the William King papers, Trinity College, Dublin. We are grateful to Dr. Philip Woodfine for drawing this to our attention.

38. George Hickes, *Linguarum Vett. Septentrionalium Thesaurus Grammatico-criticus et Archæologicus*, 2 vols. (Oxoniæ: E Theatro Sheldoniano, 1703–5), 1:XLVII.

39. Catherine Bovey's accounts can be traced in the currently surviving materials in the Gloucestershire Archives.

40. J. H. Plumb, *The First Four Georges* (London: Collins, 1968), 21.

41. Ingrid H. Tague, *Women of Quality: Accepting and Contesting Ideals of Femininity in England, 1690–1760* (Woodbridge: Boydell, 2002), 19.

42. Vickery, *Gentleman's Daughter*, 277.

43. Daniel Defoe, *A Tour Through the Whole Island of Great Britain*, 2 vols. (London: Dent, 1966), 2:40–41.

44. Harris, *Passion for Government;* Foreman, *Georgiana;* Tillyard, *Aristocrats.* See also, Elaine Chalus, "Elite Women, Social Politics and the Political World of late Eighteenth-Century England," *Historical Journal* 43, no. 3, (2000): 669–97.

45. H. G. Nicholls, *An Historical and Descriptive Account of the Forest of Dean* (London: John Murray, 1858), 186–87. See also, Crawley-Boevey, *"Perverse Widow,"* 113–14, who authenticates historical antecedents of this account.

The Limits of Sympathy: *The Histories of Some of the Penitents in the Magdalen-House* (1760)

Jennie Batchelor

> GREAT pains have been taken by philosophers, to discover from whence proceeds the pleasure we receive by having our pity excited: Some have attributed it to the tenderness, others to the cruelty of our natures; but neither have confirmed their hypothesis by answerable reasons. . . . While we participate with the distressed in their affliction, and grieve for their sorrows, we think ourselves free from all imputation of inhumanity, tho' we feel pleasure in our grief, and sometimes delight so much in it. . . . But I am not inclined to . . . think that so tender a sensation arises from cruelty or pride.[1]

So OPENS THE THIRD OF FOUR INSET NARRATIVES IN THE ANONYMOUSLY published *The Histories of Some of the Penitents in the Magdalen-House, As Supposed to be Related by Themselves* (1760). The novel, variously attributed to Sarah Fielding and Sarah Scott, has recently come to prominence in a growing body of literary and historical scholarship, which has demonstrated the decisive shifts in attitudes toward prostitution and female sexuality that occurred in the mid-eighteenth century.[2] The founding of the Magdalen House for the Reception of Penitent Prostitutes in Goodman's Fields, London, in August 1758 was central to these developments. Unlike earlier institutions such as London's infamous Bridewell, the Magdalen was not a house of correction. One of many philanthropic organizations established in London in the midcentury, the charity was founded upon a principle of benevolent rehabilitation, and relied for its success upon public goodwill (in the form of subscriptions), as well as a tractable body of potential inmates who would voluntarily admit themselves to the institution to be taught various skills and trades intended to fit them for legitimate work and wifehood upon their readmission into society. The charity's establishment followed a vigorous pamphlet debate, in which the institution's supporters sought to recast the lusty whore of the popular imagination as a victim of various socioeconomic problems and, thus, to reclaim the prostitute's degenerate body for a life of virtuous industry. The Magdalen, as she was constructed in these documents, was not only recuperable, but, by virtue of her (re)productive potential, she was also a valuable asset to the nation's political and moral economies.[3] *Histories,* while ostensibly written in support of the institution, also contained thinly veiled critiques of its principal concerns, especially those surrounding the networks of affiliation the women were encouraged to form within the House and upon their release. If the intention of the charity was, ultimately, to return the fallen woman to patriarchy through marriage, as Vivien Jones has suggested, then *Histories* offered an enticing alternative to the institution's idealized notion of heterosexual domesticity in the form of female community.[4]

To this end, the novel projected a model of sisterhood, founded upon the feelings of sympathy that the penitents' narratives aroused, which binds together the novel's author/"biographer" (90), her fallen heroines, and not-yet-fallen readers in a fellowship that can withstand the cultural, social, and economic pressures that otherwise prevent women from supporting, and fully cooperating, with one another in society at large. Once closeted in the Magdalen House, and thus free from these pressures, the penitents are shown to have no cause to "blame" or "censure" either themselves or their fellow inmates; rather, "each looks on the other with an eye of pity: Equal distress, and equal relief, begets a sort of mutual affection" between them (10). Thus, within this most unlikely setting, the confines of a female penitentiary, emerges a compassionate and egalitarian society that is offered as a model for relationships between women outside its walls.

Here as throughout the novel, the author alludes to the moral sense philosophy of Francis Hutcheson, David Hume, the Earl of Shaftesbury, and Adam Smith to counter the destructive effects of nascent capitalism on the family, marriage, and the labor market.[5] In its turn to sentimental community as a solution to the problems of female dependency and exploitation, *Histories* occupies common ground with a number of female-authored, mid-century utopian novels. Where it exceeds these texts is in its formulation of a community that can accommodate not only those who have lost their family and fortune, but those who have relinquished their chastity, something that is unimaginable in the desexualized worlds of Fielding's *The Governess* (1749) or Scott's *Millenium Hall* (1762), for example.[6] Indeed, *Histories* argues that it is politically necessary that virtuous females reach out toward fallen women, on the grounds that the former are responsible for the latter's abjection: it is not the penitents' characters, but "the affectation of too overstrained a chastity in others" that precipitates their demise. Such specious pretensions to virtue among society's middling ranks, the novel argues, "exclude" those women who have committed even a single transgression "from the means of reformation, by hunting them out of every way of obtaining an honest subsistence, till the only alternative left them, is, either to owe their support to a continuance in vicious courses, or to die martyrs to chastity" (4). Understanding prostitution itself as the result of the failure of female community, *Histories* boldly imagines a new matrix of relationships between women that, once realized, will make charities such as the Magdalen House redundant by preventing any woman "from standing in need of penitence" at all (7).[7]

This essay suggests, however, that despite the novel's attempt to refute the supposed synonymy of virtue and chastity, and its radical assertion of female solidarity, *Histories* fails fully to achieve its utopian promise, largely because, as my epigraph insinuates, the sympathetic mechanism upon which the novel's notion of community depends is unstable. As the author acknowledges, the "pleasure" that individuals might have felt in response to the penitents' suffering was difficult to police and might have served to differentiate as well as to unite women. There is, the novel indicates, an important distinction to be made between "compassion" (between "feeling for," or a more condescending feeling in spite of) and "co-respondence" (or "feeling with"), a distinction that, as Lucinda Cole has argued, was to prove a critical bone of contention in competing accounts of affective response throughout the eighteenth century.[8] And although the author of *Histories* is not "inclined" to believe that sympathy arises from "cruelty or pride," she cannot deny that the sympathetic spectators who consume the penitents' stories, within the text and without it, might derive pleasures from their narratives that are more vicarious or predatory than they are humane.

Such moments in the text expose fault lines—between, for example, relationships based on equality and a Smithian fellow-feeling, on the one hand, and so-called fellowships mediated by social or moral hierarchies, on the other—that are, of course, characteristic of mid- to late-century fictional imaginings of ideal societies more widely. The effort made by women writers to identify utopian alternatives to patriarchal capitalism has emerged in recent scholarship as a fraught and often flawed endeavor. While these authors' attempts have been tentatively hailed by some as a cause for feminist celebration, they have also provided cause for lament, particularly when their projected communities prove to be founded upon the same (and usually class-based) "strategies of exclusion, displacement, normalization, and containment" upon which patriarchy is itself established.[9] This essay aims to contribute to the ongoing debate about the scopes and limits of women's utopian writing in the mid-eighteenth century by exploring *Histories'* potentially radical conception of female community. It examines the various levels upon which notions of community resonate throughout the novel and explores the text's attempts to challenge the conventional (and misogynist) objectification of the prostitute—a representational tendency that is, I will argue, as common in the Magdalen House's official publications as it is in libertine prostitution narratives. Finally, however, I suggest that the novel's radical assertion of female solidarity is inevitably limited, not by the text's attitude to class, per se, but by what Vivien Jones has described as the "class-based mechanisms of sentimentalism": the strategies of differentiation that, paradoxically, make sympathetic identification possible and upon which *Histories'* model of community is crucially, but problematically, dependent.[10]

Labor, Narrative, and Community

It is peculiarly appropriate that a novel that champions the virtues of female fellowship was itself a collaborative enterprise, the publication of which was made possible by the Bluestocking ethoi of sociability and solidarity. The details surrounding the novel's publication history are sketchy. What is known is that in January 1759 the manuscript was presented by Lady Barbara Montagu (the author's intermediary) to Samuel Richardson, who persuaded John Rivington and James Dodsley to publish the work. Lady Barbara never divulged the identity of the novel's author, although Richardson knew her to be a "Neighbour" of her sponsor, whose "fortune being inferior to her Birth & Education[, was] desirous of reaping some benefit from the *present fondness for Novels.*"[11] *Histories'* origin in the Bath community established by Lady Barbara and Sarah Scott (a community linked to Elizabeth Montagu's London Bluestocking salons via her sister, Scott) is significant. The "political energy," as Betty Rizzo describes it, that emerged from these women, who were "useless to, even rejects of, the patriarchal system," is palpable in each of the novel's four narratives.[12] Indeed, as it is imagined in *Histories*—without men and without overseers—the Magdalen House might be read as a fictionalized extension of the all-female Bath community, in which each member was "raised . . . to a full enjoyment of virtue, prosperity, and productivity."[13] In this and the successive real-life societies that Lady Barbara and Scott attempted to establish, however, the fallen woman could not be so easily accommodated. In a letter to Elizabeth Montagu, written in June 1760, Scott asked her sister if she could find work for a "repentant sinner," a servant who, like the first penitent in *Histories,* had been "debauched by her master." Scott pitied the woman and might have taken her into her own household had she not feared the consequences of displaying "lenity for these offences" before her servants.[14] The imagined world of *Histories* achieved what the Bath society could not: the recuperation of the penitent woman as a valued member of society. No "greater reward," the novel suggested, could be claimed than that of "preserv-[ing] great numbers from a pernicious life, and an untimely death, and, by restoring them to industry and order, render[ing] them useful members of society" (7).

The vocabulary of utility the novel deploys, here, self-consciously rehearses the charity's own rhetoric about its objectives. As Jonas Hanway had argued, the Magdalen House's guiding rationale was to "employ [the women] in the most useful manner . . . and by rendering them pious, industrious, and frugal, prepare them for a comfortable settlement in the world."[15] Thus equipped, the penitents could be fully reintegrated into the domestic economy; as mistresses of a trade, they would be "a *fortune* to a husband" and might "become the *joyful mothers of children.*"[16] *Histories* similarly emphasizes the social benefits generated by the penitents' rehabilitation, yet it rigorously challenges the charity's patriarchal and protocapitalist definition of "usefulness." As if to underscore this fact, the novel opens after "the work of the day [is] past" (10), a maneuver that allows the author to assert that the women's worth lies not merely, as the institution's spokesmen claimed, in their productiveness as manual or domestic laborers, or in their reproductive capacity as future mothers, but in their generative capacity as storytellers and in their moral status as sentimental subjects. In this way, the novel valorizes narrative and the cultural work it performs as alternative, yet no less valuable, forms of female labor.[17]

Although *Histories* openly praises the "Beneficent Institutors" of the Magdalen House (182), the novel's championing of the penitents' moral subjectivity—a subjectivity formed and proven through the work of narrative composition—coupled with its rejection of heterosexual marriage in favor of female community, signals resistance to the charity's disciplinary regime and its insistent objectification of the Magdalens. That the institution problematically transformed its inmates into spectacular objects, offered up to public scrutiny at

work or in prayer in carefully managed displays designed to demonstrate the penitents' piety and the Magdalen House's efficacy, has
been well documented in recent scholarship.[18] Much less attention,
however, has been paid to the disciplinary measures the charity im-
plemented behind closed doors. For all the institution's rhetoric of
benevolent correction through training and spiritual guidance, and
for all it undoubtedly did to re-imagine the prostitute as an object
of sympathy, a residual notion of the prostitute as an appetitive and
unruly whore nonetheless informed the charity's treatment and representation of its inmates. This is perhaps most evident in the institution's complex attitudes toward labor. Although the charity
explicitly claimed that the women were taught to work ostensibly to
provide them with a means of support upon leaving the institution,
the Magdalen House's official pamphlets reveal also that labor was
implicitly conceived as a means by which to render transgressive
bodies docile. As the Magdalen chaplain William Dodd wrote in his
Advice to the Magdalens (1761), "there is an absolute necessity for
much *Industry* on your part; . . . and therefore a deficiency in industry will always be sufficient to lose our esteem, as it will too plainly
shew your want of Principles."[19] A range of disciplinary measures, at
odds with the charity's reputation for sentimental benevolence, was
introduced to ensure the Magdalens' complicity with the organization's work ethic, including the withdrawal of sustenance from those
who could, but were unwilling to, labor.[20]

Histories contests the logic and justness of such strategies by making clear that its heroines do not need to be threatened with punishment to ensure their reformation. All four of the penitents prove
themselves willing and able to work prior to their admission to the
institution, although each is prevented by social prejudice or legal
injustice from doing so. Emily, for example, is a good economist,
and establishes a successful haberdashery business after her lover
abandons her, only for her stock to be seized by bailiffs to pay off
her former lover's debts. After being coerced into prostitution by a
bawd who pays Markland's creditors and subsequently threatens to
send away the couple's child if Emily refuses to work in her brothel
to pay off her debt, the penitent once again seeks legitimate employment in service. Her efforts prove fruitless: to some she is "too handsome," to others "too genteel" to be considered suitable for such
work (43). In the world of *Histories,* the threat of starvation functions
not as the cure for unruly bodies and incentive to work that it was in
the penitentiary; rather, the author claims it is "the manifest danger
of starving" that leads active, industrious, and otherwise virtuous
bodies to prostitution (44). In this way, the novel radically figures

prostitution itself as a debased form of work, rather than as the symptom of idleness it was commonly held to be. Since the threat of poverty and hunger were widely understood by social commentators and political economists as inducements to labor,[21] the novel's understanding of the same threats as inducements to vice acknowledges prostitution's status as degraded and degrading work that the women will find an escape from through the labor of narration.

As provocative as the novel's acknowledgment of prostitution as labor is its insistence that the prostitute's virtue remains intact, despite the depths to which her poverty reduces her. Throughout, *Histories* successfully maintains a distinction—unthinkable in scandalous prostitution narratives and permanently on the brink of collapse in the Magdalen House documents—between the women's corporeal transgressions and their inviolable virtue. One of the recurrent motifs of the women's probity is their love for their children, which, as the first penitent remarks, both sustains her in a "course most odious" and makes her "anguish" all the more acute (48–49).[22] Emily would rather "suffer [her]self to die, rather than preserve [herself] in such a manner! But when [she] returned home, and saw the distress of [her] poor child, every other evil appeared light in comparison of his sufferings" (48). The prostitute's agonizing love for her child both justifies her trade and immunizes her against its taint. Thus, unlike "libertine" prostitution narratives, in which, as Laura Rosenthal argues, "the prostitute accepts," and sometimes learns to exploit, "the instrumental use of her body," "reform" texts such as *Histories* differentiate "between the mechanized body that . . . repeatedly gives over its senseless labor for the pleasure and profit of others" and the "sentimental heart" that is buried within it.[23] That the prostitute's body could be split from her character in this way, is, ironically, a consequence of precisely those socioeconomic factors that reformers, including the author of *Histories*, suggested were responsible for her fall: namely, the disintegration of the family and, as a consequence, women's increasing reliance upon alienated wage labor. As Ruth Perry has documented, concerns surrounding these matters came into sharp focus in the decade in which *Histories* was written. With the demise of the consanguineal familial, and following the passing of Hardwicke's 1753 Marriage Act, Perry argues, "women's reproductive capacities and sexual conduct had become a matter of public interest and social regulation more than ever before."[24]

The loss, therefore, that *Histories* laments and attempts to redress through its notion of community is not that of the women's virtue, but of the affective ties that have been severed as a result of the onset

of industrial capitalism. As Perry observes, narratives such as those
contained in *Histories*, which presented readers with the "spectacle
of a deracinated woman, separated from her family of origin, unable
to survive alone by waged labor," highlight "an irony of the age of
individualism" and provide a "necessary corrective to the myth of
the socially mobile individual."[25] The devastating consequences of
society's subordination of the moral to the economic are repeatedly
illustrated throughout the novel, but nowhere more movingly than
in the relationship between the first penitent and her unnamed sister. Although "not above five years older than [her]self," Emily
looks to her sister as a "parent" as well as a sibling. When the girls
are separated by their father's death, the younger is struck by an "af-
fliction" that could not have been "deeper" had her sister died
(13). The penitent's sister is a diligent worker and endures her fall
from lower-middle-class gentility to labor with dignity. Whereas
Emily enters a downward spiral of vice and whoredom after being
orphaned, her sister makes a virtue of necessity, successfully negotiating both the labor market (by establishing a profitable millinery
business) and the marriage market (by making a good match) (27).
Like her fallen sister, however, this most virtuous of workers ultimately finds only alienation in her labor. As a successful businesswoman, the milliner has the means to aid her sister financially, and
thus to rescue her from a life of vice; yet as a wife, she is powerless to
do so. Her husband has complete control over her financial affairs:
"There was such entire harmony between them, that this became
the custom as it was the easiest way; but now she regretted it extremely" (46). The milliner's marital "harmony" belies a profound
discord that reverberates through every page of *Histories:* the cultural and legal constraints that prevent women from supporting one
another. In the world of the novel, the deracinated whore and virtuous businesswoman are equally powerless. Whether they work in the
sex trade or in a legitimate occupation, women lack control over
their bodies and their laboring potential: whenever and however
they labor, they are always forced to give service to men.

If Emily's narrative reveals the devastation caused by wage labor
and the severing of familial ties, then the story of Fanny Tent, the
third of the novel's inset narratives, offers some putative solutions to
these problems. In this reworking of John Cleland's *Memoirs of a
Woman of Pleasure* (1748–49), the penitent is an illegitimate daughter of a "Lady," who pays for her child to be raised by a family of
spinners. The mother dies, unbeknownst to the young girl, and a
few years later, Fanny's surrogate "mother" dies too, upon which
the orphan is placed with an "ancient virgin" who "half starve[s]

herself, and quite starve[s] her servant," in order to preserve her family's fortune (92). Fanny's unsated appetite intensifies her hunger to find her biological mother, whom she mistakenly believes is living in London under the name of Madam Tent. Like William Hogarth's Moll Hackabout and her libertine successor Fanny Hill, the penitent arrives in the city where she is intercepted by a bawd. Claiming to be her long-lost mother, the brothel-keeper persuades Fanny to prostitute herself as a demonstration of filial obedience, and convinces her that she is married to her client, Mr. Mastin (102). When the bawd subsequently attempts to prostitute Fanny to another man, the young woman realizes that she has been duped, and is disturbed, not by her loss of virtue, but by the "melancholy" recognition that her quest for family has proven only that she is "nobody's child at all; and . . . at the same time no man's wife" (104–5). Mastin removes Fanny from the brothel and keeps her as his mistress until he falls in love with another woman, whereupon he places her in service with his benevolent sister, Mrs. Lafew, and her husband. After a happy period of service in the Lafew household, Fanny becomes her master's lover and eventually has his child. Of all the penitents' relationships with men, Fanny's with Mr. Lafew is the most complex. As Katherine Binhammer has suggested, the connections that the women form with their lovers and clients fall into two main categories: those that are loving, and thus nonmercenary, and those that are economically motivated. Indeed, one of *Histories'* innovations, Binhammer argues, is that the fallen-woman-turned-Magdalen is not motivated, in the first instance, by lust or greed: she "falls the first time for love, the second time for money."[26] Fanny's relationship with Lafew, nonetheless, complicates this account, suggesting that motives other than nonmercenary, erotic love and hopes of monetary gain drive at least one of the penitents to seek out relationships with men.

The desire that is awakened in Fanny—a "stranger to love," despite her period as Mastin's mistress—appears to be a desire for family rather than a desire for Lafew. She admires her master's wife and children "the more because [they] belonged to him," and longs to stand in one "of those near and dear relations to him." Yet, the precise nature of the relationship she covets is unclear. When she remarks that she is charmed by the little "proof[s]" of "affection" the children give their father, but envious of "their title to his tenderness," there is a clear suggestion that the servant's love for Lafew is as much filial as it is erotic (110), a possibility that is further explored when Fanny substitutes herself for her master's ailing child. When the Lafews' eldest daughter contracts scarlet fever, Fanny agrees to follow the family physician's advice and lies against the girl's "stiff" body in the hopes of "bring[ing] out the irruption again" and, thus, of saving the child's life. No other member of the household staff will undertake so dangerous an act, but Fanny's desire "to save the child" is as great as her will "to oblige the parents" (112). Fanny's willingness to sacrifice herself for the daughter—a heroic gesture that secures Lafew's love for her—cannot simply be explained by servile "gratitude"; neither can it be explained simply as an attempt to win her master. It is Fanny's desire to be bound by filial obligation that spurs the orphan here, a desire that initially prompted her descent into prostitution when she agreed to sex with Mastin to please Madam Tent.

Fanny's need to be part of a family network—regardless of whether that family is constituted biologically or affectively—is a familiar trope in eighteenth-century fiction, which, as Perry suggests, commonly manifests a need to compensate for the "psychological and social dislocations" produced by the shift from a consanguineal to a conjugal familial model. This new economy of kinship, Perry contends, was potentially democratizing, but often profoundly disabling for women, who "lost power as sisters and daughters" only to regain it, in diminished form, as "wives and mothers." The result was a "net loss of social power" for women, a loss that the novel attempted to redress through a series of compensatory fictions in which long-lost relatives are found and birthrights are restored.[27] *Histories* takes up these plotlines but refuses to indulge in the "wish-fulfillment" fantasies that Perry identifies in other fictional writing of the period. Here, family offers none of the compensations longed for or felt by heroines such as Frances Burney's Evelina. Just as Emily's brief reunion with her sister brings only pain and anguish, so Fanny's attempts to insert herself into the Lafew family lead her to "find [her] own condemnation" (127). Her attachment to Lafew, and the child she subsequently has by him, cannot endure in the face of Mrs. Lafew's love for her husband and the exemplary generosity she demonstrates when she forgives Fanny and her husband for their infidelity. "Overcome" by "guilt," and overwhelmed by the compassion she receives from a woman who not only refuses to think "with pleasure on the pain her husband suffered from his love for another" (124), but who forgives the couple and undertakes the care of their child, Fanny enters the Magdalen House. The exemplary Mrs. Lafew embodies the values of disinterested sympathy referred to in the quotation with which this essay began. Her selflessness and humanity allow her to feel a pity for the penitent that cuts across the moral and social divide that would, conventionally, make their friendship impossible. The "boundless humanity" that Fanny experiences in her relationships with Mrs. Lafew, and later the penitents, provides her with the emotional sustenance that she has sought from the moment that she first went in search of her mother, and which, in her mother's absence, she erroneously believed might be found in the heterosexual, conjugal family (128).

MORAL SENTIMENTS IN THEORY AND IN PRACTICE

The novel's argument for the ameliorative potential of female community constitutes not only an implicit critique of the charity's directive that the Magdalens be trained for work and for marriage, but further indicts the institution's efforts to police relationships between its inmates. The charity's suspicion about the Magdalens' interactions with one another was unambiguously institutionalized in its published rules and regulations, which emphasized the necessity of strict hierarchy and chains of responsibility. The charity's wards were "*classed*" according to the "superiority [of] or preference" given to individual inmates: the superior wards were occupied by women who had proven themselves to be worthy of their admission to the institution—although by what means remains unclear—while the "lower" wards housed "inferior persons" and those who could be "disregarded for misbehaviour." Each ward was presided over by a nominated representative, "accountable for the behaviour" of her fellow Magdalens and answerable to the matron, who, in turn, was responsible for maintaining order at all times.[28] *Histories* rejects such divisive measures. No "ceremony" or hierarchy structures the penitents' relationships; they tell their stories in the "order in which they arrived at the House" by way of recognition that they are a company of equals, and that no other title to "precedency" exists among them (52–53). Although they have been "brought to it by different steps," the women are all too painfully aware that they are in "the same state" (9).

Unencumbered by the regulatory technologies that affected the real-life Magdalens, the community of women imagined in *Histories* seems also to be liberated from the disciplinary mechanisms that critics have detected in other fictional utopian communities of the midcentury—particularly in *Millenium Hall*—as well as from the pessimism that inflects dystopian accounts of community, such as Fielding's *Volume the Last* (1753).[29] Yet, the penitential community's foundation in a sentimental ethic of sympathy ensures that its radical potential is nevertheless circumscribed, as I have already suggested. If *Millenium Hall* manifests a fatal inconsistency between Scott's gender and class politics, and if *Volume the Last* reveals the impossibility of a workable alternative to patriarchal capitalism,[30] then *Histories'* utopian aspirations are limited by the exclusionary and morally ambiguous mechanisms of sentimentalism itself. Considerable critical attention has focused on how eighteenth-century writings on community were, as Lucinda Cole argues, "indebted to a rapidly consolidating discourse of sensibility."[31] While much of this body of work has emphasized the fractures and fissures that (with seeming inevitability) undermine these communities from the moment they are founded, these destructive elements are commonly understood to emerge *in spite of* the egalitarian ethos of sentimentalism upon which the societies are based.[32] *Histories* suggests, however, that these destructive elements are integral to, rather than at odds with, the sentimental ethic.

Sentimentalism, as a number of critics have noted, often presented itself as universalist discourse, which seemed to augur a new model of society in which worth outranked birth as a marker of status.[33] *Histories* gestures toward such a meritocracy, proving in Fanny's story that even an illegitimate child, lacking an education and raised in poverty, can be the equal of her betters when penitence leads her to "industry and piety" (128). Yet, the novel also lays bare the exclusionary logic that underpinned sentimental ideology: the differentiation of the deserving from the undeserving without which sympathetic identification between feeling spectators and objects of compassion was impossible. Fanny's acceptance by the Magdalen community and by her readers, like that of each of her fellow penitents, comes at a price: the condemnation of other (usually, but not exclusively, laboring-class or poor) women whom the novel finds beyond redemption. The penitents emerge as the exceptions that prove the rule of working women's vice; their moral refinement is thrown into relief by the unforgiving portraits of the majority of laboring women in the text, including Markland's knowing housekeeper, who conspires in Emily's seduction, and the bogus Madam Tent, who, for her own financial ends, ruthlessly exploits Fanny's desire for maternal guidance. Entitlement to compassion is all the more valuable in *Histories* because so few of the women who appear within its pages are worthy of it.

The novel's dissociation of the penitents from other women of their class and economic standing is one of the ways in which the novel attempts to gentrify the prostitute who, as Vivien Jones has argued, was, with increasing insistence, attributed with "honorary middle-class status" in mid- to late-eighteenth-century reformist prostitution narratives.[34] By the time that Hugh Kelly wrote his *Clarissa*-inspired *Memoirs of a Magdalen* (1767), the Magdalen novel had become an entirely genteel affair. The novel's heroine, Louisa Mildmay, can boast a substantial forty-thousand-pound dowry and, although she is seduced by her fiancé before their wedding, she is never forced to degrade herself by having to sell sex for money.[35] The gentrification of the penitent, inaugurated by *Histories* and later endorsed by Kelly's novel, would eventually become embedded in the constitution of the Magdalen House itself, which from the 1780s onward, presented itself as an asylum for fallen women rather than former prostitutes. As Donna T. Andrew has argued, this development was a matter of financial necessity: as subscriptions declined and support for the charity waned, such methods were expedient.[36] However, within the specific context of *Histories,* a novel written when public support for the charity was relatively high, such efforts to elevate the penitent both socially and morally demand further explanation.

That the penitents *had* to mirror the middle-ranking sensibilities of their readers is a demand of the sentimental logic that structures the novel and from which it derives its political force. According to the Smithian sentimental formulation, sympathy provided a bridge between individuals, forged by an imaginative substitution of the sympathetic spectator for the sympathetic object. As Smith famously wrote in *The Theory of Moral Sentiments* (1759):

> As we have no immediate experience of what other men feel, we can form no idea of the manner in which they are affected, but by conceiving what we should feel in the like situation. Though our brother is upon the rack, as long as we ourselves are at our ease, our senses will never inform us of what he suffers. . . . It is by the imagination only that we can form any conception of what are his sensations.[37]

Although the transformative potential of such imaginative experimentations in sympathy is vast, it is not limitless. Class and poverty are just two of a number of factors that Smith exposes elsewhere in *The Theory of Moral Sentiments* as impeding an individual's capacity to feel with and for others. "The poor man," Smith writes, "goes out and comes in unheeded, and when in the midst of a crowd is in the same obscurity as if shut up in his hovel." Those more wealthy than he "turn away their eyes from him, or if the extremity of his distress forces them to look at him, it is only to spurn so disagreeable an object from among them." The poor man "feels" acutely the "fortunate" classes' failure to extend their fellow-feeling to him, and his internalization of the middle-ranking spectator's rejection becomes a self-fulfilling prophecy.[38] Considered undeserving of sympathy, the poor man becomes so: his spirit hardens; his unworthiness as an object of compassion is thus proven; his deracination is complete.

As this section of *The Theory of Moral Sentiments* implies, mutual sympathy does not efface differences between the sympathetic spectator and sentimental object; rather, any obstacle between these individuals (including social or economic status) must be surmounted before that exchange can be effected. The Smithian moral economy is, thus, predicated upon a familiar paradox: sentimental exchange can (momentarily and, as we shall see, cautiously) transcend physical, economic, and cultural divisions between individuals, but fellow-feeling is possible only when those divisions are not so great that they are insuperable. At the same time, however, it is vital that a certain emotional and intellectual distance is nonetheless preserved between spectator and sympathetic object. As John Mullan explains, within the Smithian model, the spectator occupies a position of privilege: "the 'spectator' must always 'know' more than the 'agent'" whose feelings he imaginatively approximates.[39] According to this paradigm, it is necessary that identification between spectator and sympathetic object is tempered by a reassuring sense of palpable though not insurmountable difference, and nowhere, it might be argued, is the preservation of difference more crucial than in the sentimental prostitution narrative where the potential stakes of identification between spectator and object are so high.

Histories is shaped by and threatens to collapse under the weight of these competing demands to elicit identification and maintain difference. The author recognizes that in order to "smooth the stern brow of rigid virtue, and turn the contemptuous frown into tears of pity" she must first paper over the divisions that stand between the readers and the penitents. Yet she knows also, as we shall see, that her readers' authority and moral integrity should not (perhaps could not) be challenged. Among the strategies the novel deploys to negotiate these contradictions are its tireless effort to establish that none of the eponymous heroines are laboring class (despite the fact that all are forced to seek work) and its determination to write out the erotic desire that the penitents feel for their lovers in favor of a more reassuringly benign maternal love. Even though the women live as mistresses or work as prostitutes, each is somewhat implausibly presented as being "ignorant of the human heart" (110), and all three of those who become mothers exhibit, as I have already indicated, the very "tenderest love" for their children (128). The sentimentalization and desexualization of the fallen women are powerful legitimizing strategies. Thus identified as "worthy object[s] of compassion," into whose position the novel's readers' might imaginatively, but safely, place themselves, the penitents' rehabilitation is sanctioned, the readers' sympathy justified, and the author's possibly indecorous literary endeavor—a novel about prostitution—vindicated. More radically, as the relationships between Fanny and Mrs. Lafew and Emily and her sister imply, this strategy suggests that sympathy might break down the cultural divide between gentle and fallen women. Yet this possibility, so fascinatingly, if problematically, explored in the four inset narratives, is emphatically closed off by the novel's paratextual apparatus, which attempts to proscribe the terms in which the text's "gentle" readers could engage with its content.

The preface, written at Richardson's behest after the novel had already been completed, and in the months after *The Theory of Moral Sentiments* was published, set out to police the "pleasure" that readers might derive from having their "pity excited" by the penitents' stories. And as in Smith's treatise, imagination is central to the novel's articulation of its moral economy. However, even more than *Moral Sentiments*, *Histories* is suspicious of the possible effects of the vicarious identification that imagination makes possible. As the author states in the novel's preface, when "imagination [is] brought in to strengthen reason" rather than to "confound it," its effects are politicizing and edifying, but when imagination is not grounded in reason it proves to be "the wildest of things" (8). In order to prevent socially useful sympathy from degenerating into solipsistic excess, or a vicarious identification that might precipitate the reader's own ruin, the novel adopts an unusual tactic: where other reformist prostitution narratives presented themselves as true and authentic accounts, *Histories*, in its opening paragraph, "acknowleges itself to be a fiction" (3).[40] This unorthodox move maintains the crucial distance between sympathetic spectator and object theorized in Smith's work: the fictionality of the penitents' stories makes imaginative engagement with their plight possible yet safe, safer even than does its emphasis on their honorary gentility and exemplary maternal characteristics. The model of sympathy the novel sanctions, here, is not a Humean reproductive sympathy—a sympathy that imaginatively copies the sympathetic object's feelings in the mind and body of the spectator—but a Smithian feeling by analogy, in which, as John Mullan writes, sympathy operates in the "space" that is the distinction between the sympathetic spectator and object, whose positions are "neither equivalent nor opposite."[41] This creation of distance between heroine and reader implies, of course,

that what is important in the novel is not the experience of the penitents, but the feelings of sympathy that these unashamedly fictionalized tales arouse in their readers. These feelings may and should
provoke readers to offer "pardon and assistance" to fallen women,
but only by reminding them that they can prove themselves more
worthy by resisting the temptations of "vanity," "indiscretion," and
"dissolut[ion]" to which the heroines succumb (8). Thus, although
Histories challenged the charity's treatment of inmates, the preface,
in its self-conscious fictionality, recapitulates one of the institution's
most effective strategies: the aestheticization of the penitent in
order to create what Ann Van Sant has described as an "illusion of
immediacy and the actuality of distance." Just as the real-life Magdalens were offered to the public as spectacles to be consumed, so the
fictional penitents are constructed in such a way that their "presentation . . . coincides with—even represents—the social distance between [the sympathetic spectator] and philanthropic object."[42]
    The effectiveness of this distancing strategy and its implications
for the novel's argument about female community can be seen most
clearly in the story of Fanny Tent. The novel's third inset narrative
is simultaneously its most radical and its most conservative. While
the friendship between Mrs. Lafew and the penitent reveals the potentially revolutionary possibilities of female collaboration, the narrative concludes by confirming the hierarchies it had earlier
appeared to challenge. Offered more than adequate financial support by her former lover and his wife, Fanny does not need to enter
the charity: "she was the only one" of the women "who was induced
to apply to that asylum merely from penitence, unaccompanied with
any distress of circumstances" (128). Fanny's voluntary and unnecessary entrance into the institution is explained in the novel as a response to the "terr[or]" induced by Mrs. Lafew's "summary
account of the Christian revelation," but closer scrutiny indicates
that she, like Smith's "poor man," has internalized the class-based
logic of sentiment to her own detriment. Fanny is finally awakened
to the feelings of sympathy and humanity denied her throughout
her short life, only to be alerted to her "indebted[ness]" to her
moral and social superior, Mrs. Lafew. Thus convinced of her
"guilt," she voluntarily admits herself to the asylum and admits her
unsuitability as a mother by committing her "dear child" to her former mistress's "care" (127). The social and moral order momentarily threatened by the friendship between the women is restored
when Fanny forsakes her life outside the Magdalen House for the
company within it. The sentimental mechanism that enables the
friendship between Mrs. Lafew and Fanny, and which underlies the

novel's putatively radical conception of female community, is thus self-regulating. Within this moral economy, women like Fanny, no matter how deserving of sympathy, find themselves perpetually in debt. Only within the confines of the Magdalen House itself can this debt be written off and the women "be a benefit [rather] than an expence" to society at large (128).

Recognizing that *Histories'* model of community is compromised in the ways described in this essay does not negate the force of the novel's reassessment of the prostitute as a "worthy object of compassion," neither does it diminish the power of its critique of sexual double standards, the demise of the family, and the onset of industrial capitalism. It does, however, force a reassessment of the possibilities of the midcentury ideal of female community, and the sympathetic mechanisms upon which such communities frequently rest. *Histories,* more dependent than many of its fictional precedents and antecedents upon sentiment to bridge the moral and cultural divide between its readers and heroines, and more potentially radical in its attempt to unite virtuous and fallen women in a sisterhood bound by fellow-feeling, provides a fascinating test case for the scope and limits of the sentimental logic that commonly underpins these communities. The "tender . . . sensation[s]" of pity the novel seeks to arouse for the penitents must be policed both to "free" readers from "cruelty and pride" and other signs of "inhumanity," and to prevent the imaginative experiment in which the reader engages from plunging the sympathetic spectator into vice. The power of the sympathetic mechanism through which the penitent is recuperated is such that it must be controlled—by the gentrification of the prostitute, the restoration of conventional social and cultural hierarchies, and the insistence upon the text's fictionality—if the novel's gentle readers are to be protected. *Histories* successfully challenged many of the disciplinary technologies inflicted by the Magdalen House upon the bodies of its inmates through its construction of redemptive female community; but it is important to acknowledge that this community is nonetheless subject to regulatory mechanisms of its own. The novel does not achieve its universalist and democratizing promise, but this failure is as much a failure of sentiment as it is of the novel. The limits of the novel's conception of community are marked out by the limits of sympathy itself.

NOTES

I am very grateful to Katherine Binhammer, Melissa Mowry, and Mary Peace for their thoughtful comments on earlier drafts of this essay.

1. Jennie Batchelor and Megan Hiatt, eds., *The Histories of Some of the Penitents in the Magdalen-House, As Supposed to be Related by Themselves* (London: Pickering and Chatto, 2007), 90. Subsequent references will be given, parenthetically, in the text.

2. On the attribution question, see the introduction to ibid., xx–xxiii. On the sentimentalization of prostitution, and the novel's role in this process, see particularly Ellis, *Politics of Sensibility,* 177–89; Jones, "Placing Jemima," 201–20; and Rosenthal, *Infamous Commerce,* 117–19.

3. On the centrality of labor to the charity's reformative process see Jennie Batchelor, " 'Industry in Distress': Reconfiguring Femininity and Labour in the Magdalen House," *Eighteenth-Century Life* 28, no. 1 (2004): 1–20.

4. Vivien Jones, "Scandalous Femininity: Prostitution and Eighteenth-Century Narrative," in *Shifting the Boundaries: Transformation of the Languages of Public and Private in the Eighteenth Century,* ed. Dario Castiglione and Lesley Sharpe (Exeter: University of Exeter Press, 1995), 55.

5. Smith's *The Theory of Moral Sentiments* was published in early 1759, at around the same time that the manuscript of *Histories* was first given to Richardson. It is possible, however, that the author knew Smith's work (or at least became aware of some of its key preoccupations and claims) before the novel's publication in December 1759, by which time changes had been made to *Histories,* including, crucially, the addition of the preface, which is discussed in more detail below.

6. On the regulatory aspects of community in *The Governess* see Sara Gadeken, " 'A Method of Being Perfectly Happy': Technologies of Self in the Eighteenth-Century Female Community," *Eighteenth-Century Novel* 1 (2001): 217–35. On the jettisoning of sexuality from the community of *Millenium Hall* see Dorice Williams Elliott, *The Angel out of the House: Philanthropy and Gender in Nineteenth-Century England* (Charlottesville: University Press of Virginia, 2002), 33–53, and Mary Peace " 'Epicures in Rural Pleasures': Revolution, Desire and Sentimental Economy in Sarah Scott's *Millenium Hall,*" *Women's Writing* 9, no. 2 (2002): 305–16.

7. In this way, the author of *Histories* shows an awareness of, and a willingness to revise, Early Modern views on prostitution as an effect of female community. On this question see Melissa Mowry, "Women, Work, Rear-guard Politics and Defoe's *Moll Flanders,*" *Eighteenth Century: Theory and Interpretation* 49, no. 2 (2008): 97–116. I am very grateful to Melissa for allowing me to read this article prior to its publication and for sharing her thoughts on women and community in this period.

8. Lucinda Cole, "(Anti)feminist Sympathies: The Politics of Relationship in Smith, Wollstonecraft and More," *ELH* 58, no. 1 (1991): 111.

9. Lucinda Cole, " 'The Contradictions of Community': Elegy or Manifesto," *Eighteenth Century: Theory and Interpretation* 36, no. 3 (1995): 197. For a more celebratory account of female fellowships, see D'Monté and Pohl, *Female Communities.*

10. This phrase is used by Jones in her discussion of Mary Wollstonecraft's *The Wrongs of Woman, or Maria* (1798). Jemima can be rehabilitated, Jones argues, because she demonstrates her capacity to feel and is thus, "recuperable for a middle-class ideal." Jones, "Placing Jemima," 212.

11. Lady Barbara Montagu to Samuel Richardson, January 31, 1759, Kroch Rare Books Collection, miscellaneous MSS: 4600, Box 42 M, courtesy of the Division of Rare and Manuscript Collections, Cornell University Library. I am grateful to Mary Peace for making available her transcript of this letter.

12. Betty Rizzo, *Companions Without Vows: Relationships Among Eighteenth-Century British Women* (Athens: University of Georgia Press, 1994), 295.

13. Ibid., 308.

14. Sarah Scott to Elizabeth Montagu, June [20?], 1760, Montagu Collection

(MO 5281), reprinted with permission of the Huntington Library, San Marino, California.

15. Jonas Hanway, *Thoughts on the Plan for a Magdalen-House for Repentant Prostitutes* (London: James Waugh, 1758), 3.

16. Jonas Hanway, *A Plan for Establishing a Charity-House, or Charity-Houses for the Reception of Repenting Prostitutes to be Called the Magdalen Charity* (London, 1758), 29.

17. See Batchelor and Hiatt's introduction to *Histories*, xiv–xv. On the mid-century novel's valorization of writing as work see Jennie Batchelor "Woman's Work" 19–33.

18. See, particularly, Ann Van Sant, *Eighteenth-Century Sensibility and the Novel: The Senses in Social Context* (Cambridge: Cambridge University Press, 1993), 31–37.

19. William Dodd, *Advice to the Magdalens*, reprinted with an *Account of the Rise, Progress, and Present State of the Magdalen Charity* (London: W. Faden, 1761), 61.

20. Ibid., 62; Hanway, *Plan for Establishing*, 29.

21. On the impact that this thinking and other "psychologies of labor" had on the midcentury charity movement, see Donna T. Andrew, *Philanthropy and Police: London Charity in the Eighteenth Century* (Princeton: Princeton University Press, 1989), 138–41.

22. Only the second penitent is childless.

23. Rosenthal, *Infamous Commerce*, 120. Some texts straddle both traditions, for example, Daniel Defoe's *Roxana: The Fortunate Mistress* (1724). In her excellent chapter on Defoe's novel, Rosenthal challenges readings of the novel that have focused on the heroine's "maternal failure" to illuminate how Roxana "becomes a relentless possessive individualist with a driving acquisitive passion that she displays for no man," yet still "harbors an inexplicable desire for her children and loses everything by acting upon this desire" (70–96).

24. Ruth Perry, *Novel Relations: The Transformation of Kinship in English Literature and Culture, 1748–1818* (Cambridge: Cambridge University Press, 2004), 279.

25. Ibid., 208.

26. Katherine Binhammer, "The Whore's Love or the Magdalen's Seduction," *Eighteenth Century Fiction* 20, no. 4 (2008): 519. I am very grateful to Katherine for making available this unpublished chapter from her forthcoming monograph.

27. Perry, *Novel Relations*, 33–34.

28. *The Rules and Regulations of the Magdalen House*, reprinted with Dodd, *Account*, 132.

29. In "Philanthropic Community in *Millenium Hall* and the York Ladies Committee," for example, Johanna M. Smith, offers a Foucauldian reading of the novel, in which she analyzes the mechanisms of "enclosure and surveillance" that reveal fissures in the utopian society. *Eighteenth-Century Studies* 36, no. 3 (1995): 266–82.

30. For a refreshingly revisionist analysis of female community in *Volume the Last* see Terri Nickel, " 'Ingenious Torment': Incest, Family, and the Structure of Community in the Work of Sarah Fielding," *Eighteenth-Century Studies* 36, no. 3 (1995): 234–47.

31. Cole, "The Contradictions of Community," 197.

32. John Mullan, for example, has influentially argued that the eighteenth-century novel found it impossible to imagine how the ideal models of sociability imagined in the philosophical writings of Hume and Smith could be "projected on to a wider society." Novels are, he suggests, commonly restricted to "a fatalistic statement" of the "value" of sympathetic community. *Sentiment and Sociability: The Language of Feeling in the Eighteenth Century* (Oxford: Clarendon, 1988), 130.

33. See, for example, Robert Markley, "Sentimentality as Performance: Shaftes-

bury, Sterne, and the Theatrics of Virtue," in *The New Eighteenth Century,* ed. Felicity Nussbaum and Laura Brown (London: Methuen, 1987), 210–30.

34. Jones, "Placing Jemima," 205.

35. For a more detailed discussion of this novel see Ellis, *Politics of Sensibility,* 185–89.

36. Andrew, *Philanthropy and Police* 191.

37. Adam Smith, *The Theory of Moral Sentiments,* ed. Knud Haakonssen (Cambridge: Cambridge University Press, 2002), 11.

38. Ibid., 62.

39. Mullan, *Sentiment and Sociability,* 44.

40. Indeed, in a maneuver that demonstrates that fact is certainly stranger than fiction, when the first of *Histories* was reprinted in 1783, it was entirely repackaged as a real-life account. See William Dodd and M. S. *The Magdalen, or History of the First Penitent Received into that Charitable Asylum; in a Series of Letters to a Lady. With Anecdotes of Other Penitents, by the Late Rev. William Dodd* (London: W. Lane, [1783]).

41. Mullan, *Sentiment and Sociability,* 44.

42. Van Sant, *Eighteenth-Century Sensibility,* 37.

Changes in Roles and Relationships: Multiauthored Epistles from the Aberdeen Quaker Women's Meeting

Betty Hagglund

IN 1993, THE LITERARY CRITIC MARGARET J. M. EZELL CRITICIZED PREVALENT depictions of women's literary history, particularly in relation to the early modern period. She argued that:

> By unconsciously permitting our perceptions of the past to be shaped by unexamined ideologies, perhaps unwittingly carried over from certain privileged texts or theories, we may have infused the values and standards of those texts and theories in our constructions of the past. The result could be that we have unintentionally marginalised or devalued a significant portion of female literary experience.[1]

By privileging printed texts over manuscript and single-authored texts over collaborative works, we risk silencing a large proportion of early women's voices. By making the assumption that women writers in the sixteenth, seventeenth, and eighteenth centuries "shared certain innate values and desires with women in the nineteenth century and with us," we risk devaluing those texts which seem at odds with that assumption.[2] By esteeming fiction and poetry over other genres and by relying on nineteenth-century concepts of "public" and "private" literary forms, we risk misinterpreting significant groups of "nonliterary" texts such as letters and diaries.

This paper looks at one such group of manuscript "nonliterary" texts, a set of seventeenth-century letters written collaboratively by groups of Scottish Quaker women. Between 1675 and 1700, a number of multiauthored letters known as epistles were sent from a group of Quaker women at Aberdeen to the Quaker Women's Meeting in London. Four of the epistles survive, although it is likely that there would have been at least one letter sent each year and possibly more. In these epistles we can trace two important sets of changes over the twenty-five-year period: firstly, the changing role of women

137

within Scottish Quakerism and corresponding changes in their textual self-representation; and secondly, the changes in the relationships between the two groups of women.

Women's multiply authored texts have received little critical attention. Received notions of authorship and the primacy of publication have marginalized early modern women's collaborative
writings. Only a few of the signatories of this group of letters stand
out as notable in their own right, although a number of them are
known to have played central roles in the fledgling Aberdeen
Quaker movement. Two are known to have written and published
more widely. Lilias Skene, née Gillespie (1626/27–97), circulated
poetry in manuscript, wrote and delivered a prophetic warning to
the inhabitants and magistrates of Aberdeen, and published a theological postscript to a polemical work by the scholar and theologian
Robert Barclay (1648–90).[3] Christian Molleson (ca. 1651–1724),
who married Robert Barclay, wrote a number of influential letters
which were circulated among groups of Quakers throughout Scotland.[4] Many of the other women are relatively unknown. But as Catie
Gill has argued, in the only critical study to discuss seventeenth-century Quaker women's multiauthored texts in any detail,

> Multiple-authorship is significant in that it shows that Quakerism sought
> to give voice to many "ordinary" believers through its varied collective
> and collaborative modes of writing. . . . Through the collaborative efforts
> of Quakers writing multiply-authored texts, lines of horizontal alliance
> were drawn. In terms of their form, collectively authored texts produce
> an impression of community, since they implicitly unite Friends around
> an issue, or series of concerns, within a single work. The effect of such
> writing is that it offers a way to explore women's relationship to the
> wider Quaker body. . . . Since women were present as writers from the
> earliest days of the Society, they helped to shape the public definitions
> of Quaker beliefs, even as they were emerging. . . . These texts . . . show
> how shared accounts produce a sense of community through print.[5]

The letters under consideration show an awareness of writing both
as women and as Quakers. The collective norms and values of the
Quaker movement changed and shifted during the twenty-five years
between the first and last epistle being considered here. The writers
of Quaker multiauthored works both responded to those changes
and helped to shape the movement.

In his 1993 monograph, *Scribal Publication in Seventeenth-century England,* Harold Love explored the uses of manuscripts in seventeenth-
century England, suggesting that printed publication was in fact the
exception and that most writings were circulated in manuscript, a

practice which he called "scribal publication." He argued that "we now need to consider how handwritten texts are to be classed as published or unpublished within a culture in which scribal transmission might be chosen without any sense of its being inferior or incomplete."[6] Love's definition of "publication" does not necessarily require wide circulation of the text beyond a defined group, since within his classification he includes texts which circulated within a particular community such as a family, a tightly knit group of officials, or a group of courtiers.[7] Love, however, concentrated on the circulation of "literary" texts and on texts circulated via professional copyists; as Margaret Ezell has convincingly argued, despite his focus on manuscript copies, he still privileges print and "is less interested in the dynamics of . . . manuscript authorship than in the ways in which an older authorial practice is adapted to the uses of the new."[8] Nonetheless, the Quaker epistles under consideration in this paper do fit with Love's model of scribal publication and we need to understand them as public documents meant for circulation and multiple readership, not as "private" letters in the modern sense.

As the feminist critics of the Personal Narratives Group writing as a multi-authored collective contend,

> [Contexts play] an essential role in grounding and validating the interpretation of women's personal narratives. They show the importance of the interpersonal relationships within which the life story emerges; they illuminate the significance of the intersection of individual life and historical moment; they address the importance of the frameworks of meaning through which women orient themselves in the world; and they allow us to explore the ways in which the interpreter's own context shapes both the formation and interpretation of a personal narrative.[9]

One of the contexts in which we can begin to understand the four epistles is that of Scottish Quaker history and, in particular, the history of the movement in Aberdeen.

Quakerism began in Aberdeen approximately fifteen years after it had become established in England. While English Quakers had visited Aberdeen as early as 1658, it was not until the English missionary Friend,[10] William Dewsbury (ca. 1621–88), arrived in 1662 that there began to be conversions and the establishment of Quakers in Aberdeen.[11] The date is significant. It is usually agreed that English Quakerism originated in 1647, the year in which George Fox began his work as a preacher in England. By 1662, the date of Dewsbury's visit to Aberdeen, English Quakerism had changed considerably from its early ecstatic and apocalyptic form. A major scandal in 1656 had shaken many Friends' belief that following one's sense of the inward dwelling light would always guide one in correct ways.[12] English Friends became much more quietist directly after the scandal and there was a dropping off of public actions such as the disruption of church services. The corporate understanding shared by a congregation became more important than the working of the light as it appeared to an individual Friend. The emphasis in pamphlets published at this time in England shifted from prophetics to apologetics and Friends became increasingly concerned about their public image.

Other factors had also moved English Friends toward becoming a more inward-looking body. The belief that the Kingdom of God on earth was imminent had receded. An increasing number of respectable business people had joined the movement. After the Restoration in 1660, Quakers were considered suspicious and, in large sweeps, thousands of English Quakers were arrested and Quaker businesses investigated. Many Quaker historians have argued that in response to the persecution, Quakers were pushed into an attempt to be seen as nonthreatening, but this argument does not hold when we look at Scottish Quaker experience.

The Quakerism that William Dewsbury brought to Aberdeen was a post-Restoration Quakerism, coming from an English movement which was far more inward looking than it had been at the beginning. Many of the early Aberdeen converts were well connected and prominent citizens, including baillies, kirk elders, and the City Treasurer. Given that, it is interesting to note that early Aberdeen Quakerism did in fact have a strong public and prophetic element, which lasted about seventeen years and which included public preaching, prophesying, the disruption of church services, and the public acting out of symbolic signs by both women and men. Although severe persecutions of the movement began almost immediately and between 1676 and 1679 virtually every Quaker man spent weeks or months in harsh conditions in the Tollbooth, Aberdeen Friends did not move to a more inward-looking position until after the persecutions had stopped.

A large number of the early Aberdeen converts were women, many of them becoming convinced years before their husbands did. While the men were imprisoned, the women kept the movement going, managing businesses, holding meetings, delivering meals to the jail, circulating their own writings, and lobbying for the release of the prisoners. Since the authorities would not arrest Quaker women, although they frequently increased the fines imposed on the men for "their wives' transgressions," the women were able to take on significant leadership roles and tasks.[13]

As the English Quaker movement developed formal organizational structures, one of the outcomes was the creation of separate women's and men's business meetings and the gradual redefinition of women's roles and tasks within the movement. Similar organizational changes took place in Scotland, despite the different social and political context in which Scottish Quakers were operating. Critics differ substantially on their interpretation of the wider effects of the establishment of women's meetings: Phyllis Mack, for example, asserts that the establishment of the women's meetings was "in reality an extremely radical solution to the problem of reconciling emotion and spirituality with the new political order," concluding that "on balance . . . the separate women's meeting was good for women."[14] Margaret Hope Bacon argues that the separate women's meetings gave women the opportunity to "develop their talents for speaking, for raising money, for keeping minutes, for writing epistles, and for influencing their brethren."[15] In contrast, Christine Trevett has argued that women's meetings channeled Quaker women's service "into more conventional spheres" and that "what is most remarkable about the Women's Meetings . . . is the *lack* of power associated with them."[16] Regardless of the political dimensions, however, it is clear that the women's meetings provided cooperative spaces in which women could find and provide spiritual and emotional support, and their establishment led to a network of women who corresponded regularly and visited each other whenever possible.[17] They also gave women the chance to develop a variety of administrative and practical skills.[18]

It has been suggested that the epistle is a distinctive Quaker form of writing. The Swarthmore collection of manuscripts contains hundreds of letters and epistles sent by Friends, both to those inside and outside the movement. [19] While letters were generally addressed to individuals, the epistle was a public form, designed to be circulated and read by groups of people.[20] Taking the epistles of Saint Paul and the writings of the Old Testament prophets as models, Quaker women wrote prophetic warnings to those in authority who were oppressing them, answers to those who attacked them, warnings of judgments to come, and letters of comfort and inspiration to other groups of Friends.

Looking specifically at those epistles addressed by Friends to other groups of Friends, Margaret Benefiel has suggested that:

> Letters and epistles formed the backbone of the young Quaker movement. . . . Through letters Friends offered encouragement and exhortation to individual meetings and also kept meetings in touch with one

another. . . . Quakerism was not an individualistic faith. . . . The individual became fully herself only as she experienced her connection to the
community. To be cut off from the body was to lose one's source of life
and to wither and die spiritually. [Letters and epistles] conveyed this
message and thus served to weave the web of spiritual community among
early Friends. . . . Women took seriously their roles as weavers and mend-
ers of the fabric of community.[21]

Epistles could be written either by individuals or by groups. Some
were printed and circulated, others were circulated in manuscript.
The custom of groups writing and sending epistles survives to the
present day and it is still common for groups of Quakers to send
multiauthored epistles to other groups of Quakers.

Extrapolating from twenty-first-century Quaker experience and
practice and connecting that with what we know of seventeenth-century Quakers, we can, I think, make certain assumptions. The first
assumption is that every woman who was a signatory to the letter
would have felt, to a significant extent, that she "owned" that letter,
and that the letter represented or expressed her personal beliefs
and ideas as guided by God. This would be true whether she had
actually composed any part of it or not.

Secondly, and running alongside this assumption, is the fact that
the letter would have been composed at a meeting or series of meetings in which practical affairs and worship were intertwined. Even
today, meetings at which Quaker business is transacted are titled
"meetings for worship for business" and silent worship forms part
of the decision-making process. An epistle from the Women's Yearly
Meeting at York in 1688 begins: "We, being met together in the fear
of the Lord, to wait upon him for his ancient power, to order, and,
in his wisdom and counsel to guide us in our exercise relating to
church affairs."[22] Su Fang Ng has argued that Quaker acceptance of
women's prophecy and speaking by divine inspiration led directly to
an acceptance of women taking an active role in church administration, and that during the 1670–1700 period "the result of God's
spirit manifesting itself in women and authorising their speech
[was] not spontaneous and enthusiastic prophesying but rather de-
liberative policy-making suggested by the terms 'exercise' and
'church affairs.'"[23] Although, as argued above, the period of prophecy and public manifestations ended at a later date in Aberdeen
than in England, it is evident that both women and men in Aberdeen were involved in the administration and development of the
Quaker movement and that the "business" was deeply rooted in the
practice of silent worship.

The four epistles to be considered here were all sent from the Women's Meeting in Aberdeen to the Women's Meeting in London. The first one was written in 1675; the other three are from 1694, 1697, and 1700. The first one, therefore, was written just before the great offensive against the Aberdeen Quakers began in 1676 and at a time when Friends' meetings were being repeatedly disrupted, Friends were being arrested, imprisoned, and fined, and Friends' corpses were being repeatedly dug up for reburial in the kirkyard. The other three epistles were written after the persecution had ended and at a time when Aberdeen Quakers had largely withdrawn from the public arena.

The first epistle is dated February 15, 1675, twelve years after the first conversions and within only a few years of the convincement of some of the signatories.[24] Twelve women have signed it, many of them women who are known to have played significant roles in the movement. The epistle is written in Standard English and there seems to be no instance of local dialect words in any of the epistles.

The image we are given in this epistle is that of a young group placing themselves in relation to the larger and more experienced group of women in London. The Aberdeen women describe themselves as a little flock, few in number, and speak of having "a sense of weakness and unfitness to answer the obligations we are under." They talk of being "your friends & fellow travellers: in our Measures," implying a comparison in which they are the lesser.

Three times the women refer to themselves as a remnant. This term, which derives from several Old Testament texts, had become common among Friends in England from the 1660s and carried the idea of a small group which God would preserve from the persecution surrounding them.[25] Given the relatively small numbers of Friends in Scotland, this term seems to have had particular resonance for Aberdeen Friends and we find it used repeatedly in the women's writings. It underlines the women's concern for the preservation of the community, a concern which indicates the prioritizing of group experience over individual experience.

The epistle refers to the London women as caring for the Aberdeen women "as tender hearted parents, have held out an hand, for help to Children." By doing so, the writers of the epistle place themselves in the role of children. This is later reinforced by the phrase "a Liveing Cry from our hearts . . . to your father: & our father that wee may abide & grow up in him." In wider Quaker writings we find "the family model . . . employed to describe leading Quaker figures." The female role of the "mother of Israel" was assigned, for example, to Margaret Fell (1614–1702) and to Ann

Whitehead (1624–86); letters from the Fell family to George Fox (1624–91) after their convincement address him as "our dear nursing father," a term subsequently used to denote Richard Samble (ca. 1644–80) and Giles Barnardiston (1624–80).[26] These representations are clearly intended to underline the sense of familial closeness between Quakers, but also in this epistle position one group of women in relation to the other. At the same time, however, the Aberdeen women describe themselves as having "true unity" with the London women and say firmly that "wee have a place in the body; wee know the meanest member in its place: is made Instrumentall to Refresh the whole."

The epistle is steeped in biblical allusion and imagery, typical of Scottish Quaker writings of the time. The allusions are mostly Old Testament—Quakers saw direct parallels between their own experiences and those of the biblical Israelites and saw themselves as inspired by the same spirit that had inspired the prophets. The biblical references are allusive rather than direct quotation. While Quaker writers do quote directly on occasion, it was more common to write "a continuous flowing paraphrase in which biblical phrases from different sources were run together along with the author's own comments."[27]

The focus of the 1675 epistle is on the women's own experience and desire to go on in that experience. They pray that they themselves may not "outlive the tendernesse, freshnesse: zeale: & Love" that they had felt and that "not one upright in heart may turn back." This is clearly an epistle written by first-generation converts, cognizant of what they have received.

The three later epistles are much shorter and quite different in emphasis. The epistle of 1694—nineteen years later—is signed by nineteen women. Only three of the signatories signed both the 1675 and the 1694 epistles—Lilias Skene, Jean Williamson, and Jean or Joan Sumervell. Some of the women who had signed the 1675 epistle had died by then, but others appear again as signatories to the 1697 epistle, and may just have been absent from that particular meeting.

In 1694, the Aberdeen women no longer position themselves as children in relation to London. This is a letter sent to equals, to sisters, although a letter received from London is described as having contained "motherly counsel." Nonetheless, the sense of this epistle is of a group that has reached adulthood or even old age—and many of the signatories, of course, would be elderly by this time.

The earlier epistle talked of new and living discoveries of truth, of fervent love, of "freshnesse" and "zeale." The 1694 epistle, in contrast, speaks of being "helped to walk up to that holy principle and good order that is amongst the faithfull." It describes local Friends as "generally well" and the meetings as "peaceable" and goes on to say: "many can say it was a good time wherein God made his Truth known unto us," praying that "all may be kept in that meek and Lowly Spirit in which wee may be ready to receive of his counsel."

Significantly, a substantial portion of the epistle focuses on young people within the Aberdeen Meeting. The women write: "That wee may be good Examples to the youth among us is our desire and blessed be our God severall of our young ones begin to taste of his goodness and many times their young hearts are tendred thereby, and we have a good Hope that the Lord will preserve them from the evill of those times that others runn into." This is a movement in transition from the first to the second generation, with those born into the movement not having had the same experience of mystical convincement that the first group did. Male Quaker writers of the 1680s and 1690s also show concern for children and young people, but the subject is mentioned much more often in letters and epistles sent between women.[28] There is supporting evidence from other Aberdeen Quaker women's writings that keeping the youth on the right path becomes a local central concern in the 1690s and early eighteenth century.

The 1697 and 1700 epistles are very similar to that of 1694 and reinforce the reader's sense of an aging population. In 1697 the women write of going "on in Our Journey towards the holy land where Rest from our Labours is Witnessed" and pray that "you with us and we with you may feel the Rock that upholds and the ankor that will stay our Souls . . . untill the Kingdom of our Lord be over all"—a long way from early Quaker apocalyptic hopes for a Second Coming in their lifetime. Again a section of the epistle deals with children and young people: "(Blessed be the Lord) our young ones are Growing up in some Measure in the love of truth, and are beginning to see the Vanity and Emptiness of the foolish Customs and fashions of this world so that we have good Ground to hope well Concerning them . . . Let Your Cry Dear Sisters [be] with ours that they may be preserved pure and Clean from the polutions of the world." While earlier Friends saw the world as a place which would be transformed in their lifetimes, later Friends increasingly see the world as a corrupt and corrupting place with particular hazards for the young.

The 1697 epistle also mentions the visit of "our dear and Worthy sister Margaret Monro," who will carry the Aberdeen letter back to the women in London, a reminder of the importance of both corre-

spondence and intervisitation in sustaining the relationships between groups of Quaker women in different parts of Britain and
beyond. In the 1700 epistle the London women are addressed as
"mothers and sisters"—but this is, I think, a description of their social and familial roles, not a description of their relationship to the
Aberdeen women. This foregrounding of women's traditional roles
is something that did not exist in the first epistle, where the London
women were referred to as friends, friends of God, fellow travelers,
and parents—all terms without gender reference. In 1700 the Aberdeen women refer to themselves as "wee who have known the truth"
and pray to be preserved and kept faithful unto the end. Again the
issue of youth is raised: "We have good hopes of our Young Generation that the Lord will make many of them instrumental in his hand
for the carrying on of the work."

In conclusion, the changes that we see in the Aberdeen Women's
Meeting epistles reflect both changes in the perception of women's
roles during the first half century of the movement and a maturation
of the relationship between two geographically separated but spiritually and emotionally linked groups of women. How much those
changes were brought about by external factors and how much they
represent a natural development from charismatic movement to
classic religious sect and from first-generation convincement to sec-
ond-generation inheritance has still to be investigated.

Notes

1. Ezell, *Writing Women's Literary History*, 7.
2. Ibid., 27.
3. "It has [also] been plausibly claimed, but cannot be confirmed, that she assisted her husband in compiling the two manuscript accounts of the history of
Quakerism in Aberdeen which he produced in the early 1680s." For this and previous information on Lilias Skene, see Gordon DesBrisay, "Skene, Lilias (1626/7–
1697)," *Oxford Dictionary of National Biography* (Oxford: Oxford University Press,
2004), http://www.oxforddnb.com/view/article/69911 (accessed May 2008).
4. A large number of letters and epistles by Christian Barclay are held by Aberdeen City Archives.
5. Gill, *Women in the Seventeenth-Century Quaker Community*, 7–8, 183–84.
6. Love, *Scribal Publication*, 35.
7. See ibid., 44–45.
8. Ezell, *Writing Women's Literary History*, 17.
9. Personal Narratives Group, eds., *Interpreting Women's Lives: Feminist Theory and
Personal Narratives* (Bloomington: Indiana University Press, 1989), 23.
10. The terms "Quaker" and "Friend" are used interchangeably in this paper.
"Friend" is the name they usually called themselves.
11. See Joseph Besse, *A Collection of the Sufferings of the People Called Quakers*, 2 vols.

(London: Luke Hinde, 1753), 2:496; John Barclay, "Memoirs of the Rise, Progress, and Persecutions, of the People Called Quakers, in the North of Scotland," in *Diary of Alexander Jaffray* (London: Harvey and Darton, 1833), 232–35.

12. This was the 1656 Bristol scandal in which James Nayler (1618–60), a leading male Friend, together with a group of women, publicly reenacted Christ's entry into Jerusalem with Nayler taking the role of Christ. The event itself and Nayler's subsequent arrest and trial for blasphemy led to splits in the movement.

13. Gordon DesBrisay, "Lilias Skene: A Quaker Poet and her 'Cursed Self,'" in *Women and the Feminine in Medieval and Early Modern Scottish Writing*, ed. Sarah M. Dunnigan, C. Marie Harker, and Evelyn S. Newlyn (Basingstoke: Palgrave, 2004), 162.

14. Phyllis Mack, *Visionary Women* (Berkeley: University of California Press, 1992), 288, 349.

15. Margaret Hope Bacon, *Wilt Thou Go on My Errand? Journals of Three 18th Century Quaker Women Ministers* (Wallingford: Pendle Hill, 1994), 4.

16. Christine Trevett, *Quaker Women Prophets in England and Wales, 1650–1700* (Lewiston, New York: Edward Mellen, 2000), 12; Trevett, *Women and Quakerism*, 81.

17. The London Women's Meeting corresponded, for example, with women Friends in England, Wales, Scotland, Jamaica, Barbados, and the American mainland. See Irene L. Edwards, "The Women Friends of London: The Two-Weeks and Box Meetings," *Journal of the Friends' Historical Society* 47, no. 1 (1955): 5.

18. There is little information about the setting up of the Aberdeen Women's Meeting. A separate Men's Meeting "for affairs, in administering true and righteous judgement . . . and taking care of the poor, &c." is recorded as having been established at the beginning of 1672; see Barclay, "Memoirs of the Rise, Progress, and Persecutions," 299. The record of that decision, however, does not mention a Women's Meeting and it is likely that it was established some time later. Given that one of the Women's epistles is dated 1675, there obviously was a Women's Meeting in Aberdeen by that date and that first epistle includes a section justifying separate Men's and Women's Meetings, indicating, perhaps, that this had been a recent development.

19. This collection of over 1,400 original letters, accounts and other papers from the seventeenth and eighteenth centuries is held at Friends House Library, Euston Road, London NW1.

20. Some early Friends do seem to use the terms "letter" and "epistle" interchangeably. Nonetheless, the distinction usually applies.

21. Margaret Benefiel, "'Weaving the Web of Community': Letters and Epistles," in *Hidden in Plain Sight: Quaker Women's Writings, 1650–1700*, ed. Mary Garman et al. (Wallingford: Pendle Hill, 1996), 443–44, 450.

22. York Women's Yearly Meeting, *Epistle from the Womens Yearly Meeting at York, 1688 and An Epistle from Mary Waite* (York, 1688), reprinted in Garman, et al., *Hidden in Plain Sight*, 530.

23. Su Fang Ng, "Marriage and Discipline: the place of women in early Quaker controversies," *Seventeenth Century* 18, no. 1 (2003): 123.

24. Complete texts of the four epistles will be found in the appendix to this essay. Reproduced with the permission of the Library of the Religious Society of Friends in Britain.

25. For example, Isa. 11:11 and Mic. 2:12.

26. Gill, *Women in the Seventeenth-Century Quaker Community*, 164; Ng, "Marriage and Discipline," 134.

27. Moore, *Light in their Consciences*, 53.

28. See, for example, Steven Crisp, *An Epistle of Tender Counsel and Advice* (London: Benjamin Clarke, 1680), 14–15; John Crook, *An Epistle to Young People Professing the Truth* (Luton, 1686); John Banks, *An Epistle to Friends* (London: T. Sowle, 1693), 16–20; William Dewsbury, *A general epistle to Friends, from that ancient servant of Christ William Dewsebury* (Warwick, 1686); Richard Bauman, *Let Your Words Be Few: symbolism of speaking and silence among seventeenth-century Quakers* (London: Quaker Home Service, 1998), 151–53.

Appendix

Note—in all four manuscripts long s has been silently changed to s and abbreviations (yt, ye, etc.) have been expanded.

1675

[Outside: A Paper from the womens meeting at Aberdeen in Scotland
This is Coppied in the booke
1675 Meeting—
to The Women Friends of Truth at Aberdeen to the Women Friends
of Truth in London]

From the Women's Meeting of Friends of truth at Aberdeen
the 15th Day of the 2d mo: 1675

Dearly Beloved Friends,
   Wee dearly salute you all in the fervant Love of our heavenly father, which he hath Graciously & freely shed abroad in your hearts, & ours; A sweet savor of his tender love: & care: for the preservation & prosperity of his Little flock: in this Nation: & Corner, we have Received a fresh Impression of: upon the late occassion of Receveing some papers from you: Which was unto us very encouraging: & seasonable as all the vissitations: of the precious Love of our God: hath been from the beginings: whether Mediately or Imediately: unto the hearts of A Remnant: And though wee are but a small number: & some much exercised: and on the sense of Remaineing weaknesse: & unfitnesse to Answer: the Manyfold obligations wee are under: to serve, & love the Lord: And to Answer the weightie Testimonie of truth: in absolute and universall obeydiense thereonto; Yet is it the Joy: & Refreshment of our souls: to know, & feel that the Lord hath a Large gathering amongst you:. In whose hearts he hath established, the Love of truth: & every Conformment

thereof: Yea it is unto us a token for good, that he who hath begun to gather us: will go on to gather us thorowly; from all that hurts the precious Life, & all that hinders the progresse of truth in the particular & in the generall:—

And dear Friends; haveing felt your tender Love: & Care towards the Lords work: & us: as therein Interested, & as tender hearted parents, have held out an hand, for help to Children; have Communicated your experience: & severall services for our example: whosowith wee have true unity; & Can say: as face Answereth face in water: there is an Answer in the hearts of A Remnant here: according to our Capacities and occasions:—It is in our hearts Likewise, to desire your aid & [word crossed out] hand for help: In travelling in spirit: with: & for the goods sake: that the Remnant in this Nation, whom the Lord hath gathered may be preserved: that the Enemie prevaile not to pluck us out of his hand: even to the worlds observation for this is a winnowing hour here: an hour wherein the Lord is observablie at the work; to fan & to clense & to seperate: betwixt the precious & the vile, & is goeing to the bottom; to bring up: what lyeth, and hath Laine hid there; It is even feelt to be a day: wherein the Lord is risen openly to lead such forth, with [?out] [word crossed out] the workers of Iniquity, as have been secretly turning aside to Crooked waies, that which yet Remaines Lame: will yet turn others from the way; O Deare friends travell with us: that while Sathan is seeking to have us in his power to winnow: wee may not faill through Discouragment: nor Insencsbilitie of our hazard: and that none of us: who hath followed the Lord, in severall professions: according to the measure of his Manifestations, may outlive the tendernesse, freshnesse: zeale: & Love: that sometime was felt: that not one upright in heart: may turn back from following the Lord fully: neither follow the Lord, in the new & Liveing Discoveries of truth, in the Dispensation of this day; haveing some of Babylons wards in there Company: Dear friends: feell our burthens: our love: our freedom: & nearnesse through the one Everlasting truth, in this opennesse:: Many occasions are given us: of further searching of heart, further watchfulnesse: & working out our salvation, in fear, & trembleing: but never any occasion to Repent: our turning our backs upon the fleshpots of Egypt: nor hath the Lord suffered it: to enter into our hearts: to desire to turn back againe, though many particulars should fall in the wildernesse & but a few be permited to enter in, & possesse the Good Land: because we have received many precious Seals & Confirmations in our hearts, that the work is the Lords: And the testimonie & principle of truth Clearly: pure: & precious; & lives a witnesse, against all transgression: And transgressors:

As also: that over all the workings, of the spirits of violence; & deceit, & after all that the Lord hath done; or shall doe to prove, & try his people; he shall bring forth a pure people, to worship him in spirit: & in truth:—

And Friends: in a measure of the blessed presence: & Love of our God: which hath opened & enlarged your hearts towards us: and wee moved to a freedom: with you: touching our Condition; haveing found the benefit of your following the Lord therin, & that rather some account from us. wee finde necessary upon this occasion, that friends who live remote from us: & know our state, but in part, have not so fully informed you, as wee Judge were meet: for the greater Increase of your Joy on our behalfe although wee be few in number [word crossed out]: & diverse waies weak in Respect of you; yet feelling wee have a place in the body; wee know the meanest member in its place: is made Instrumentall to Refresh the whole since the Lord Gathered us by his arme of Almighty power, & seperated us from the world, both Inwardly, & outwardly: our very warmest Desire hath been to follow him fully, through tryals & temptations of all sorts: that befall us, for the exercise of our faith: & patience, the which if they were fitting to be particularly mentioned here wee know would not seem strange unto you; who / noe doubt / have known many Tribulations for your so doeing: wee may not say the Lord hath failed; to lead as wee might goe: to his praise wee mention it & for our Mutuall Refreshment: he appeared among us: & stood for us: when wee were few in number, & to the eye that looks out very dispiceable, he strengthened us to stand: till he gathered more: & added to us men of upright hearts on whom the Confornment of truth: from the Greatest matter to the least particular: was laid so weightie, that for some yeares together: wee did not see, such need of distinct meetings from them; but when we came further to see; as truth; & its affaires: had an increase: & progresse; there was an usefulnesse: & need of such meetings: wee with one Consent set about [word crossed out] it; & a few there were, & Continues to be of upright hearts: [crossed out: (on whom the Conformnent of truth)] whom the Lord Joyned to himselfe: & to one another: some of whom are taken from us by death: who were zealous, & very encourageing, while they remained among us: & others outwardly seperate as to distance of place: which for a season: made some Interuption, of the freequancie of our womens meeting; But the Lord is ariseing: & wee hope: more & more: will; to gather & raise, & build us up: in his holy power: upon the sure foundation: against which the Gates of hell Cannot prevaile, And unto him who can, &

will establish us together: with you be the praise ascribed: [crossed out: & the Glory] & the Glory over all:—

And now deare Friends of God: & his unchangable truth: wee bid you farewell feelling a Liveing Cry in our hearts: to your God: & our God: to your father: & our father: that wee may abide & grow up in him, in the sincerity & Intirenesse of Love, towards one another: that in the simplicity of truth: every eye may be single & the whole body may be full of Light: that so we may more & more, come to a perfect discerning of all: that wee are to leave behinde us: & of what yet Remaines to be attained: & experimentally witnessed, in the full accomplishment, of the Great & precious promisses: to the Gospell Church in the latter daies

Wee are your friends & fellow travellers: in our Measures in the work of the Lord: & the testimony of Jesus:

For the womens meeting of friends of truth at: London:
Hellin Skene
Christin Barcley
Elizabeth Johnston
Lillias Skeen
Anna Forbes
Elizabeth Smith
Christin Jaffrey
Jone Summervell
Isabell Cowie
Jane Williamson
Margaret Fursite
Jane Lopall

1694

[Outside: For Our Dear Friends of the Womens Meeting Att London

These are—]

Aberdeen in Scotland
the 21:4th/mo. 1694

Dear Friends & Sisters in the Lord.

Your Letter we received dated the: first month which was read in our womens meeting and it was indeed both usefull and seasonable; your good advice and motherly counsel was very acceptable to us, O! that we may be helped to walk up to that holy principle and good order that is amongst the faithfull in the Church of our God, which is the earnest desire of a Remnant, whom (blessed be his holy Name) he hath given to taste of his goodness.

Now our dear friends it is the breathing of our Souls for you as for our selves that we may all be keept in that meek and Lowly Spirit in which wee may be ready to receive of his counsel, and willing to give up our all unto him who giveth all good things and doth call for them again at his pleasure; That so we may go up hand in hand to the Mountain of our God that there wee may know his minde and will and may be helped to answer it whatever it may be, tho' it may look a little hard, yet he can make rough wayes smooth and hard things easie, a Remnant there are who have given up their names and listed themselves under his banner with a full and firm Resolution, (thro' his assistance) to follow him wheresoever he shall lead them

And now Dear Friends and wellbeloved Sisters we hereby let you understand that Friends here (at present) are generally well and our Meetings are peaceable, and many Sweet Visitations of our Fathers Love and tender streams of his never failling Mercy do runn amongst us and many can say, it was a good time wherein he made his Truth known unto us, and have cause to bless the day in which we were acquainted with him, for to the praise of his worthy Name a Remnant Can Say his mercy failleth never.

That wee may be good Examples to the youth among us is our desire and blessed be our God severall of our young ones begin to taste of his goodness and many times their young hearts are tendred thereby, and we have a good Hope that the Lord will preserve them from the evill of those times that others runn into, we have given them up unto him and he hath accepted of them if they will but be willing to Receive him on his own terms to take him for their Leader and director, then he will perfect his own work that he hath begun in them and he shall have the glory whose alone right it is.

Wee are very Sensible of your Love to us ward and wee know your Labor of Love will not want its Reward, even a double reward be returned into your bosoms Saith our Souls — And Dear Friends our desire is that we may frequently hear from you as you finde any thing in your hearts to write unto us that you may be helpfull to us in the Lord in that weighty service which we are called unto that we may grow up to gather in the fellowship of the blessed Truth, and be edified in the unchangeable Love of our heavenly Father in which we Remain — Your Friends and Sisters

Anna Skene
Rachell Gellie

Anna Leask
Isobell Galloway
Jannet Gerard
Jean Robisones
Joan Gaw
Eliza: Hall
Eliza: Stiven
Eliz: Taylour
Margaret Gordone
Margaret Tayllor
Elizabeth Glennie
Lilias Skeen
Isobell Gerrard
Isobell Gray
Jean Williamson
Jean Somervell
Mary Leslie

1697

[Outside: For the Women's Meeting Att London]

Dear and Wellbeloved Sisters In the Lord

Your Letter Dated the 31 of the 3 month 1697 Came to our Hands some days agoe and was Read in Our Womens Meeting it was Very Acceptable, unto us and great Encouragement we have to Goe on in Our Journey towards the holy land where Rest from our Labours is Witnessed and praises Returned to Our God who so Largely Hath let forth of his Mercys and is daily Giveing us New Draughts of his love, the Righteous will be Glad and Rejoyce for Our God is worthy, worthy is he Can A remnant Say and with Love unfeigned doth our Souls Dearly Salute you our Dear friends Mothers and Sisters Even with a measure of that pure Love which our Lord Jesus Christ hath bestowed upon us, of which Love and Goodness you hath he made Large shearers of and his Right hand hath a Remnant Known to be A Supporter and Refuge in the day of trouble, so that many times when the wicked one hath sought to destroy our hope his power hath been near to uphold, O Can we not say he is our God and we will trust in him, Dear Sisters truth [crossing out] prospers in this place and our meetings are peaceable and quiet and fresh, and the Living springs of our fathers love doth Run Amoungst us and (Blessed be the Lord) our young ones are Growing up in some Measure in the love of truth, and are begining to see the Vanity and Emptiness of the foolish Customs and fashions of this world so that we have good Ground to hope well Concerning them which is matter of great Joy to us who are Mostly Concerned in them, Let Your Cry Dear Sisters be with ours that they may be preserved pure and Clean from the polutions of the world, and Now haveing the Occation of this our dear and Worthy sister Margaret Monro whose Visit to us in the love of God and true Regard to his blessed truth in Visiting the seed of God in this place was very Acceptable, we did judge it a very fit Opertunity to send this by her who Can Give you a more full account of the Affairs of truth here away unto whome we refer You, and do hope She shall Return with a plentifull reward in her Bosom And now dear Sisters our Cry in our small measure is that you with us and we with you may feel the Rock that upholds and the ankor that will stay our Souls which will never fail but will Endure to the End of all temptations and troubles, untill the Kingdom of our Lord be over all, unto whome we Dearly Commit and Recommend you all, and bids you fare well Dear Sisters we Rest your Friends and Sisters in the truth

Aberdeen In Scotland the

14 of 5th month 1697———

Anna Leask
Christian Jaffray
Margared Forbes
Issobell Summervell
Margaret Gray
Katheren Barclay
Christian Barclay younger
Margaret Fallconer younger
Anna Skene
Janet Gerrard
Jane Williamesone
Anna Seatoune
Christian Barclay
Margaret Fallconer
Issobell Gerard
Issobell Leaske
Elizabeth Hall
Anna Burnet
Mary Bennerman
Elizabeth Barclay

1700

[Outside: For The Meeting of women Friends att London]

To our Friends & sisters of the Womens Meeting at London

Dear Friends:

Mothers & Sisters whome we do Esteem & Honour in the Lord & in the Everlasting Covenant of light & life do we Dearly salute you all.

Yours we received Dated the 19th: 4/mo: 1699: & were greatly refreshed in the reading of the same feeling the Divine fountain of the love of our God to runn so plentifully through you our Dear Sisters towards us, & we may say many Testimonies & tokens of his love do we receive from time to time of which this is not the Least that he brings us to your remembrance so as to Visit us with a few lines for our comfort & Strengthening as well as for our Instruction & O it is the breathing of our Souls that we may walk worthy of & answer his great love, who is our God & our trust is in him, that he will carry on the work that he hath begun, yea he is Carrying of it on Sweetly Blessed be his holy name for ever; for he is reaching to the hearts of many Even in this our Nation, & causing them to see the Vanity & Emptiness of all Will worship & leting of them see the Great want there is of true & Spirituall Religion.

O that wee who have known the truth & have been partakers of the life & Virtue thereof may be preserved in the same & be Examplary to them in our lives & conversations; Blessed be the Lord truth is prospering amongst us & our meetings quiet & peaceble; & we have great hopes of our Young Generation that the Lord will make many of them Instrumentall in his hand for the carrieing on of his work many have been our cries and Supplications to the father of all our Mercies on their behalf, which we hope will not be Ineffectuall yea he hath in a measure answered the same, praised be his holy name for ever

And Dear Friends & webeloved [sic] in the Lord we do earnestly desire the help of your prayers as ours are often for you & we hope shall be that our God may preserve & Keep us all faithfull unto him Even unto the End, so to the Lord do we recommend you with our own Souls Earnestly Desireing that you may more & more, tast feel & enjoy of his soul comforting & refreshing presence to whome be Glorye honour & praises, rendered & ascribed now & for Evermore

Signed by your Dear Friends & Sisters in the unchangable truth.

From our womens meeting Held at Aberdeen in Scotland the Sixth day of the 2d month 1700

Heline Corbes
Issobel Gerard
Mary Banerman
Isobell Galloway
Helen Gellie
Lillias Glennie
Jannett Gerard
Margaret Gellie
Jane Williamssone
Joane Gae
Christan Jaffery
Elizabeth Hall
Margaret Forbe
Margret Taylor

Elizabeth Carter and Modes of Knowledge
Judith Hawley

Eᴌɪᴢᴀʙᴇᴛʜ Cᴀʀᴛᴇʀ (1717–1806) ᴡᴀs ᴛʜᴇ ᴍᴏsᴛ sᴜᴄᴄᴇssꜰᴜʟ ᴏꜰ ᴛʜᴇ ꜰɪʀsᴛ generation of Bluestockings. Her translation of the works of Epictetus (ca. 55–ca. 135)—the first complete English translation of this Stoic philosopher—garnered praise and earned her financial independence.[1] She was celebrated in public as the most learned English woman of her day. In private she collected round her a sustaining circle of affectionate friends.[2] There are apparently two sides to Carter's life and works: she challenges both her contemporaries and modern readers by appearing in contradictory guises: as "Epictetus Carter" the rational Stoic on the one hand, and as "my Dear Miss Carter," the sentimental Bluestocking friend, on the other.[3] These contradictory guises are evidence of the difficulty learned women faced in achieving public recognition. One assumption made then and now is that in order to acquire knowledge, a woman had to suppress her feelings. Romance and marriage are perhaps incompatible with the life of the mind. Indeed, there is an explicit association between the Bluestockings and repression. They have been seen, largely correctly, as conservative, pious, and socially conformist. However, recent work on the Bluestockings in general and Carter in particular has opened gaps in this rigid casing and revealed greater complexity in their conservatism. In the stimulating collection of essays edited by Nicole Pohl and Betty Schellenberg, scholars have reconsidered the Bluestockings in a number of fruitful ways.[4] Some address issues to do with their relationship to the Establishment. In different ways, Emma Major and Susan Staves address the relationships between the Bluestockings and the church. Other essays in this collection explore more private and emotional aspects of Bluestocking relationships. Deborah Heller examines how Carter and Elizabeth Montagu (1718–1800) both celebrated the free-spirited persona of the "Sylph," Elizabeth Vesey (1715?–91), and counseled her to regulate her feelings. Susan Lansing suggests that the regulation of feelings or "economy of desire" was a screen for Sapphic

longings. I want to suggest that Carter experienced a conflict between her rational public persona and her private affections, yet
found ways to resolve these tensions. For her, feelings were a mode
of knowledge. More specifically, her sentimental feelings for her
dear friends gave her knowledge of the afterlife. While feeling reinforced her Christian piety, her rationally held orthodox belief reconciled her to separation from her friends.

We should begin by acknowledging the difficulties the burden of
her knowledge imposed on Carter. As well as causing her literal
headaches, knowledge was difficult to carry off. The term "learned
lady" was something of an oxymoron. Yet it is inaccurate to assume
that Carter's personal quest for knowledge and her public reputation as a learned lady were met with widespread opposition and patriarchal suppression. Carter was very much supported in her studies
by her father and she was not unique in this respect, as Miriam Ler-
enbaum reveals.[5] Harriet Guest convincingly demonstrates that Carter was actually celebrated as an icon.[6] In the 1760s and '70s, she
was revered both for her own achievements and for making learning
respectable for other women. Carter's exemplary success, rather
than bringing her opprobrium, was a source of national pride. Or
to be more exact, argues Guest, Britain prided itself on having produced a learned woman like Carter (and unlike the French *femmes
savantes*). Not that it then went to any lengths to provide a system
of primary and secondary schools to educate other women. Indeed,
Guest notices that Carter's hard-won advances were soon lost: with
the French Revolution and subsequent wars, a conservative backlash
once again made the learned woman a transgressive figure because
she threatened the gender balance on which the whole social hierarchy depended. Hannah More's (1745–1833) *Strictures on the Modern
System of Female Education* (1799) and *Hints Towards Forming the
Character of a Young Princess* (1805) can be taken to exemplify the
conservative attitudes which prevailed when Montagu Pennington
(1762–1849) published the body of work that brought Carter to a
wider audience.

Whether in spite of or because of this paternal support, Carter
internalized opposition to learned women. She expressed com-
plexly ambivalent feelings about how she appeared in public, and
how she passed her time in private. Often, she tried to present herself in public as very ordinary, sitting quietly knitting in a corner at
social gatherings.[7] At the same time, she relished anecdotes about
how other people saw her as a freak: some of her country neighbors
thought that she was either a witch or destined to become a Member
of Parliament; the London papers jested that she and the other

Bluestockings should be awarded honorary degrees or Oxbridge Fellowships.[8] In private, she indulged in both intellectual and trivial pursuits. Those who know her as "Epictetus Carter" would think it entirely in character to come across her studying astronomy, mathematics, Latin, Greek, Hebrew, French, Italian, Spanish, Portuguese, Arabic, and German. They would be surprised to find that she boasted in her letters of her enjoyment of dancing, flirting, buying clothes, taking snuff, and going on long country rambles.[9]

Carter posed conundrums (partly deliberately) for her contemporaries as well as for later readers. Even a cursory glance at the range of modes of knowing and being she experimented with, as well as at the range of genres she worked in, indicate the difficulty of accommodating her in a simple scheme. She demonstrated her abilities in original composition by producing poetry and in foreign languages by publishing both modest and ambitious translations of learned works. In her roles first as poetic prodigy in the pages of the *Gentleman's Magazine* and then as Epictetus Carter, she demonstrated what might be possible for women. She was a powerful advocate for women's education and women's writing. Montagu Pennington in his *Memoirs* of his aunt rather apologetically mentions "her extreme partiality for writers of her own sex" (line 447–48). Yet some questions remain: why did Carter not champion learned women in a more forthright way in her public life, and why did she feel ambivalent about her learning even when, or especially when, she received widespread support? Unlike the younger Bluestockings, Hester Chapone (1727–1801) and Hannah More, she did not publish any treatises or conduct manuals on women's education. Her modestly worded but subtly incisive statement about the possibility that women might equal men intellectually if they were granted the same educational opportunities was rather hidden in *Sir Charles Grandison* (1753–54) by Samuel Richardson (1689–1761), in a debate in which Grandison's own views about the different natures of men's and women's minds is given more prominence (242–51). Why did she hide behind the roles of, on the one hand translator, and on the other sympathetic correspondent, rather than setting out her own philosophy in a systematic way? And why are her poems more orthodox than her letters?

The difference between public and private might provide a clue about Carter's decisions to promote the orthodox or the sentimental, the rational or the emotional. There has been much discussion about the Bluestockings' ideological positioning in recent debate about the formation of public and private spheres.[10] In her discussion of Carter and other Bluestockings, Harriet Guest focuses on the public perception of their contribution to national life.[11] The Habermasian public/private divide seemed for a time to help make sense of gender and culture formations in the eighteenth century. It now seems to complicate more than it clarifies and to lead to some rather contorted reasoning. Rather than trying to position Carter and the Bluestockings in general on one or other side of the binary opposition, it would be more helpful to recognize that there are relative grades of publicity from, at one extreme, the privacy of silent thought, through personal conversation, correspondence, and general conversation at a Bluestocking assembly to print publication at the other extreme. Individuals can perform in different roles in different moments in their lives and even occupy overlapping positions. Carter had an identity as a private and as a public individual. Not surprisingly, she presents herself differently in different contexts. These differences are ones of nuanced degree more than differences of kind, but still, in her published writings she deals with general knowledge and in her familiar letters she deals with particular and relative knowledge. That is, she tempers her pronouncements to her perception of the needs of her audience.

It is possible to test this claim about how Carter employs different modes of knowledge in different contexts because she frequently treats the same themes (such as solitude, the world of sense, the afterlife, friendship, natural scenes, history, particular people and places) in rather different ways in her poems and letters.[12] The comparison is, of course, compromised because, in preparing Carter's private correspondence for publication, her nephew Montagu Pennington exercised a heavy editorial hand. Nonetheless, by analyzing a series of letters and a poem addressed to Elizabeth Vesey on the subject of the role of the imagination and the existence of an afterlife, we can assess how far Carter reserves particular and experiential knowledge for private communication.[13] In her poem "To Mrs Vesey," dated 1766, Carter seems to present herself as keen to transcend the trammels of the physical universe and to look forward to the coming of the archangel who will signal the end of the world. Her letters, I will suggest, are rather more attached to this world and are enthusiastic about the knowledge to be gained from experience. As is typical of many of her poems, especially those published in her second collection, *Poems on Several Occasions* (1762), she begins the poem by dimming the senses in order to withdraw from the world of sense perception. In this poem she walks at the close of day in a shady grove and visits a grand Gothic structure, probably an abbey or cathedral:

SILENT and cool the dews of ev'ning fall,
Hush'd is the vernal music of the groves,
From yon thick boughs the birds of darkness call,
And mark the walk that Contemplation loves.

(lines 1–4)

Other poems begin at nightfall or midnight and locate the poet in a marginal place such as the seashore or a graveyard to which she has withdrawn to enjoy the melancholy pleasures of solitude. Typically she describes the fading of the light and argues that the extinction of the senses and the apparent disappearance of the gaudy and vain world allow the philosophical powers of reason to awaken. She imagines talking to a friend whose absence she laments, and some lost pleasures recalled. The friend's virtues will be contrasted with the folly of the world and she will be counseled to reject the labyrinths of the passionate world and to pursue the paths of virtue. Finally, and perhaps to figure the process of transcendence more vividly, Carter imagines the death and ascension to heaven of her friend, looking forward to the heavenly dawn of resurrection.[14]

"To Mrs Vesey" seems to be no exception to this typical pattern. It seems at first reading to lament the vanity of human wishes. In this awe-inspiring Gothic pile, "The various schemes of busy care repose" (line 18): the "moon's pale beam" (line 20) casts its gloomy light on the tombs of the dead, ironically highlighting the failure of their grand ambitions and the nothing to which their schemes of pleasure have come. Similarly, in her "Ode to Wisdom," she notes that "fortune drops her gay Parade, . . . Pleasure's transient Roses fade, / And wither in the Tomb." (lines 43–45). And in her "Ode to Melancholy," she asks whether "wild Ambition" (line 43), "ill-got Wealth's superfluous Store" (line 44), or "pleasure's more bewitching Charms" (line 46) can avert "the Dread of Death" (line 45). These poems have a shared structure of renunciation and employ similarly abstract poetic diction.

However, "To Mrs Vesey" is mounting a more complex argument than first appears. Rather than being a monologue on the vanity of human wishes, it is actually dialogic in structure.[15] Carter voices and then challenges the melancholy nihilism of the Sylph: "Yet check that impious thought, my gentle friend, / Which bounds our prospects by our fleeting breath" (lines 37–38). Mrs. Vesey's nervous character had always made her an amusing but a high-maintenance friend. She was such a mental butterfly that she interested herself in everything but settled nowhere. The best aspect of this characteristic was that it allowed her, as Montagu enthused, to harmonize differences and to make her drawing room into a paradise where opposing forces could be reconciled.[16] The worst was that she fretted about everything and was often transported to a dark realm of her own imagining. What particularly disturbed Carter was that Vesey rejected the assurances of religious faith. This poem is just one of Carter's many attempts to comfort Vesey by either chiding or persuading her toward faith. Perhaps because of sensitivity to her friend's feelings, or in acknowledgment of the difficulty of always suppressing doubt, Carter does not structure the poem as a dialogue with a clear-cut distinction between Vesey's impious thoughts and Carter's correct ones. Rather, the poem allows the gloomy thoughts to arise out of the Gothic shade and to develop for a while. The "dubious shade" (line 5) in stanza 2 casts a shadow over "th'astonish'd mind" (line 8) so that it imagines how successive generations of artists, philosophers, and public or fashionable figures have busied themselves only to end up mouldering in their tombs. These thoughts are only checked when they despair even of Affection: "E'en Virtue sighs, while poor *Affection* mourns / The blasted comforts of the desert heart" (lines 35–36). At this point, a separation opens up between what we might call the "Sylphic" and the "Carterian" voices in the poem. Here the Carterian voice intervenes to check the impious thought that there is no life after death. Crucially it is Virtue and Friendship, the two qualities which the Sylphic voice had most despaired about, that the poet insists are evidence of the afterlife:

> Ah! what is Friendship, if at once disjoin'd,
> The sympathetic tie unites no more?
> Ah! what is Virtue, if below confin'd?
> The fruitless struggle of a toilsome hour.
>
> (lines 41–44)

Again and again, Carter argues that the experience of friendship demonstrates the existence of heaven. When she is separated from a friend, whether by absence, marriage, or death, she reflects that the intensity of their feeling and the virtues that are activated in their relationship prove to her that there must be a God and that God must intend to reunite friends after death.[17] Her feelings for her friends are a mode of knowledge. The lesson they teach her and which she feels it is her duty to pass on is that this present moment is evidence of an eternity in which they will never be separated.

The final stanza of the poem raises Mrs. Vesey's eyes from the gloomy graveyard and directs her heavenwards to see the end of the world revealed:

> To Nature rescu'd from Corruption's pow'r,
> The glad Archangel lifts his awful voice:
> He swears that Time and Change shall be no more;
> Hear Earth and Heav'n! and Earth and Heav'n rejoice!
>
> (lines 57–60)[18]

The ending is truly apocalyptic, but Carter does not always preach transcendence. She rejects Epictetus's argument that we should pay no heed to the things of this life.[19] From the point of view of a Stoic or an Ecclesiastes, all is vanity, but Carter's belief is that to a Christian, earthly experience is valuable in itself and necessary as a preparation for the future. In stanza 4, she had argued that human endeavor is not rendered meaningless by death, but that artists and philosophers are elevated because they think of the future.

Similarly, Carter's "Ode to Wisdom" ends on a note of renunciation, but in the middle, as Harriet Guest notices, Carter celebrates the public activity of moral and social reform.[20] Virtuous individuals only go into retirement so that they can return to their duties refreshed. Plato retreated to "the peaceful Groves" (line 58) to fine-tune his philosophy in order to reclaim Athens's "wild licentious Youth" (line 67). The poet, patriot, and domestic being are all associated with both retirement and with social improvement brought about by the triumph of virtue over the passions.

> Thy Breath inspires the Poet's Song,
> The Patriot's free unbiass'd Tongue,
> The Hero's gen'rous Strife:
> Thine are Retirement's silent Joys,
> And all the sweet endearing Ties
> Of still, domestic Life.
>
> ("Ode to Wisdom," lines 73–78)

So wisdom is found in retirement and in the privacy of domestic life, but equally it is found in the public lives of poets, politicians, and heroes. Her advice to Elizabeth Vesey is to come down from her flight of gloomy fancy and to recognize the value of engagement with the world.

The genre of this poem, or more precisely the public presentation of all Carter's poems, poses another interesting conundrum: they are "occasional" poems that maintain a distance from the experience that occasioned them. Carter published two collections of poems, the first called *Poems on Particular Occasions* (1738) and the second entitled *Poems on Several Occasions* (1762). The "occasional" poem, still a genre that survives in, for example, commemorative verses by the laureate, was a very common form in the eighteenth century, encompassing such things as dedications and other liminal verses, epigrams, toasts and valentines, funerary or hymeneal poems, poems on affairs of state, national disasters, and military exploits. Much poetical magazine fodder was occasional in orientation; between 1735 and 1744, Carter herself contributed epigrams, elegies, replies to, and poems "on" someone or something to the poetry department of the *Gentleman's Magazine*. Several of the works published in her first slim collection are clearly occasional. One commemorates a private occasion, the poet's birthday ("In Diem Natalem"), two are public: "On the Death of . . . Queen Caroline"; "To Mr Duck, occasioned by a Present of his Poems." The poems in her second collection are more devoted to private friends and personal occasions. The occasions include a thunderstorm, a walk on the seashore, the gift of a watch, the death of a child, and a visit to an oratorio. More than twenty are addressed to friends and relations, but only one is addressed to a named friend: the Earl of Bath. The majority of them are addressed "To BLANK," i.e., to unnamed friends and private individuals, most of them young women about whom nothing is now known.[21] In both of Carter's volumes of poetry, particularity is downplayed: most of the names are replaced by blanks, dates and places are rarely specified, darkness and solitude reduce the opportunity for engagement with places and people. Moreover, the tone of her poems is not worldly. The language does not encourage a direct knowledge of the world through the senses, although engagement with the world is what she usually recommends for her friends.

Carter's correspondence is much more particular than her poems as we can see by comparing the poem to Mrs. Vesey with some of Carter's letters to her. Pennington reproduces this poem and the letters in rather misleading ways in the *Memoirs*. He dates the poem 1766 and the letter 1770, but because the letter seems to refer directly to a letter Vesey sent to Carter in which she sketched out a fantasy about a Gothic retirement, I suggest that the poem might have been written shortly after the letter and thus be a different working out of the same complex of ideas.[22] Pennington's editorial interference is also misleading in the way he supplies titles to Carter's poems and letters: he makes the poems more particular and the letters more general. "To Mrs Vesey. 1766" was one of the poems Carter added in the third edition (1776) and she did identify the addressee, but the names of most of her friends were not made public until Pennington reprinted her poetry in the *Memoirs*. The letter he treats as if it were an essay on a specific topic by supplying the title: "ON THE INDULGENCE OF FANCY. &C. &C. TO MRS. VESEY. 1770." He also puts together a series of extracts from letters to Mrs. Vesey and to another unidentified correspondent under the title "ANSWERS TO OBJECTIONS CONCERNING THE CHRISTIAN RELIGION."[23] He went against his aunt's wishes in publishing her correspondence and tried to protect her reputation by perpetuating an image of her as a pious moralist. I do not mean to deny that she was pious or moralizing—she was—but I need to indicate that he deliberately excluded from view aspects of the private Carter by excising from the letters what he called "trifling chit chat and confidential communications" (*Memoirs*, 5). Thus the letters he printed do not give us a full indication of how she came across to her friends, but still they represent a marked contrast between the works she intended for publication and the works she did not.

In the letter to Vesey, she refers to the Gothic vision as an example of the Sylph's characteristic magic and a fantasy in which she is happy to indulge: "I am inexpressibly delighted with your Gothic retirement, which I shall certainly visit every moonlight evening; and I hope you will advance to meet me with the first ray, which you discover gleaming through your cathedral window" (2:158–59). She imagines herself and Vesey like witches summoning the inhabitants of the ruined abbey: "When the twilight aids the visions of contemplation, and the owl begins his melancholy serenade, we will conjure up the Lady Abbess, and fix her in her niche in the wall. We will summon together a long series of the successive tenants of this venerable fabric, and we will make them recount to us the adventures of former days" (2:159).

Although she does not recount the adventures, these tenants are considerably more embodied than the personifications in the poem who appear only in the form of "limbs" (line 12) and "heads" (line 12) and abstractions such as the Passions of the "giddy throng" (line 27). Moreover, she uses the letter to draw her friend's mind from both her own imaginary visions and the generalities of history. Listening to these stories from the past will bring them back to the present reality. Dissatisfaction with our lives might draw us into fantasies about the past, but "the telescope through which we survey the actors on the theatre of past ages, can give us only a general view; while the distance conceals from us the whole play of those little interests and passions, which . . . form most of the business and bustle of general and private life" (2:159–60). The particularity of biogra-

phy makes it a much better mode of knowledge than history because
the detail allows one to assess life more realistically. She reinforces
this lesson with an example from her own recent study: she has been
reading Plutarch's lives and finds it so vividly detailed that she col-
lapses the distance between past and present:

> I find very little difference between what passed among the inhabitants
> of Athens and Rome, and the news of the day in London; and when I
> read of Cicero's and Pompey's appointment to sup with Lucullus, it is
> no more than hearing that my Lord Lyttelton and Mr. Pitt had engaged
> themselves to dine with Sir Laurence Dundas, on condition that he
> would not set all his six men cooks to work for their entertainment.
> (2:160)

The parallel between the Romans and the Londoners is certainly
pertinent and has a tighter grip on reality than the broad references
to Ambition and Pleasure in the poem. Pompey the Great (106–48
BC) and William Pitt the Elder (1708–78) are a good match; George
Lyttelton, first Baron Lyttelton (1709–73), famous as both a man of
letters and a major player in Patriot politics, is an apt avatar for the
orator and statesman Cicero (106–43 BC); and Lawrence Dundas
(1710–81), who had amassed a fortune supplying the army with the
necessaries of life and spent it lavishly, lines up with Lucullus
(118–56 BC), the retired general notorious for his luxurious appe-
tites. But it is significant that Carter describes them in their private
lives (if a meeting between political grandees could ever really be a
private matter) and juxtaposes the grandeur of the political figures
with the hubris of Dundas's domestic arrangements. Feigning surprise that her disquisition on antiquity and fantasy could have led
her in this direction, the classical scholar famous for her culinary
abilities asks: "Do pray tell me, for it is past my comprehension, how
the subject with which I sat out could possibly lead me to Sir Laurence Dundas and his six men cooks [?]" (2:161).

The letter achieves an impressive balance between public and private, political and emotional, imaginative fancy and moral lesson.
Friendship is at the heart of it: Carter's friendship with Lyttelton
gives her a link to high politics; friendship for Vesey allows her to
join with her in fantasy but also gives her a moral duty to try to bring
the Sylph down to earth. Friendship, too, is her evidence for the existence of an afterlife in which we will no longer require the bodies
which are necessary both for knowledge of the world and for living
the life which earns a place in heaven.[24] Thus in a letter to Vesey
adapted by Pennington, Carter responds to Vesey's apocalyptic fan-

tasy of universal ruin by assuring her that death is not the end; life is "a kind of preparation to a state of undecaying life, unwearied activity, and uninterrupted order" (2:402). The climax of her argument anticipates the end of her poem to Vesey: "Thus amidst the wasters of mortality, the havoc of raging elements, and the dissolutions of consuming years, the thoughts look forward to a period of restoration, and anticipate the voice of the Archangel proclaiming to a renovated world 'that time shall be no more'" (2:402).

The recurrence of this prophetic phrase suggests how much comfort it provided to Carter herself. She possessed the paradoxical certainty of a Christian: the end of her knowledge is to know the thing that cannot be known until she is no more.

Carter saw her role as a learned woman as teaching what she believed to be the great lesson in life: the truth of the revelation, a truth derived from the Book. In her version of Anglican orthodoxy, this truth might be borne out by experience and apprehended in the feelings, but it is independent of personal discovery or rational deduction. Knowledge, then, is transcendent and learning life's great lesson is more important than secular learning. Yet secular knowledge is not to be neglected and, in Carter's case, it was intimately connected with feelings. Carter's translation of Epictetus was undertaken as an act of friendship, therefore her learning was conducted in an affective context. It was molded by the advice she received from Catherine Talbot (1721–70) and her guardian, Archbishop Secker (1693–1768), both of whom encouraged her to point out the errors and dangers of the Stoic philosophy from a Christian point of view. It brought her friendship with Elizabeth Montagu, a friendship which led her to articulate her belief about the relations between reason and feeling, mind and body.

Carter's orthodox Christian belief underlies much of her ambivalence about her reputation as Epictetus Carter. However, while it underpins a strong current of conservatism in her writing, it might also open up the possibility of both intellectual and spiritual equality and a balance between reason and feeling. At the same time as fitting her into an institutional identity, Carter's beliefs could be read as a way of sidestepping the gender binary, thus of escaping social restrictions. Like the Cartesianism of Mary Astell (1668–1731), Christianity provided a way of asserting that the mind has no sex; all souls will be equal in the sight of God. Maintaining a respectable persona and refusing to marry were both ways of avoiding being in thrall to social expectations. Much of the advice Carter gives to her friends has this air of liberation rather than of restriction. She urges the flighty Vesey to come down to earth to exchange the experience of physical satisfaction for imagined miseries; she coaxes the melancholy and darkly pious Talbot to get out more and to enjoy the "trifling" and "bustle" of the "worky-day world."[25] The anxiously wealthy Montagu needed to be advised to think better of herself intellectually and to aim higher than the top of the social echelon. In each case, she fits her prescriptions to the particular needs of her friends rather than imposing on them a general model. She wishes to reconcile them to themselves to release them into self-development.

NOTES

1. See Judith Hawley, ed., *Elizabeth Carter,* vol. 2, *Bluestocking Feminism: Writings of the Bluestocking Circle, 1738–1785,* general ed. Gary Kelly (London: Pickering & Chatto, 1999), 1–3.

2. This chapter is based on a paper delivered to the Women's Studies Group 1558–1837 Day School on Women and Learning in April 2002. I was very pleased to participate in this event because a meeting of WSG is the perfect forum for a discussion of the subject of women and learning. I was even more pleased to be invited to revise my paper as part of a tribute to Mary Waldron whose life and career exemplify the best traditions of the acquisition and dissemination of knowledge about and among women. It was a tradition earlier exemplified by Elizabeth Carter. Waldron and Carter would have a lot to say to each other about the challenges faced by independent women scholars. I would like to feel that they are now enjoying a stimulating conversation in a Women's Study Group of the afterlife. I have also incorporated material from a paper I gave at another congenial gathering: "The Bluestocking Circle: Muses and Amazons," a conference held at the Henry E. Huntington Library, May 2001.

3. Elizabeth Montagu addressed her as "my Dear Miss Carter" when she first came to know her in 1758; her form of address changed to "My Dear Friend" as their intimacy grew. See Elizabeth Carter, *Letters from Mrs. Elizabeth Carter to Mrs. Elizabeth Montagu,* ed. Montagu Pennington, 3 vols. (London: F. C. and J. Rivington, 1817).

4. Pohl and Schellenberg, *Reconsidering the Bluestockings.* See, esp. Harriet Guest, "Bluestocking Feminism," 59–80; Susan Staves, "Church of England Clergy and Women Writers," 81–103; Emma Major, "The Politics of Sociability: The Public Dimensions of the Bluestocking Millennium," 175–92; Deborah Heller, "Subjectivity Unbound: Elizabeth Vesey as the Sylph in Bluestocking Correspondence," 215–34; Jane Magrath, "'Rags of Mortality': Negotiating the Body in the Bluestocking Letters," 235–56; and Susan S. Lanser, "Bluestocking Sapphism and the Economies of Desire," 257–75. For other insightful studies of Carter, see Williams, "Poetry, Pudding and Epictetus," 3–24; Clarke, *Dr Johnson's Women;* Guest, *Small Change;* Thomas, "Th'Instructive Moral and Important Thought," 137–69; Freeman, "A Dialogue," in Armstrong and Blain, *Women's Poetry,* 50–63.

5. Miriam Leranbaum, "'Mistresses of Orthodoxy': Education in the Lives and Writings of Late Eighteenth-Century Women Writers," *Proceedings of the American Philosophical Society* 121 (1977): 281–301. See also Staves, "Church of England," in Pohl and Schellenberg, *Reconsidering the Bluestockings.*

6. See Guest, *Small Change,* esp. 95–151. For national pride, or possibly relief, in the fact that England had finally produced a woman capable of matching the erudition of the French Anne le Fevre Dacier (1654–1720), see Staves, "Church of England," in Pohl and Schellenberg, *Reconsidering the Bluestockings,* 96.

7. See Elizabeth Sheridan, *Betsy Sheridan's Journal: Letters from Sheridan's Sister, 1784–1786 and 1788–1790,* ed. William LeFanu (Oxford: Oxford University Press, 1986), 40; Carter to Talbot, September 14, 1754, Elizabeth Carter, *A Series of Letters between Mrs. Elizabeth Carter and Miss Catherine Talbot, from the Year 1741 to 1770. To which are Added, Letters from Mrs. Elizabeth Carter to Mrs Vesey, between the Years 1763 and 1787,* ed. Montagu Pennington, 2 vols. (London: F. C. and J. Rivington, 1808), 2:182.

8. See Montagu Pennington, *Memoirs of the Life of Mrs. Elizabeth Carter, with a New Edition of her Poems . . . to which are Added, some Miscellaneous Essays in Prose,* 2 vols. (London: F. C. and J. Rivington, 1816), 1:48, 246. See also Harriet Byron's compliment to Carter in her discussion about women, learning, and modes of knowledge in Richardson, *Sir Charles Grandison,* 49.

9. See her letters to Catherine Talbot January 1, 1743, January 20, 1748, May 24, 1744, in Hawley, *Elizabeth Carter,* 381, 388–89, 384, and the introduction to this volume, 14; and Pennington, *Memoirs,* 1: 9.

10. See, for example, Pohl and Schellenberg, *Reconsidering the Bluestockings,* 6–7, 11–13, 62–63, 77–80, 181–82.

11. Guest, *Small Change,* esp. 95–151; and Guest, "Bluestocking Feminisms" and Emma Major, "The Politics of Sociability," in Pohl and Schellenberg, *Reconsidering the Bluestockings.*

12. Cf., e.g., "To Miss Sutton. 1762" and letter to Miss Sutton, October 27, 1762, in Pennington, *Memoirs,* 1:416–20; "Ode to Wisdom" and letter to Catherine Talbot, January 20, 1748, in Hawley, *Elizabeth Carter,* 387–90 and letter to Talbot, April 28, 1750, in Carter, *Series of Letters,* 1:336–40; "To Miss Lynch. 1743" and letter to Talbot, May 24, 1744, in Carter, *Series of Letters,* 1: 56–60; "To Miss Talbot" and letter to Talbot, July 20, 1744, Carter, *Series of Letters,* 1: 43–45; "To Mrs Montagu" ("Where are those Hours, on rosy Pinions borne"), "To Mrs Montagu" ("No more, my Friend, pursue a distant Theme"), and Carter, *Letters from Mrs. Elizabeth Carter to Mrs. Montagu,* letters 30–31, September 1, 1761 and September 25, 1761, 1:116–24; letter 35, October 28, 1761, 1:136–41; letter 68, October 2, 1764, 1:241–44; letter 78, October 14, 1765, 1:279–81; letter 119, October 1, 1769, 2:36–38; "To Dr Walwyn," 358–59 in my edition and letter to Talbot, August 8, 1745, *A Series of Letters,* 1:70–72.

13. Compare "To Mrs Vesey. 1766." and the letters to Mrs. Vesey extracted in Pennington, *Memoirs,* 2:158–62, 402.

14. Compare "To Miss Hall. 1749.," "To [Miss Talbot]," "To [Miss Margaret Carter]," and "To Mrs. [Montagu]." Whereas in most "retirement" poems written by men the subject is truly solitary, in Carter's she imagines having her friends with her and pays tribute to their social virtues.

15. Carter's "A Dialogue," although somewhat untypical of her verse, has attracted most critical attention. Critics also emphasize the complexity of Carter's argument in this poem; see Williams, "Poetry, Pudding and Epictetus," in Ribeiro and Basker, *Tradition in Transition;* Freeman, "A Dialogue," in Armstrong and Blain, *Women's Poetry,* and Magrath, "Rags of Mortality," in Pohl and Schellenberg, *Reconsidering the Bluestockings.*

16. See Major, "Politics of Sociability," in Pohl and Schellenberg, *Reconsidering the Bluestockings,* 180–82, 191.

17. See, for example, "To [Miss Lynch]"; "To Miss Hall"; "To [Miss Talbot]"; "To Mrs. [Montagu]"; "To Mrs Montagu"; "To Viscountess Cremorne"; letter to Vesey, January 15, 1770; letter to Matthew Montagu, August 28, 1770, in Hawley, *Elizabeth Carter* 354–56, 361–62, 368–69, 370, 372–74, 374, 405–6, 407. See also letters to Vesey in Carter, *Series of Letters,* 3:217, 269, 286, 334–47, 372, 380, 384–85.

18. Pennington points out the excellencies of this final stanza in his edition: "It is worthy of observation how the author's style rises with her subject: in this last stanza it is elevated above the generally equal elegance of her poetry, almost to sublimity. See the same idea expressed in Prose, Letter V. Second Paragraph, near the end of this vol. It is not known which is the original." It looks as if Carter is directly alluding to the scriptures in this final stanza, but I have not traced exact verbal parallels. The closest I have found are Rev. 10:6 (Authorized Version) "there should be time no longer"; Rev. 22:5 "And there shall be no night there"; Rev. 12:12 "Therefore rejoice, ye heavens, and ye that dwell in them"; 1 Chron. 16:31 "Let the heavens be glad, and let the earth rejoice: and let men say among the nations, The LORD reigneth." Perhaps Carter is imitating the mode of prophecy rather than quoting a specific scriptural saying. For a fuller discussion of the Bluestockings' investment in apocalyptic ideas and imagery, see Major, "Politics of Sociability," in Pohl and Schellenberg, *Reconsidering the Bluestockings,* 175–92.

19. See headnote to *Epictetus* in Hawley, *Elizabeth Carter,* 5–6.

20. See Guest, *Small Change,* 147–50.

21. Pennington supplies the names of addressees and dates of composition in the edition he includes in his *Memoirs* of his aunt.

22. The letter also refers to "Mr Pitt"; William Pitt (1708–78) was elevated to the peerage in the summer of 1766 so the letter might date from before then.

23. Pennington, *Memoirs,* 2:158–61.

24. See, for example, the extract from a letter written in 1770 after the death of Catherine Talbot, entitled by Pennington "On the Duration of Friendship" (ibid., 2:162).

25. Ibid., 1:5, 2:160, 158.

III
Adventurous Women

"The best freind in the world":
The Relationship between Emma Hamilton and Queen Maria Carolina of Naples

Julie Peakman

Emma Hamilton (baptized 1765–1815) has always been a celebrated figure in British history but generally seen as an appendage to the life of Horatio Nelson (1758–1805) rather than as a successful person in her own right.[1] She is usually thought of as the epitome of the classic "rags-to-riches" tale of an eighteenth-century woman whose attractiveness to men enabled her to drag herself up from an impoverished background to become the wife of the British ambassador to Naples, Sir William Hamilton (1730–1803), and mistress to the most famous naval commander in history. Yet, as this chapter will show, important historical consequences also flowed from her friendship with a member of her own sex, Queen Maria Carolina of Naples (1753–1814). Emma was attacked by her contemporaries, and more recently by her biographers, for being a drunk, a whore, and a pretentious socialite. She was perhaps all these things, but she was also a genuine friend to those who needed her. Emma has been described as "at best a rather silly woman" who "brought little dignity to her husband's career and ended by becoming rather ridiculous."[2] Yet Emma's relationship with Maria Carolina gave her opportunities to prove her worth by providing valuable assistance to Britain in its war with France, and assisting the Neapolitan royal family to escape a potentially disastrous situation.

To arrive at this stage, Emma had to overcome her illegitimacy, her lack of education, and her torrid reputation as a whore. While Nelson and her husband Sir William were both commended for their actions in Naples, Emma has been denied adequate recognition for her contribution to Britain's eventual victory. Maria Carolina, too, has been overlooked, yet she played an important role, taking over from her boorish, uneducated husband King Ferdinand IV (1751–1825), allying her country to the British at a pivotal time

An engraving of Emma Hamilton at 30, after a portrait by George Romney.
Reproduced from A. T. Mahan, *The Life of Nelson*, vol. 1. Boston, MA: Little, Brown,
1897. Courtesy of the Albert Sloman Library, University of Essex.

in the war, and avoiding the fate of her sister Marie Antoinette
(1755–93).

The cooperation between Emma and Maria Carolina was unusual
for its period, and some features, particularly the disparity between
their social backgrounds, may have been unique. Few women had
managed to become involved in political action, particularly commoners. Elizabeth I (1533—1603) and Anne (1665–1714) managed
to wield power as sovereign queens; and high-ranking noblewomen

such as Georgiana, Duchess of Devonshire (1757–1806), and Sarah, Duchess of Marlborough (1660–1744), tried to exert political influence; these, however, were exceptional cases. It was, after all, not a time when women were expected to express political opinions. It has been suggested that the idea of "political culture" is perhaps more appropriate than "politics" for feminist historians as a framework for women's involvement in "dispensing patronage, influencing decision-makers and elections, petitioning, demonstrating, gift-giving, entertaining, haranguing, reporting seditious conduct, writing and disseminating ideas in print form."[3] The language of politics used by women was frequently based on power and privilege.[4] Yet Emma and Queen Maria Carolina stand out as examples of women operating at the very heart of military activities during a pivotal time of war. Their letters went much further than mere rhetoric; they not only spoke in warm tones of sincere friendship but also contained orders for meting out punishment to rebels, and undertakings to assist Nelson in carrying out the planned retribution.

Although there have been some explorations into the importance of female friendships over the last few decades of feminist history, there have been relatively few in the context of British eighteenth-century history, and they have been mainly casting light on relationships between women writers, or supporting an investigation into lesbian relationships.[5] Fewer still have examined political friendships between women.[6] None of Emma's biographers attributes great importance to the friendship between Emma and the Queen, mostly concentrating on Emma's relationship with Nelson and Hamilton.[7] Yet the relationship between Emma and Maria Carolina offers insights not only into intimacy between a queen and a commoner, but also into the strong political influences these women exerted in a realm where women were less known for their involvement. This essay aims to shed light on the little-known story of two of the most fascinating women in history.

The trajectory of Emma's life up to 1805, when Nelson died, is generally charted in terms of her relationships with men, but, on closer examination, women appear to be of crucial importance, too. Emma's life began in obscurity: even the date of her birth is uncertain.[8] Her father died soon after her birth, and her mother returned to her own mother's cottage in Harwarden, near Chester. From then on, Emma was brought up by her mother and grandmother, both major influential figures in her life. It was probably because of these early relationships that later she would find it easy to form close ties with another older woman, Maria Carolina. Impoverished and uneducated, Emma was a prime target for seduction, and in 1781 a country gentleman, Sir Harry Fetherstonhaugh (1754–1846), whisked her off to his country estate at Uppark in Sussex. Nobody could have realized it at the time, but this was the point at which Emma's circuitous route to high favor in the Neapolitan court began. Before the year was out, she was pregnant and abandoned, a "fallen woman" cast out from respectable society. Luckily, Charles Francis Greville (1749–1809), whom she had probably met through Sir Harry, was on hand to rescue her. He agreed not only to look after her on the condition that she handed over her child to be brought up elsewhere, but also to take on her mother as house-keeper. He became a major step in Emma's social rise, providing the basis of an education that would serve her well at court. His most valuable service, however, was to tire of her, and arrange for his uncle, Sir William Hamilton, to take her off his hands.

Emma first met Hamilton when he visited his nephew at their house in Edgware Row, London, in the spring of 1783; he had re-turned from Naples to bury his first wife. Hamilton had been British ambassador to the court of Naples since 1764. He was an amiable old soul, described as "tall, with a dark complexion, an aquiline nose, and an air of intelligence, blended with distinction."[9] Greville urged Sir William to invite Emma to Naples for a trial visit, telling him, "You will be able to have an experiment without any risk."[10] Once she understood that Greville had no intention of continuing his relationship with her, the ever-pragmatic Emma decided to make the most of her current situation, and began to exploit her opportu-nities. Naples was a glorious town full of opera, pomp, and splendor and, as Hamilton's consort, she was surrounded by riches and glam-our. She had a chance to mix with royalty as well as to socialize on a grand scale that she had previously only dreamed of. Hamilton pro-vided her with her own apartment in his home, the Palazzo Sessa, overlooking Naples Bay. He did everything he could to make her happy, taking her to the opera, and holding regular concerts for guests.

Emma's status, however, remained insecure. In order to be fully recognized by polite society, she must be formally received by ladies of the highest rank at their own homes. The necessary degree of re-spectability could be achieved only by making Hamilton marry her. Sir William, however, hesitated; he admitted to his friend Sir Joseph Banks (1743–1820), "I assure you that I approve of her so much that if I had been the person that made her first go astray, I wou'd glory in giving her a public reparation, and I would do it openly, for in-deed she has infinite merit and no Princess cou'd do the honours of her Place with more care and dignity than she does those of my house."[11] At this stage, Emma was entertaining up to fifty guests a night, including nobles and visitors on their Grand Tour. Emma had made her place so well in Naples that Hamilton recognized he had found a potential lifetime companion and finally married her, returning to England for the ceremony. On her return to Naples, she was officially received at court, and met Maria Carolina.

At this time, Naples was not just a city but a state which took up a third of (as yet) nonunified Italy, part of "the Two Sicilies," ruled by Ferdinand, a younger son of the Spanish royal family. As the eldest daughter of Maria Theresa of Austria (1717–80), Maria Carolina was a political asset; her sister Marie Antoinette was to marry King Louis XVI of France (1764–93). Maria Carolina had been duly married to Ferdinand when she was only fifteen and he seventeen, to cement a political union between Austria and Spain. Ferdinand, lacking a proper education in his youth, grew into an uncouth, boorish young man, chiefly interested in hunting, drinking, and whoring. As a result, the task of ruling the country was left to his wife. Educated and astute, she rose to the challenge, taking over the everyday political decisions with efficiency and flair, and introducing the liberal reforms favored by the most enlightened despots.

Emma, now formally recognized as wife to the British ambassador, immediately made herself agreeable to the Queen, and the Queen, as it seems from Emma's letters, made herself equally accessible to Emma. In December that year, Emma wrote to her old friend George Romney (1734–1802), "I have been received with open arms by all the Neapolitans of booth sexes, by all the foreigners of every distinction. I have been presented to the Queen of Naples by her own desire, she as shewn me all sorts of kind and affectionate attentions; in short I am the happiest woman in the world."[12] No doubt Emma's affable nature worked its charms, and the Queen probably liked her unpretentiousness. Emma, in turn, was to devote most of her time to the Queen and delight in her newly established position of confidante to royalty. Both would benefit from the friendship. Maria Carolina was politically shrewd enough to recognize that the new wife of the British ambassador could act as a mediator between the court of Naples and Britain. Emma, although politically unsophisticated, was cunning enough to see this as a chance to advance her prospects at court. They were also sincerely attached to each other. Sir William recognized Emma's efforts to compensate for her lowly beginnings and was very proud of her. Writing to Horace Walpole (1717–97) on April 17, 1792, he remarked, "Lady H. who has had also a difficult part to act & has succeeded wonderfully, having gained by having no pretensions, the

thorough approbation of all the English ladies. The Queen of Naples, as you may have heard, was very kind to her on our return and
treats her like any travelling lady of distinction. . . . She goes on im-
proving daily. . . . She really is an extraordinary being."[13]

Life in Naples, however, was to alter radically as the Napoleonic
Wars unfolded. By 1793, Britain had joined the alliance fighting revolutionary France, and Nelson's arrival marked a turning point in
the lives of both Emma and Maria Carolina. Britain needed a strong-
hold in the area to protect it from the French. Reinforcements were
urgently needed and Nelson was under orders to recruit troops from
Turin and Naples to help maintain the British occupation of Tou-
lon. With those instructions, Nelson sailed into Naples on the *Aga-
memnon* on September 10 with his British fleet. Naples was officially
neutral, but Hamilton and Sir John Acton (1736–1811), the Neapolitan prime minister, had negotiated a secret treaty between Britain
and Naples earlier that year in July, forming an Anglo-Neapolitan
alliance. Nelson, seen as the savior of Naples, was offered six thousand troops. He also received desperately needed provisions for his
crew. "My poor fellows have not had a morsel of fresh meat or vege-
tables for near nineteen weeks," Nelson complained to his wife,
"and in that time I have only had my foot twice on the shore of
Cadiz." [14] He devoted much of his time to discussions with Hamilton, Acton, and the King. On the fourth day of his visit, he made a
dramatically abrupt departure, in pursuit of a French man-of-war,
and did not return to Naples for five years. Despite the brevity of
Nelson's stay, the first meeting between himself, Emma, and Sir William, as well as with the royal family, must have had a great impact
on all of them, as they were to keep up a correspondence thereafter.

Maria Carolina was now living in fear that Naples, like France,
would become a republic. By June 1793, Naples had become so volatile that the royal family decided to move temporarily to their palace
in Caserta. Emma wrote to Greville, "For political reasons we have
lived eight months at Caserta, that is, making this our constant resi-
dence & going twice a week to town to give dinners, balls etc and
returning here at 2 or 3 o'clock in the morning."[15] Despite the tur-
bulent situation, guests continued to drop in at the villa on a regular
basis. The Hamiltons continued to give dinners for fifty or more and
suppers for three hundred people and kept up their routine of din-
ing with the royal family at midday on most days. Emma would
spend up to three hours most evenings talking with the Queen, tête-
à-tête. Nonetheless, Emma retained her level head and resisted any
temptation to presume on their intimacy in public; her discretion
increased her popularity with the ministers' wives, and confirmed

the Queen's favor. She wrote to Greville, "I had been with the Queen the night before alone *en famille* laughing and singing etc. but at the drawing room I kept my distance, and pay'd the Queen as much respect as tho' I have never seen her before, which pleased her very much."[16]

By now, Emma had become the Queen's closest confidante. In 1794, she wrote to Greville,

> She is everything one can wish—the best mother, wife, and freind [*sic*] in the world. I live constantly with her, and have done intimately so for 2 years, and I never have in all that time seen anything but goodness and sincerity in her & if you ever hear any lyes about her contradick them & if you shou'd see a cursed book written by a vile French dog with her character in it don't believe one word . . . if I was her daughter she cou'd not be kinder to me & I love her with all my soul.[17]

Their feelings were mutual and the Queen took every opportunity to show her concern for Emma. When Sir William lay ill of a bilious fever, she wrote a note to Emma telling her to "put confidence in God . . . who never forsakes those who trust in Him," and confirmed her "sincere friendship."[18] Emma confirmed that "my ever dear Queen as been like a mother to me since Sir William as been ill: she writes to me four or five times a day, and offered to come and assist me; *this is friendship*."[19] Hamilton indicated that the Queen was increasingly susceptible to Emma's influence: "The Queen of Naples seems to have great pleasure in her society. She sends for her generally three or four times a week. . . . In fact all goes well *chez nous*."[20]

Emma was now well placed to enter into political maneuvers. With the Queen's encouragement, she began to play a significant diplomatic role in Naples. When King Ferdinand's brother, Charles IV of Spain (1748–1819), wrote him a series of clandestine letters urging him to ally himself with France as Spain was planning to do, the Queen "borrowed" the letters, made copies and placed them in Emma's hands, along with confidential papers "which may be used by your husband."[21] These were hastily couriered to London to inform the government of the latest political developments. Emma reported to Greville on April 19, 1795, "Against my will, *owing to my situation here* I am got into politicks, and I wish to have news for my dear beloved queen whom I adore nor can I live without her, for she is to me a mother, friend & everything . . . She is the first woman in the world, her talents are superior to every woman in the world and her heart is the most excellent and strictly good and upright."[22] In February 1796, Emma wrote to Lord George Macartney (1737–

1806) about political affairs in the Neapolitan court; the King was
having some difficulty in deciding what to do, or whose side to take,
while the Queen was doing everything in her power to prevail upon
him to throw his allegiance behind the British. Emma reported, "I
have this moment received a letter from my adorable Queen. She is
arrived with the King. She has much to do to persuade him; but he
approves of all *our prospects*. She is worn out with fatigue. Tomorrow
I will send you her letter."[23]

The situation in France was increasingly dangerous and Naples
was becoming affected; Emma, Sir William, and the royal family
were now in the thick of political unrest. By June 1796, Sir William
was becoming increasingly concerned, conveying his doubts to Greville as to the safety of Naples: "I must own to you that I think Italy
is in great danger of being completely plunder'd and ruin'd unless
some unforeseen accident shou'd operate in her favour, and that
very soon."[24] Emma relayed to Greville the intrigues in which she
was involved, while emphasizing her role in the drama:

> We have not time to write to you as we have been 3 days and nights writ-
> ing to send by this courier letters of consequence for our government.
> They ought to be grateful to Sir William & *myself in particular,* as my situa-
> tion at this Court is *very extraordinary,* & what no person as yet arrived at;
> but one as no thanks, & I allmost [*sic*] sick of grandeur. We are tired to
> death with anxiety, and God knows where we shall soon be, and what
> will become of us, if things go on as they do now.[25]

Maria Carolina was quick to realize that any protection she might
gain for herself and her family against the encroaching French lay
solely with the British and made various gestures to signal her new
allegiance. She asked Emma to say to the company, "God save great
George our King," and declared she loved the British prince as she
did her son.[26] As the French attacked British ships in the Mediterranean, allies dropped off one by one, and the British began to recall
their ships from the area. Nelson, annoyed at the withdrawal of British support, complained bitterly to the Hamiltons in October, "Till
this time, it has been usual for the allies of England to fall from her,
but till now she never was known to desert her friends while she had
the power of supporting them."[27] Meanwhile Maria Carolina despaired; spies were everywhere and capital sentences were being
handed out; all the prisons were full of traitors and massacres were
occurring in the streets. The King and Queen demanded contributions from the monied Neapolitans as they poured their own jewels
and money into the battle against the French.

Emma's relationship with Nelson, and the Queen's relationship with Emma, were integral to the dynamics of these political machinations. They affected the Queen's decisions and the movements of Nelson, Emma, and the royal family. Emma's relationship with Nelson allowed the Queen to place her trust in him, while Emma acted as intermediary between the Queen and Nelson. News of Nelson's victory at the Battle of St. Vincent on February 14, 1797, cheered his friends back in Naples. Maria Carolina now felt confident enough to backtrack on her harsh policies, releasing all her captives. She was cheered on by the Lazzaroni, but Emma was perturbed. She complained to Nelson, "These pretty gentlemen *that had planned the death of their Majesties* are to be let out in society again. In short, I am afraid all is lost here; and I am grieved to the heart for our dear Queen, who deserves a better fate . . . I hope you will not quit the Mediterranean without taking us . . . I trust in God and you, that we shall destroy those monsters before we go from hence."[28] The Queen was well aware that all her hopes lay with the British fleet. Nelson, loyal to the core, was stirred by Emma's letter: "The picture you draw of the lovely Queen of Naples and the Royal Family would rouse the indignation of the most unfeeling of the creation . . . I am bound—by my oath of chivalry—to protect all who are persecuted and in distress."[29] In May 1798, Nelson's storm-damaged ship, the *Vanguard,* was anchored off Elba, in urgent need of harbor and restocking; he relied on the assistance of the King to allow him to dock in one of the Sicilian ports. Emma hastily dashed off a letter to Nelson after a meeting with the Queen, and reassured him, "The Queen desires me to say everything that's kind, and bids me say with her whole heart and soul she wishes you victory."[30] Nelson replied, "I have kissed the Queen's letter. Pray say I hope for the honour of kissing her hand when no fears will intervene, assure her Majesty that no person has her felicity more than myself at heart and that the sufferings of her family will be a Tower of Strength on the days of Battle, fear not the event, God is with us, God Bless you and Sir William."[31]

Emma was playing a pivotal role in reinforcing the Queen's reliance on the British fleet. Without Emma, it is doubtful whether the Queen would have so easily been persuaded to form an alliance between Naples and Britain. Indeed, Emma was to add to her list of claims that it was due to her influence that the Queen, without the King's knowledge, had provided a letter instructing all governors of the islands to give Nelson the assistance he needed and allow him to dock at their ports. Nelson, with his ships restocked at Syracuse and his crew rested, was ready for battle again. He wrote to Hamilton,

"Pray, present my best respects to Lady Hamilton. Tell her I hope to be presented to her crowned with laurel and cypress."[32] The royal family was delighted by the news that Nelson had won the battle of the Nile at Aboukir Bay on August 1; Nelson had, at least for now, protected them and made the capital safe. In gratitude, the Queen sent Nelson a letter of congratulation accompanied by casks of wine and a guinea for every man on board.

The *Vanguard* landed back in Naples victorious on September 22, 1798. Emma had been faithful to Hamilton, now sixty-eight, for twelve years, but it was inevitable she would be attracted to Nelson, since they both aspired to adventure and glory. The trust Maria Carolina placed in Emma allowed her to rely on Nelson; her political maneuverings were, to a large extent, influenced by Emma's relationship with him. Staying in Naples would put the royal family in an increasingly dangerous situation; Emma had to urge them to plan their escape. The threat came from the nobility and bourgeoisie, who were considering allying with the French in the hope they would be allowed to retain their privileges and rights; and from the poor who were tempted by the Liberty, Equality and Fraternity that France purportedly offered. Emma employed various strategies to induce the Queen to leave. She explained to Nelson, "I translate from our papers for her to inspire her or them, I should say, with some of your spirit and energy—how delighted we British were to sit & speak of you."[33] She outlined the hideous possibilities which might befall them all if the Queen did not make her move soon:

> I flatter myself I did much whilst the passions of the Queen were up and agitated, I got up, put out my left arm, like you, spoke the language of truth to her, painting the drooping situation of this fine country, her friends sacrificed & her husband, children, and herself led to the Block, and eternal dishonour to her memory, after for not having been active, doing her duty in fighting bravely to the last to save her country, her Religion from the hands of the rapacious murderers of her sister [Maria Antoinette] and the Royal Family of France, that she was sure of being lost if they were inactive and their was a chance of being saved if they made use of the day, and struck now while all minds are imprest with the Horrers [*sic*] their neighbours are suffering from these Robbers.[34]

The King and Queen could see that it was time to flee before they suffered the same fate as Marie Antoinette and her husband, Louis XVI. After holding a council meeting, the royal party agreed it was time to remove what valuables they could and make for Sicily. All details for their departure had to be made in the utmost secrecy to allay any potential hysteria from the mob. The slightest suspicion by the populace of the royal family's impending disappearance would inevitably lead to looting and rioting. With increasing unrest in Naples, it became evident that the royal family and the Hamiltons had to evacuate. Emma was keen to play out her role and began organizing their escape, under cover. She declared that if the Queen were to die at her post, she would remain with her to the last: "I feil [sic] I owe it to her friendship uncommon to me."[35] Promising unswerving loyalty, she scribbled a note on the envelope of her letter to Queen Maria Carolina, "Emma will prove to Maria Carolina that an humble-born Englishwoman can serve a queen with zeal and true love even at the risk of her life."[36] Although Emma's declaration might appear theatrical, she possessed a strong loyalty to the Queen. She also recognized that she was embarking on a quest which, if the situation turned out as planned, would elevate her to the status of a true heroine.

The escape was to be executed during a soiree given in Nelson's honor by Selim III (1761–1808), Sultan of Turkey. Prior to the night of the escape, Emma acted as messenger between Nelson and the royal family. Dispatches from Maria Carolina to Emma show a desperate queen clinging to the hope that Emma and Nelson would be able to carry out the plan. At a time when she saw herself as "the most unfortunate of women, mothers, Queens," she saw Emma as her "sincerest friend."[37] Both the Hamilton and royal households had to take as many valuables as possible through secret tunnels between the embassy, the palace, and the shore. The royal family smuggled out linen, silver, jewelery, and other possessions, using Emma as courier. Nelson wrote to Lord St. Vincent (1753–1823), "Lady Hamilton from that time [December 14] to 21 every night received the jewels of the royal family and such clothes as might be necessary for the large party to embark."[38] Emma was in constant fear of being caught and torn apart by the ferocious mob.

The intention was to board the *Vanguard* on December 21 to set sail for Palermo. Ten of the royal family went down to the quay in the dark. Emma reported to Greville,

> On the 21st at ten at night, Lord Nelson, Sir Wm., Mother & self went out to pay a visit, sent all our servants away, & ordered them in 2 hours to come with the coach, & ordered supper at home. When they were gone, we sett off, walked to our boat, & after two hours . . . to the *Vanguard*. Lord Nelson then went with armed boats to a secret passage adjoining to the pallace, got up the dark staircase that goes into the Queen's room and with a dark lantern, cutlasses, pistols etc, brought off every soul, ten in number, to the *Vanguard* at twelve o'clock. If we had remained to the next day, we shou'd have all been imprisoned.[39]

The ship finally sailed out of Naples Bay at seven in the evening of December 23, a worse night than Nelson had seen in thirty years. Emma was to write to Greville, "all our sails were torn to pieces, and all the men ready with their axes to cut away the masts."[40] Pitched fiercely about, everyone was violently seasick except for Emma and her mother, Mrs. Cadogan. The sickest was the Queen's six-year-old Prince Carlo Alberto who became gradually worse. Despite Emma's constant nursing, he convulsed and died in her arms on Christmas Day. Emma reported to Greville, she had "not a soul to help me, as the few women her Majesty bought on board were incapable of helping her or the poor royal children."[41] After landing, the Queen was inconsolable with grief at the funeral service. Emma lamented, "My adorable Queen whom I love better than any person in the world is allso unwell, we weep together & now that is our onely comfort."[42] The King and Queen moved into the Colli Palace, while Hamilton set up a temporary embassy at the Villa Bastioni.

Emma's role in the enterprise had been favorably reported back to England and she was praised for her courage in the escape and onward journey. The *Times* for January 28, 1799, announced, "We are informed from a very respectable authority that the Queen owed her safety much to the address of Lady Hamilton, who assisted in her getting away." Hamilton confirmed to Greville the central role Emma had played. He wrote, "Emma has had a very principal part in this delicate business as she is, and has been for several years the real and only confidential friend of the Queen of Naples."[43] Even Lord St. Vincent commended her "magnanimous conduct."[44] Yet these contemporary tributes were forgotten as time went by. Despite her impressive display of courage, resourcefulness, and diplomatic skill, Emma's role at this time has been consistently played down, most probably because she was a woman, and, worse still, a woman of dubious reputation.

The Queen had, by now, come to rely on Emma to a considerable extent. Emma, in turn, did not take her role lightly. Sir William praised Emma's political acumen in a letter to Greville: "Emma makes a great figure in our political line, for she carries on the business with the Queen, whose abilities you know are great."[45] But by June, Emma was sick with worry. She had been supporting her royal friends and her husband through illness. Nelson complained that she was "fretting" her "guts to fiddle-strings"[46] as a result of her concern for Maria Carolina. The Queen once again relied on Emma's relationship with Nelson to persuade him to consider retaking Naples. Emma offered to go with him (along with Sir William), ostensibly to act as translator; this was perhaps the time when they first consummated their love. Nelson's ships pulled into Naples Bay on June 24. In a letter to Emma, Maria Carolina gave instructions that immediate and severe punishments should be inflicted on the rebels, including the women involved.[1] Meanwhile, Emma recognized the importance of her position, boasting in a letter to Greville, "The Queen is not yet come. She sent me as her Deputy; for I am very popular, speak the Neapolitan language, and [am] considered, with Sir William, a friend of the people."[48] But it was a sad time for Emma as she surveyed the destruction which had been wrought: "I saw at a distance our despoil'd house in town & Villa Emma that had been plunder'd & Sir Wm's new apartment, a bomb burst in it but it made me so low-spirited I don't desire to go again."[49] Fourteen days after the trio's arrival, the King joined them in Naples but would not come ashore, preferring to remain on the *Foudroyant,* while the Queen remained in Palermo.

After regaining some control of the situation in Naples, the party landed back in Palermo in triumph on August 8, and here, too, Emma received recognition for her exploits, along with her husband and her lover. The streets were thronged with crowds welcoming them; cries of *Viva Nelson! Viva Miledi! Viva Hamilton!* rang out in honor of the conquering heroes. In appreciation for their loyalty, the Queen showered the trio with presents; Emma and Sir William were given jewelery worth approximately six thousand pounds for their help during the ordeal; Emma received a fine gold chain with the Queen's miniature; Hamilton received a huge yellow diamond ring; Nelson was given a diamond-encrusted sword owned by Louis XIV. The British government at last rewarded his endeavors with two thousand pounds and a gift of ten thousand pounds from the East India Company for defending their route by his victory in the Battle of the Nile. In April 1800, after more than three decades of serving his country, Hamilton was recalled. Nelson was also told to come home. By this time Emma was pregnant with Nelson's child. The trio finally set off to England via Austria in summer, accompanying the royal party; this comprised not only Maria Carolina, but three princesses, two princes, and fifty of her retainers. By the time they reached Vienna, news of their imminent arrival had preceded them and celebrations were in place to welcome them; the court threw banquets on their behalf, concerts were arranged for them, and firework displays filled the skies.

Realization of the imminent separation from Emma distressed the Queen, a situation Hamilton had foreseen; writing to Greville, he lamented, "the Queen is really so fond of Emma that the parting will be a serious business."[50] Emma also acknowledged, "I am misera-

ble to leave my dearest friend. She cannot be consoled."[51] Maria
Carolina gave Emma a gift of a diamond necklace carrying tresses of
the hair of the royal children made into initials, by which to remember her. Her gift to Sir William was a golden snuff box, with a lid
inlaid with portraits of herself and the King. Emma was never to see
her beloved Queen again. Emma went on to have at least two children by Nelson (and possibly a third, a twin who died along with
Emma's second child), and continued to share her life with the two
men she loved, and her one surviving child, Horatia. Maria Carolina
continued in power until her husband abdicated in 1812 in favor of
his son Francis (1777–1830), upon which the Queen was exiled to
her homeland of Austria. She died in 1814.

Although others may have neglected or forgotten Emma's achievements in these dangerous times, Emma herself was fully aware of
their significance and value. Eventually, she would claim that her
actions entitled her to a pension from the British government. She
asserted that, due to her deliberate manipulation of her relationship
with the Queen, Britain obtained vital information about the shifting alliances of Spain toward France, and its declaration of war
against England:

> By unceasing cultivation of this influence [with the Queen] and no less
> watchfullness to turn it to my country's good, it happened that I discov-
> ered a courier had brought the King of Naples a private letter from the
> King Of Spain. I prevailed on the Queen to take it from his pocket un-
> seen. We found it to contain the King of Spain's resolution to withdraw
> from the Coalition, and join the French against England. My husband at
> this time lay dangerously ill. I prevailed on the Queen to allow my taking
> a copy, with which I immediately dispatch'd a messenger to Lord Gren-
> ville, taking all the necessary precautions; for his safe arrival then be-
> came very difficult, and altogether cost me about £400 paid out of my
> privy purse.[52]

Both Nelson and Hamilton recognized that without Emma's help
Nelson might not have obtained the supplies which enabled him to
go on to conquer the French fleet. Nelson was to write seven years
later, on the morning of Trafalgar,

> The British fleet under my command could never have returned the sec-
> ond time to Egypt had not Lady Hamilton's influence with the Queen
> of Naples caused letters to be wrote to the Governor of Syracuse, that he
> was to encourage the fleet being supplied with everything, should they
> put into port in Sicily. We put into Syracuse and received every supply;
> went to Egypt and destroyed the French fleet.[53]

This is a remarkable instance, not merely of an eighteenth-century female friendship, but one which took place in the political realm and had a direct influence on international politics at the highest level. British military history might well have been different if Emma and Maria Carolina had not felt such strong affection for each other. Yet Emma also exploited the situation to fashion herself as a heroine; she grabbed every opportunity that life presented to her, finding herself a well-connected husband, educating herself, and setting herself up as confidante to the Queen; then she rose to the occasion by rescuing the royal family when it was demanded of her. But there can be little doubt that her actions were also those of a fiercely loyal friend. The Queen, for her part, helped Emma achieve acceptance into high society, something she would never achieve back in England.

NOTES

1. See Julie Peakman, *Emma Hamilton* (London: Haus, 2005). NB the British Library Manuscripts Collection contains most of the letters of Emma Hamilton, the Queen of Naples, Greville Hamilton, Horatio Nelson, William Hamilton, and various other key characters. These can easily be accessed by using the British Library Manuscripts Catalogue. Many of the letters have been printed in the Alfred Morrison Collection, as *The Collection of Autograph Letters and Historical Documents Formed by Alfred Morrison: The Hamilton and Nelson Papers*, 2 vols. (London: Printed for Private Circulation, 1893–94), BL shelf mark LR 4 e 1. For ease of reference in the endnotes, I have cited this printed collection wherever possible, using the short form *Morrison MS*, although I have examined the original manuscripts.

2. Brian Fothergill, *Sir William Hamilton: Envoy Extraordinary* (London: Faber and Faber, 1969), 219.

3. Lois G. Schwoerer, "Women's public political voice in England: 1640–1740," in *Women Writers and the Early Modern British Political Tradition*, ed. Hilda L. Smith (Cambridge: Cambridge University Press, 1998), 57–58.

4. James Daybell observes that the basis upon which women laid claim to this language was "founded for a large part on material power, social status and influence," and points to the fact that this mainly applied to aristocratic women, usually within the family but sometimes on the wider political stage. This rhetoric was often deployed in patronage letters. James Daybell, "Women's Letters of Recommendation and the Rhetoric of Friendship in Sixteenth-century England," in *Rhetoric, Women and Politics in Early Modern England*, ed. Jennifer Richards and Alison Thorne (London: Routledge, 2007), 179. On the eighteenth century, see Amanda Vickery, ed., *Women, Privilege and Power: British Politics, 1750 to the Present* (Stanford, CA: Stanford University Press, 2001).

5. On writers, see Norma Clarke, *Ambitious Heights. Writing, Friendship, Love: The Jewsbury Sisters, Felicia Hemans and Jane Welsh Carlyle* (London: Routledge, 1990); and Pauline Nestor, *Female Friendships and Communities: Charlotte Brontë, George Eliot, Elizabeth Gaskell* (Oxford: Clarendon, 1985). On lesbians, see Elizabeth Susan Wahl, *In-*

visible Relations: Representations of Female Intimacy in the Age of Enlightenment (Stanford, CA: Stanford University Press, 1999) and Faderman, *Surpassing the Love of Men.*

6. One of the few parallels which might be drawn with the relationship between Emma and Maria Carolina might be that which subsisted between Sarah, Duchess of Marlborough, and Queen Anne, but Sarah was a noblewoman serving as handmaid to her queen, employed in a position in court as Groom of the Stole, Mistress of the Robes and Keeper of the Privy Purse. See Ophelia Field, *The Favourite: Sarah, Duchess of Marlborough* (London: Hodder & Stoughton, 2002). Also see Kate Davies, *Catharine Macaulay and Mercy Otis Warren: The Revolutionary Atlantic and the Politics of Gender* (Oxford: Oxford University Press, 2005), but this is mainly in relation to American politics.

7. One of the best biographies is still Walter Sichel, *Emma Lady Hamilton* (London: Archibald Constable, 1905); see also Kate Williams, *England's Mistress* (London: Hutchinson, 2006); Tom Pocock, *Nelson's Women* (London: André Deutsch, 1999); Roger Hudson, ed., *Nelson and Emma* (London: Folio Society, 1994); Flora Frazer, *Beloved Emma* (London: Weidenfeld and Nicolson, 1986); Colin Simpson, *The Life of Lady Hamilton* (London: Bodley Head, 1983); Nora Lofts, *Emma Hamilton* (London: Book Club Associates, 1978); Patricia Jaffé, *Lady Hamilton in Relation to the Art of her Time* (London: Arts Council, 1972); Mollie Hardwick, *Emma, Lady Hamilton* (New York: Holt, Rinehart and Winston, 1969); Jack Russell, *Nelson and the Hamiltons* (Harmondsworth: Penguin, 1969); Edward Bishop, *Emma, Lady Hamilton* (London: Heron Books, 1969); Hugh Tours, *Life and Letters of Emma Hamilton* (London: V. Gollancz, 1963); Oliver Warner, *Emma Hamilton and Sir William* (London: Chatto and Windus, 1960); Gerald Hamilton and Desmond Stewart, *Emma In Blue* (London: Allan Wingate, 1957); Edmund B. D'Auvergne, *The Dear Emma* (London: George G. Harrap, 1936); O. A. Sherrard, *A Life of Emma Hamilton* (London: Sidgwick and Jackson, 1927); Julia Frankau [Frank Danby, pseud.], *Nelson's Legacy: Lady Hamilton. Her Story and Tragedy* (London: Cassell, 1915); E. Hallam Moorhouse, *Nelson's Lady Hamilton* (London: Methuen, 1908); J. T. Herbert Bailey, *Emma, Lady Hamilton: A Biographical Essay with a Catalogue of her Published Portraits* (London: W. G. Menzies, 1905); W H. Long, *Memoirs of Emma, Lady Hamilton* (1815; repr., London: Gibbings, 1899); John Cordy Jeaffreson, *Lady Hamilton and Lord Nelson: An Historical Biography* (London: Athenaeum, 1897).

8. Although Emma always gave 1765 as her birth date, it is possible she was born earlier: she may have wished to conceal her illegitimacy, as her parents did not marry until 1764. See Peakman, *Emma Hamilton,* 4.

9. Sir Nathaniel Wraxall, *The Historical and the Posthumous Memoirs of Sir Nathaniel William Wraxall, 1772–1784,* ed. Henry B. Wheatley (London: Bickers and Son, 1884), 1:163–64.

10. *Morrison MS* 142, December 2, 1785.

11. Add. MS 34048 fols. 61–62, April 6, 1790.

12. *Morrison MS* 199, December 20, 1791.

13. *Morrison MS* 208, April 17, 1792.

14. T. J. Pettigrew, *Memoirs of the Life of Vice-Admiral Lord Viscount Nelson* (London: Boone, 1849), 1:40.

15. *Morrison MS* 221, June 2, 1793.

16. Ibid.

17. *Morrison MS* 250, December 18, 1794.

18. Egerton MS 1615 fol. 18, April 17, 1795.

19. *Morrison MS* 263, April 19, 1795.

20. Add. MS 34710 fol. 23, November 17, 1795.

21. Egerton MS 1615 fols. 20–22, April 17, 1795.

22. *Morrison MS* 263, April 19, 1795.

23. *Morrison MS* 274, n.d. [February 1796].

24. *Morrison MS* 282, June 7, 1796.

25. *Morrison MS* 287, September 21, 1796.

26. Egerton MS 1615 fols. 8, 69, June 4, 1795, December 3, 1796.

27. *Morrison MS* 290, December 1, 1796.

28. Horatio Nelson, *The Letters of Lord Nelson to Lady Hamilton. With a Supplement of Interesting Letters by Distinguished Characters* (London: T. Lovewell, 1814), 1:181.

29. Pettigrew, *Memoirs,* 1:119.

30. Add. MS 34989 fol. 3, September 8, 1798.

31. Geoffrey Rawston, ed., *Nelson's Letters* (London: J. M. Dent, 1960), 182, June 17, 1798.

32. *Morrison MS* 320, June 18, 1798.

33. Add. MS 34989 fol. 15, October 20, 1798.

34. Ibid.

35. Add. MS 34989 fol. 20, October 27, 1798.

36. Egerton MS 1616 fol. 38.

37. Egerton MS 1615 fols. 8, 129.

38. *Memoirs of Lady Hamilton* (London: Henry Colburn, 1815), 195–96.

39. *Morrison MS* 370, January 7, 1799.

40. Ibid.

41. Ibid.

42. Ibid.

43. *Morrison MS* 369, January 6, 1799.

44. Pettigrew, *Memoirs,* 1:187, January 17, 1799.

45. *Morrison MS* 381, April 8, 1799.

46. Sichel, *Emma Lady Hamilton,* 284.

47. Fothergill, *Sir William Hamilton,* 359.

48. *Morrison MS* 411, July 19, 1799.

49. Ibid.

50. *Morrison MS* 444, January 25, 1800.

51. Nelson, *Letters of Lord Nelson to Lady Hamilton,* 1:272.

52. *Morrison MS* 1046, n.d. [March 1813].

53. Sherrard, *A Life of Emma Hamilton,* 186.

Founding Mothers: Religious Communities in New France

Tanis Hinchcliffe

The founding story of new france in canada includes women among the main actors, so that together with the names of Jacques Cartier (1491–1557), Samuel de Champlain (1567–1635), and Sieur de Maisonneuve (1612–76), we find those of Marie Guyart (1599–1672) and Marguerite Bourgeoys (1620–1700). Should we be surprised that these women also belonged to religious communities as well as being founding mothers of the fledgling colony? Perhaps not, when we come to understand the context within which they lived their lives as women in seventeenth-century France, and subsequently in the very different environment of New France.

In recent years, women's engagement in religious communities has become studied seriously as an area of gendered activity, demonstrating some very interesting behavior outside the roles of wife and mother. In *Society and Culture in Early Modern France* (1975), Natalie Zemon Davis noted that Catholic women of the seventeenth century engaged in "organized group action among women."[1] In this context she mentions the Ursuline order of nuns, one of whose number was the subject of an essay in Davis's more recent *Women on the Margins* (1995), in which she tells the story of Marie Guyart, Marie de l'Incarnation in religion, who traveled to Canada in 1639 to establish the Ursulines in the distant French colony.[2] The context for such action is provided in the work of Elizabeth Rapley. For example, in *The Dévotes: Women and Church in Seventeenth-century France* (1990), Rapley gives a useful overview of the communities established by women, and something of their spiritual origins.[3] More recently there have been studies by Laurence Lux-Sterritt and Susan E. Dinan on specific religious orders and their significance in the spiritual and practical lives of seventeenth-century French women.[4] What emerges from all these studies is that the early modern period opened fresh opportunities for women to act in the world through their commitment to religious communities, an opportunity which,

however, had to be fought for against both lay and clerical convention. Within the Counter-Reformation Catholic Church there was an
underlying contradiction which on the one hand led the clergy to
encourage women's piety, but when the spiritual life inspired
women to adopt an apostolic role among the poor, the hierarchy
sought to confine them to the family home or to the cloister.

It might be assumed that the women who came as religious to New
France were simply replicating an already existing and well-orga-
nized system in France, but this would not be strictly true. The
women and their religious organizations were a product of a particular period, during which women fought for and won permission to
work in the wider community outside the home both in France and
elsewhere. Their religious status both aided and hindered their
work, but in the end made it possible at a time when opportunities
to work outside the family were dwindling. Alongside the story of
how religious women achieved and maintained their autonomy is
the account of how their spirituality supported their struggles, and it
is the conjunction of these two elements of the story of the Canadian
founding mothers that I will discuss here.

Today, particularly in Anglo-Saxon cultures, the main characteristic of the religious life is often assumed to be that of enclosure. We
talk about women being "shut up" in a convent, or being "im-
mured" behind convent walls, and not without reason when we discover the struggle that went on during the seventeenth century over
the issue of enclosure. Olwen Hufton in *The Prospect Before Her*
(1995) has given a vivid picture of life in a European convent of the
early modern period, where primarily aristocratic women, either
through their own or their families' choice would enter at a young
age or later in life as widows.[5] On profession a woman was required
to present a dowry to the convent, but once she had taken her solemn vows she was financially dead to her family as far as inheritance
went. These vows ensured that she made no further financial claim
on her family, but despite enclosure professed nuns would periodi-
cally be allowed to visit their home for extended periods.

The main activity of the cloistered nun was prayer and contemplation, formalized through the recitation of the daily office. Although
cloistered communities continued, the general quickening interest
in religion and in spirituality in the sixteenth century resulted in
some women looking for an alternative religious life, which would
allow them to live in the wider community as teachers or carers of
the sick and infirm, while developing a shared spiritual life. Personal
piety, fostered through the growing prevalence of books and
through charismatic preachers, spread an awareness of a type of

mysticism which fostered empathy with the poor as exemplars of the suffering Christ. Despite their desire to do good in their local areas, however, these women found the church authorities reluctant to give them permission to venture out into the world while claiming conventual status. There was, however, an existing model, since from the twelfth century women in the Low Countries had been able to form lay associations, living in the world without vows, whose members were called "beguines." In 1535 in the northern Italian town of Brescia, Angela Merici (1474–1540) brought together a group of women under the patronage of St. Ursula to teach and to tend the sick. They did not take solemn vows, but lived in their own homes, wearing their own clothes, and in this way they hoped to sidestep the enclosure required of women's religious orders and the restrictions that that entailed. In 1582 under Charles Borromeo (1538–84), the Archbishop of Milan, the Ursulines, as they were called, started to live a communal life and to take simple vows, but continued to maintain their freedom of movement.[6]

Some years earlier the Council of Trent (1545—63) had been called by the church to establish strategies to counteract the effects of the Protestant Reformation, and to dispel the perception that the church was corrupt and lax. The result was that steps were taken to regularize many practices that had arisen over time, and to take more control into the central administration. There was a great suspicion of devotions beyond the influence of the hierarchy, with a strong desire to uphold convention. One area where the hierarchy insisted on conformity was over the issue of cloister.[7] They insisted firstly that women in religious life accept solemn vows, and a rule, based on one of the monastic orders, and as a part of the rule, it was necessary to accept enclosure. There was a practical and worldly aspect to this, which was that if women were not bound by solemn, religious vows, there was nothing stopping them from returning to their families and claiming their inheritance, a right they renounced when they entered the cloister. A further restriction on female orders was that they had a duty of obedience to their bishop, which meant that each convent remained autonomous without connections in any official way to other convents, even of the same order. This arrangement ensured that the influence of women's religious orders remained local, unlike the orders of men, such as the newly formed Jesuits.

These restrictions imposed by the church attacked the very root of the new associations of women, who wished to dedicate their lives to work in the wider community. The first group of Ursulines in France formed themselves in Avignon in 1592, and another group formed in Paris at the turn of the century. Their particular mission was the education of young girls and the care of the sick. Both these activities depended on mobility outside the confines of home or convent, but pressure was exerted on the women to accept solemn vows and the resulting enclosure. When they finally gave in to enclosure in 1612, they retained a vow to teach along with the other solemn vows of poverty, chastity, and obedience, and they overcame the problem of teaching the laity by an elaborate system of locking doors. At the beginning of the teaching day the nuns and children would gather in a dedicated part of the convent building, when the communicating internal door and that leading to the exterior would be closed, thus preventing the contamination of enclosure.[8] This was the beginning of the association of girls' schools with convents in Catholic countries which has had such a long-reaching cultural influence.

Along with the desire for practical service in the world went an increased interest on the part of women in mysticism.[9] Surprisingly, there seems to have been a sympathy between the two. The model mystic for women was the great St. Teresa of Avila (1515–82), a Spanish Carmelite. Her mysticism was well known through her books, her *Vida* (autobiography), *The Road of Perfection,* and *The Interior Castle,* and emphasized the relationship of the individual soul with the divine. Despite her intense mysticism, Teresa demonstrated her organizational abilities, by traveling about central Spain, establishing houses of discalced Carmelites, which followed her particular version of reformed cloistered life. Soon after her death there appeared an account of her life by Francisco de Ribera which was quickly translated into French, and which provided the inspiration among women for a spiritual regeneration already underway.[10]

In Paris, at the turn of the seventeenth century, the homes of certain women became the gathering places for those interested in mysticism, rather in the style of the later literary salons. Mme Acarie (1566–1618), a married woman with six children, was one of these. She was instrumental in bringing the reformed Carmelites from Spain to France, and was also involved in establishing a community of Ursulines in Paris. She ended her days in the Carmelite convent, but before that her salon was a meeting place for ardent reformers, such as Pierre de Bérulle (1575–1629), the founder of the French order of Oratorians. François de Sales (1567–1622), the Bishop of Geneva, and therefore in exile, associated with de Bérulle and Mme Acarie when he was in Paris. He was interested in promoting the spiritual life among the laity, and produced some influential devotional books, such as *Introduction à la Vie Dévote* (1609), written with lay women in mind. It was writing such as this which helped develop a sense of self among women, further nurtured by the growing practice of regular direction by a spiritual advisor. As Olwen Hufton has pointed out, regular confession with a spiritual director gave women access to self-knowledge and "shaped their capacities for thought."[11] After years of neglect by the church, women—even from the ranks of the artisans—were being encouraged to develop their own spirituality.

A practical outlet for female spirituality lay in the social sphere, where increasingly there were opportunities appearing for the kind of work that had traditionally fallen to women, albeit in the home. Rapid growth in urban populations from the sixteenth century, and the deteriorating conditions of the poor, led to increased incidence of ill health and poverty among the working people, as well as social disturbance. At the same time, rising aspirations among artisans and the petty bourgeoisie drove their desire to educate their daughters. Women who had become awakened to a new sense of self, through spiritual awareness, felt themselves called to work in the wider community, often among the poorest and most ignorant. It was this sense of being special, fostered by mysticism, which led to the formation of groups who managed to maintain their autonomy, often in the face of continued opposition, but also with the help of wealthy lay women and progressive priests.

Not all efforts turned out as the women hoped. We have seen how the Ursulines were transformed back into the more conventional enclosed order, although they managed to maintain their vow to teach. A similar fate awaited the Visitation order, founded by Jeanne de Chantal (1572–1641) in collaboration with François de Sales (1567–1622), whom she met in 1604.[12] Chantal was also married with six children, but was widowed in 1601. When she started her congregation of women in 1610 their purpose was to visit the poor and sick, and for this reason she wished her associates to be unenclosed, as were the Ursulines at that time, but unfortunately, as with the Ursulines, this freedom was short-lived. Although the activities within the community of religious orders such as the Visitandines were curtailed, there was a perceived need within French society for the services religious women were willing to carry out.

By calling themselves a "congregation," women were able to avoid, for a time at least, the pressure to become cloistered. In Lorraine the Congregation de Notre Dame, formed like the Ursulines with the express mission to instruct girls, had their work approved by Papal Bull in 1628.[13] Under their organization they were able to maintain an interchange between houses, and they soon had schools in many of the local towns. They proved so successful that the daughters of the elites filled the schools, and the parents, rather than the clergy, put pressure on the congregation to become a fully fledged religious order with solemn vows and the resulting enclosure. However, when the congregation moved into the French provinces, they established an associated group of secular helpers, or *externes*, who were able to continue work outside the convent, one of whom, Marguerite Bourgeoys, was prefect of the group in the congregation at Troyes.[14] Marguerite's superior, mère Louise de Chomedey, was the sister of Paul de Chomedey (1612–76), Sieur de Maisonneuve, governor of Montreal, who, on a visit to his sister, was able to persuade Marguerite to travel to Montreal in 1653 and set up a secular community there, along with three companions.[15]

New France in the seventeenth century was for the French the promise of a utopian society, where it would be possible to establish a perfected version of the old country. Mixed up with this desire for a pure beginning was competition with the Dutch and English in the colonies they were establishing further south, along the eastern coast of America. In New France the language would be French and the religion Catholic; the society would be run on the best principles devised at the time. When it came to dealing with the peoples native to the lands claimed as New France, hearts and minds were sought as well as subjugation through military means. The native populations were too large for the small French communities to overcome their resistance purely through arms. Hearts and minds were the job of the church, and for this purpose the Jesuits and later the Sulpician Fathers came from France to the New World.

Because the French wanted to establish not just military outposts, or plantations in New France, but a utopian colony, they needed facilities which would foster the welfare of women and children. Life was also physically difficult in the new settlements, with a great deal of disease and hardship, conditions magnified beyond even the most taxing in France. A fully rounded French, Catholic society could not be expected to form on its own under such circumstances, therefore conditions were ripe for the introduction of women able to take on the roles of teacher and nurse, those roles being assumed in France at this time by the innovative religious communities.

In the first half of the seventeenth century, New France acted upon the imagination of the French people, as Joyce Marshall says, "like a breeze coursing through France."[16] Nearly fifteen years before Marguerite Bourgeoys's arrival in Montreal, Marie Guyart, Marie de l'Incarnation, arrived in Quebec to set up an Ursuline community in the New World. Marie de l'Incarnation, who joined the Ursulines in Tours in 1633, credited her call to Canada to the Virgin Mary, whom she encountered in a dream of a fog-enshrouded land.[17] As noted above, the strong spirituality which inspired many women to join religious orders, and to dedicate themselves to teaching and nursing, should not be underestimated. Not only did their spirituality sustain them in their work and help forge the bonds of community, but it could also silence the objections of relatives.[18] In Marie de l'Incarnation's case she needed her spiritual strength to overcome objections not just from her relatives, but also from her young son, who was still a child when she entered the convent. Later, when she decided to go to Canada, her reasons had to be even stronger.

Marie de l'Incarnation was a widow with an eleven-year-old son when, at the age of thirty-one, she entered the recently established Ursuline convent in Tours. At the age of twenty-one she had had a "conversion" and under the direction of her confessor had lived a life of mortification, with mystical interludes, while she was working for her brother-in-law in his carting business. This experience of conversion was, according to Anya Mali, ongoing and dictated the direction of her spiritual life in France and later in Canada.[19] Once professed, Marie de l'Incarnation received spiritual advice from one of the Jesuits, newly arrived in Tours. When she had her dream of the Virgin in a vast land of fog, he identified the land as Canada. This led Marie to read the Jesuit *Relations*, which gave a yearly account of their missionary activities in New France, and from this reading she devised a resolve to go to Canada to undertake the education of native girls and women.[20]

The obstacles to such a plan were enormous. The practicalities of the journey and the resources needed to set up a convent so far from France seemed beyond one nun in the middle of the Loire Valley, but with the help of the Jesuits, Marie made contact with Madeleine de La Peltrie (1603–71), a wealthy and influential lay woman, who also believed that she had been called to missionary work in Canada. Mme de La Peltrie was as extraordinary as any of the other women encountered here.[21] Although widowed at the age of twenty-two, she avoided the pressure from her family to remarry, eventually arranging a marriage of convenience with a pious man. When it was made known to the Jesuits that Mme de La Peltrie was interested in financing a party of religious women to go to Canada to instruct native girls, they put her in touch with Marie de l'Incarnation. The Company of New France promised land if Mme de La Peltrie would put up the money for the passage from France to Canada and for the Ursuline house in Quebec. After a short sojourn in Paris, on May 4, 1639, Marie de l'Incarnation set sail from Dieppe with her companions, including Mme de La Peltrie, and landed at the Isle d'Orléans in the St. Lawrence River on July 31. Not long after that, the Ursulines were established in Quebec.

Marie de l'Incarnation began writing letters back to France, which now form a vivid account of her life in Canada. There is a telling incident in her description of a fire which devastated her convent in 1650, where she says: "I intended to go up to the room where I had placed the cloth and other reserves of provision for the Community, but God made me put this thought aside to follow one he gave me to save the business papers of our community. I threw them out of the window of our room, and with them whatever came to my hand."[22] This was someone who in France had numerous mystical experiences, but who, at the same time, also helped her brother-in-law run a successful business. Here we have a good example of a woman in whom practicality and mysticism could exist side by side. Marie had also found writing an important part of her spiritual life, and she continued to write in New France, both in French as well as in the languages of the Native Peoples. This was a woman defining herself and her experience through writing, making life in Canada "real" through the written word she sent back to France. Each year she wrote a torrent of letters, and she maintained a faithful correspondence with her son, who edited and published her writings after her death in 1677, thus bringing them to a wider metropolitan audience.

From Marie de l'Incarnation's letters we learn not just about the work of the Ursulines with the native girls and women, but also about the events which concerned the small French community in Quebec. These were dominated by the Iroquois wars, and the steps taken by the authorities in France to establish a viable colony in Quebec. When the houses of religion were vacated in 1660 in preparation for an expected Iroquois attack, Marie de l'Incarnation remained with three companions in order to oversee the welfare of the convent while under military control. Her role was not passive as she notes in her letters: "All our doors were barricaded anew and I armed all our soldiers with what was necessary."[23] Her description is far from what we have come to expect from the cloister, and yet the issue of enclosure did arise in relation to French opinion over the effectiveness of the Ursulines in New France. In 1668 she wrote to her son, outlining the successes they had in teaching both French and native girls, but this was never noted in the Jesuit *Relations*, the main source of information on life in Quebec. As she says: "our enclosure covers all, and it is difficult to speak of what one does not see."[24] As a result, unfair rumors were spread about the uselessness of the Ursulines in the New World.

Although the Ursulines were cloistered in Canada as they were in France, Marie de l'Incarnation's experience demonstrates that there was a certain amount of latitude, since conditions did not lend themselves to strict observance of enclosure. This was even more true of the mission of Marguerite Bourgeoys when she arrived in Montreal in 1653. In 1640 there had been set up in France a Société de Notre-Dame de Montréal, with the intention of establishing a new colony on the Island of Montreal, dedicated to the ideals of what they understood as the primitive church. By 1642 the settlement of Ville Marie had been founded on the island, with de Maisonneuve the governor of this new venture, and in this capacity he recruited Marguerite Bourgeoys in 1653 to set up a secular congregation in the new colony. Marguerite had joined the Congregation de Notre Dame in Troyes as a secular helper after she had experienced a vision of the Virgin during a procession of the rosary; thus she too emerged from the highly charged mystical milieu of French women in the first half of the seventeenth century.[25] She also came from the hardworking, bourgeois, and artisanal background of so many of the women who wished to work among the poor, in the New World as well as in France.

After five years in Montreal engaged in general charitable work, in 1658 Marguerite Bourgeoys was given a stone stable for use as a school for girls, but by 1669 Marguerite and her companions had been able to build a large stone house where they taught up to one hundred pupils. In 1669 Bishop Laval gave the congregation permission to teach throughout the whole Montreal area, a task made possible by the unenclosed status of the sisters. Despite the occasional relaxation of the Ursulines' enclosure, they were nevertheless confined in Quebec City to their convent, and their pupils had to come to them. The inhabitants of Montreal were pleased to welcome a community of women willing and able to work throughout the new parishes around the whole island of Montreal. And yet during the 1670s the prelates of New France would have preferred a cloistered order, with both Laval and his successor Saint-Vallier pressing for the congregation to join the Ursulines.[26] This they managed to avoid and in 1697 they were able to obtain a new rule as the Congregation de Notre Dame with simple vows and without enclosure.

The Congregation de Notre Dame were very successful, supporting themselves through their enterprise and the acquisition of property. They had allies in the Sulpician fathers who owned most of the Island of Montreal, and by 1693 the Congregation themselves owned seven hundred acres and five separate houses.[27] They taught and recruited from the principal families of Montreal, and remained the main teachers of girls in the Montreal area until the nineteenth century. There were two other early orders in Montreal, the Sisters Hospitalières de Saint-Joseph at the Hôtel Dieu, brought from France in 1659 by Jeanne Mance (1606–73), and the indigenous Sisters of Charity of Montreal, founded in 1737 by Marguerite d'Youville (1701–71).

The French Sisters of Charity had been started in the early decades of the seventeenth century, with the help of St. Vincent de Paul (1581–1660). In 1629 a network of confraternities of women devoted to visiting the sick and poor was united under the general care of Louise de Marillac (Mme Le Gras, 1581–1660), and she introduced the innovation of dividing the confraternity into the Ladies of Charity, consisting of elite society women, and the Daughters of Charity, women of peasant and artisanal background who were capable of actually helping the poor.[28] This confraternity managed to maintain their unenclosed status, and went on to establish themselves as a vital element in the French system of poor relief and nursing provision. Historians have noted that in the seventeenth century the destitute, orphans, the blind, and the mentally ill were no longer tolerated in society as they had been during the Middle Ages, and needed removal from the streets or asylum, depending on the point of view.[29] The institutions opened for these people required staffing, and secular religious orders provided the appropriate skills, while largely funding the charitable works themselves through unpaid labor and fundraising.

When Marguerite d'Youville came to establish the Sisters of Charity of Montreal in 1737, the French confraternity had already proved their benefit to society. Like their French counterpart, the Sisters of Charity of Montreal, or the Grey Nuns as they were called, took on the care of those abandoned by the rest of society (such as the orphans, the destitute, the elderly, and the mentally ill), and in 1747 they were asked to take over the Hôpital Général in Montreal which had fallen into ruin. Marguerite d'Youville was another young widow, but unlike Marie de l'Incarnation and Marguerite Bourgeoys, she was born in New France, and she had received some of her schooling with the Ursulines in Quebec. Her path was not an easy one, and some objections to her conduct were raised by those around her, but there does not seem to have been difficulty about enclosure. This may have been because the social good these women were able to perform had at last validated their autonomy in the wider community, as it had with the secular confraternities in France.

What can we draw from this brief account of early modern French religious life and the women who were inspired by it to work in the new colony of Quebec? One issue I wanted to raise was that the mystical and practical seemed to be firmly entwined in the experiences of many of these women. The current religious rhetoric emphasized the individual self in relation to God, and many of these women expressed the belief that they had been called to an extraordinary task, a conviction which gave them the strength of will to override objections from church hierarchy as well as from parents and relatives. The rhetoric of "visions" and portentous dreams gave explanations for their actions, needed by the women themselves as much as by their reluctant families. To silence objections to entering religious life, and then to disappearing to Canada, the women needed a language which would stop argument. According to Natalie Zemon Davies this rhetoric troubled Marie de l'Incarnation's son when he came to publish her letters and autobiography in 1677.[30] By this time mysticism had acquired a bad reputation in France, and her account of her life appeared irrational and overemotional. The language of the mystics can be extreme indeed, with a strong sexual undercurrent, perhaps preparing the way for a more thoroughly elaborated sexual consciousness for women in the eighteenth century.

Along with the language of the mystic went a practical attitude to service in the community, and the ability to undertake the sort of tasks required by society in both France and Canada. This indicates a trend established when women from bourgeois and artisan backgrounds began to enter religious life in numbers not hitherto seen, since the traditional convent had been inhabited by aristocratic choir nuns with lay sisters to do the work within the cloister. Teaching, nursing, and caring for the unfortunate in the wider community needed a range of skills based on practical experience more readily found in the middling orders of society, but it was the mysticism of the seventeenth century which focused these skills and made them available within an understanding of a public sphere suitable for women to inhabit.

The definition of this notional public sphere posed a problem, for the hierarchy who wished to keep women within the cloister, and for the women who saw their vocation out in the world. Again it was more likely that bourgeois women, such as Marie de l'Incarnation, would already have experience of work in a secular environment, so that they did not necessarily associate religious life with enclosure. The church feared women doing men's work, and it was this fear that brought down the ambition of Mary Ward (1585–1645) to set up a female religious order, along the lines of the Jesuits, with a mission to reconvert England.[31] Now, as far as the church was concerned, women could follow a religious life as long as they did it within the privacy of the cloister. At the same time, many lay people, whether private individuals or officials, could see that religious women performed invaluable work in an increasingly complex social sphere, where there were more demands for the sorts of services the women could perform, such as the education of girls from bourgeois and artisanal backgrounds. This was especially the case in New France where cloistered aristocrats would simply be a burden on a fragile society.

One area where religious women's autonomy was noticeable in New France was in the amount of building they were able to do. Both the Ursulines and the Congregation of Notre Dame built substantial houses, often the most substantial residential buildings in the town.[32] The frequency of fires in the new colony also meant that they often had to build over again, as their convent yet again was destroyed. Rebuilding required a renewed search for resources and all the organizational upheaval such a disaster entailed, not just for the religious women, but also for their charges. These buildings, however, were a potent symbol of the institutions they housed, and also of the wider culture embodied in the religious and secular order represented there.

When viewing the achievement of religious women in New France, it is worth considering first the effect their actions had on the native peoples they came to teach. Karen Anderson has argued that the Jesuits sought to establish gender relations among the indigenous people which reflected the asymmetry of those in France, but which were antithetical to the traditions of the native peoples.[33] The Ursulines, according to Marie de l'Incarnation, had mixed success in their attempt to Frenchify the native girls. As she wrote to her son: "Others [native girls] are here only as birds of passage and remain with us only until they are sad, a thing the Savage nature cannot suffer; the moment they become sad, their parents take them away lest they die. . . . There are still others that go off by some whim or caprice; like squirrels, they climb our palisade, which is high as a wall, and go to run in the woods."[34] After coming to Canada ostensibly to teach the native girls, the Ursulines found themselves increasingly teaching the children of the growing number of colonists.

Secondly, what was the long-term effect on New France of religious women founding many of the cultural institutions for education and care of the sick? Were they able to achieve what they did because they were in a colonial situation, perceived as necessary, perhaps temporarily, by the male authorities? They certainly carried out essential work, and they were able to achieve a professional status within the confines of their jurisdiction, that is, within the sphere of teaching girls and women, nursing, and care of the poor. It could be argued, however, that women in Quebec, having achieved this professional space in the seventeenth century under the specific conditions of that time, found it more difficult to break into the traditionally male professions later on in the nineteenth and twentieth centuries. But this issue belongs to a later period of history, which does not concern us here.

The heroic efforts of the religious women in New France have secured for them, along with the founding fathers, a place as founding mothers of the French culture within Canada. The particular religious sensibility of seventeenth-century France and the social conditions within France and Quebec opened for them an opportunity to work and travel not granted to many before them. In Olwen Hufton's words: "Further than they went, in both the geographical and the professional sense, it was impossible for women in the early seventeenth century to go."[35] And yet, as Marguerite Bourgeoys maintained, it was only by working together and maintaining their unity that these women were able to overcome the prejudicial objections of the church to their chosen life.

NOTES

1. Natalie Zemon Davis, "City women and Religious Change," in Davis, *Society and Culture*, 92.
2. Natalie Zemon Davis, "New Worlds, Marie de l'Incarnation," in Davis, *Women on the Margins*, 63–139.
3. Rapley, *Dévotes*.
4. Laurence Lux-Sterritt, *Redefining Female Religious Life. French Ursulines and English Ladies in Seventeenth-Century Catholicism* (Burlington, VT: Ashgate, 2005); Susan E.Dinan, *Women and Poor Relief in Seventeenth-Century France: the Early History of the Daughters of Charity*. (Burlington, VT: Ashgate, 2006).
5. Hufton, *Prospect Before Her*, 367.
6. Lux-Sterritt, *Redefining*, 3.
7. Rapley, *Dévotes*, 27–28.
8. Ibid., 45.
9. Marie-Florine Bruneau, *Women Mystics Confront the Modern World* (Albany: State University of New York Press, 1988), 8; see also Michel de Certeau, *The Mystic Fable*, vol. 1, *The Sixteenth and Seventeenth Centuries*, trans. Michael B. Smith (Chicago: University of Chicago Press, 1992), ii–x.
10. Davis, *Women on the Margins*, 68.
11. Hufton, *Prospect Before Her*, 375.

12. Rapley, *Dévotes,* 35.

13. Ibid., 45.

14. Ibid., 103.

15. Louise Chomedey's certificate of baptism "has never been located," and all we know of the date of her death is that she survived her brother. *Dictionary of Canadian Biography,* s.v. Marie-Claire Daveluy "Chomedey de Maisonneuve, Paul de" (by Marie-Claire Daveluy), "Chomedey de Maisonneuve, Paul de" http://www.biographi.ca/EN/ShowBio.asp?BioId = 34251&query = chom edey%20AND%20 de%20AND%20Maisonneuve (accessed June 14, 2008).

16. Joyce Marshall ed., *Word from New France: The Selected Letters of Marie de l'Incarnation* (Toronto: Oxford University Press, 1967), 1.

17. Ibid., 51–53.

18. Anya Mali, *Mystic in the New World: Marie d'Incarnation (1599–1672)* (Leiden, Netherlands: E. J.Brill, 1996), 7.

19. Ibid., xvii.

20. Davis, *Women on the Margins,* 78.

21. Marshall, *Word,* 55–65.

22. Ibid, 197.

23. Ibid., 244.

24. Ibid., 337.

25. Rapley, *Dévotes,* 97.

26. Ibid., 109.

27. Ibid., 106.

28. Susan E. Dinan, "Spheres of Female Religious Expression in Early Modern France," in *Women and Religion in Old and New Worlds,* ed. Susan E. Dinan and Debra Myers (New York: Routledge, 2001), 80.

29. Rapley, *Dévotes,* 77.

30. Davis, *Women on the Margins,* 130.

31. Lux-Sterritt, *Redefining,* 29–38.

32. Marshall, *Word,* 128–30.

33. Karen Anderson, *Chain her by one Foot: The Subjection of Women in Seventeenth-Century New France* (London: Routledge, 1991), 6.

34. Marshall, *Word,* 336.

35. Hufton, *Prospect Before Her,* 379.

"On *Boadicea* think!":
In Search of a Female Army

Carolyn D. Williams

SINCE AMAZONS COULD BE REGARDED AS AN EXTREME INSTANCE OF women's ability to work together, it is not surprising that they provoked controversy in the eighteenth century. Incredulity and horror collided with admiration in responses to accounts of female communities whose members not only survived without men to organize and control them, but administered independent polities, waged successful wars against masculine armies, and felt no need to conceal their sex. Most research on eighteenth-century images of the female warrior has concentrated on women who fought as individuals, generally in male disguise, and whose exploits were often both recent and reliably attested.[1] Such solitary figures might also be referred to as "Amazons."[2] The term was also applied to fighting women who might or might not have had female military support, including Boadicea (d. ca. 62), who was credited with organizing a formidable coalition of ancient British tribes in a rebellion against Roman rule, and who, according to some versions of her story, was supported by other female figures, including her own daughters.[3] It appeared that she was still recruiting female followers, being associated with eighteenth-century women's quests for various forms of recognition and empowerment. Yet, like other Amazons, Boadicea and her followers did not inspire universal approval: references reveal a wide variety of attitudes toward female cooperation and its practicability, promises, and perils. She figured as heroine, villain, religious bigot, ancient British Bluestocking, shrewd tactician, and raving lunatic. Her sex was generally used to heighten whatever effect the author was seeking to create, making her courage and wisdom all the more miraculous, or her cruelty all the more monstrous. Women who tried to follow her example might be laudably inspired, or fatally misled.

Throughout the period covered in this book, European scholars were confronted by substantial bodies of ancient testimony to the existence of Amazons. However reluctant they were to believe it, they might be equally reluctant to contradict their sources: they lacked the knowledge and theoretical perspective that enabled subsequent researchers to pronounce them mythical.[4] Recognition of the Amazons' achievements was expressed by the distinguished constitutional lawyer Bulstrode Whitelocke (1605–75), who said they were "most warlike and wise women, as the historians report them; and without the counsel of any men they vanquished great armies, subdued large countries, provinces and cities."[5] A believer from the middle of this period was Samuel Johnson (1709–84): in his brief "Dissertation on the Amazons," based on the *Histoire des Amazones Anciennes* (1740) by Claude-Marie Guyon (1699–1771), he said the first Amazons were Scythian women who were forced to defend themselves after their husbands died in battle, and "soon discovered that they had no need of the Government of Men for the Sake of their Protection." But Johnson's sympathy waned when he recorded that their fighting, begun from necessity, continued from choice. He found their views were dangerously independent: they realized "they had lived hitherto in subordination, for want of examining into their own Abilities." They were not only proud but cruel: of their male babies, some were strangled, others maimed, and "some, whose Mothers had not wholly divested themselves of Tenderness, sent to their Fathers." As for the girls, they "deprived them of their Right Breasts," a mutilation which not only marked them out as victims, but suggested a potential lack of maternal tenderness to their own offspring.[6]

Johnson returned to the subject of female warrior communities in the *Idler,* no. 87, Saturday, December 15, 1759, concluding with some satirical speculations on the kinds of English women most likely to revive this institution. He associated Amazons with two groups of women regularly vilified and satirized in contemporary writing and visual imagery: old maids and gamesters. Assuming that warfare against men would not appeal to women conventionally regarded as socially successful and emotionally fulfilled, he began with a group often considered to be despised and rejected by men: "The old Maids seem nearest to independence, and most likely to be animated by revenge against masculine authority," but they seldom have any "settled hatred" for men, and "it is yet more rarely observed that they have any kindness for each other."[7] Since sexual desire endangered an Amazonian community, its members must be incurably addicted to something else, if the group was to hold together. Johnson says, "The Gamesters, if they were united," would be "a formidable body," since they consider men only as "beings that are to lose their money," but if men kept away, the female gamblers "would perish in a few weeks by a civil war."[8] Johnson regarded the Amazonian lifestyle as an experiment whose failure showed "that men and women live best together."[9] He could not, or dared not, envisage a community of women living together from choice.

The anonymous author of "The History of the Amazons" in *The Britannic Magazine* goes a step further than Johnson in expressing disbelief in the existence or possibility of such communities. He concedes that individual women might be strong and brave enough to make good soldiers, but refuses to believe that women were capable of efficient political and military organization: "That there should have been women, who, without the assistance of men, built cities and governed them, raised armies and commanded them, administered public affairs, and extended their dominion by arms, is undoubtedly so contrary to all that we have seen and known of human affairs, as to appear in a very great degree incredible."[10] Yet the Amazons had not lost all their champions: those in quest of support for a protofeminist cause might consider the name of Cesare Mussolini (b. 1748 or 1749) rather unpromising, but his eloquent defense of female abilities is supported by references to many fighting women, including "Mirina, a famous warrior, who with an army of thirty thousand women on foot, and two thousand on horseback . . . conquered the greatest part of Lybia."[11] He adds the inspiring tale of Archidamia, who, "in company with her female citizens in the temple, was assaulted by Aristomenes and his soldiers, who went on purpose to ravish them. Archidamia and her companions with cutlasses repulsed the enemy, and made Aristomenes prisoner."[12] He also refers to women who may have fought without female support, including "the valiant and famous Boadicea."[13]

Boadicea's name was familiar to eighteenth-century readers who knew their British history; James Thomson (1700–48) airily referred to her "well known" story, thus eschewing further explanation.[14] Today's readers might require more information. According to the *Annals* of Gaius Cornelius Tacitus (ca. 58–122), she was the widow of Prasutagus, King of the Iceni, who had left his estate jointly to his two daughters and the Emperor, in an attempt to ensure the welfare of his family and kingdom. The callous Romans looted his property, enslaved his relatives, lashed his widow, and raped his daughters. The Iceni joined forces with other tribes, and rebelled against the Romans, under Boadicea's leadership. They sacked Camulodunum, Londinium, and Verulamium (Colchester, London, and St. Albans), destroyed a substantial contingent of the Ninth Legion, and brutally slaughtered seventy thousand Romans and their British allies. Only

Suetonius Paulinus, governor of Britain, was capable of standing against her. Before the final battle, Boadicea rode about her war-host in a chariot, with her daughters before her, making stirring speeches, in which she declared that she was resolved to conquer or die: the men, if they preferred, might live in slavery. Her army was routed by the more disciplined Romans, who killed eighty thousand Britons: a major factor in their destruction was a ring of wagons installed around the edge of the battlefield, from which British women were watching the fight. To avoid capture, Boadicea took poison and died (*Annals,* 14.31–37). A century later, further vivid details appeared in the *Roman History* of Dio Cassius (164-ca. 235), but their credibility is doubtful: significant deviations from Tacitus will be mentioned later in this chapter.

Before discussing Boadicea's possible collaborations with other women, it is necessary to consider opinions on whether she was capable of efficient cooperation with anybody. Warfare and politics are not solitary arts, and her initial successes suggest that, somehow or other, perhaps by taking the advice of an experienced male commander in chief, she was doing something right. Her ultimate defeat, however, could be taken as evidence either that her forces were not sufficiently organized to withstand real opposition, or that there had been some disastrous breakdown within the British command structure, for which she might be responsible. A third possibility, more flattering to Boadicea's generalship, is that the Britons' defeat had not been so final as Tacitus implies: Dio says they were planning further action, but gave up when she fell sick and died (Dio, 62.12.6).

The first theory, that her forces were not well organized, was taken up by John Milton (1608–74) and also by Richard Glover (1712–85). John Milton maintains in his *History of Britain* (1670) that from the moment the Britons had accepted female leadership, they were doomed: "In this Battel, and whole business, the *Britans* never more plainly manifested themselves to be right *Barbarians;* no rule, no foresight, no forecast, experience or estimation, either of themselves or of thir Enemies; such confusion, such impotence, as seem'd likest not to a Warr, but to the wild hurrey of a distracted Woeman, with as mad a Crew at her heeles."[15] Richard Glover provides a similar estimate of female strategic potential in his tragedy, *Boadicia* (1753), but his heroine began by recognizing her limitations and entrusting the campaign to her brother-in-law and ally Dumnorix. This accounted for the early victories. Later on, however, she quarreled with Dumnorix, because he refused to allow her to hand over innocent Roman prisoners to be sacrificed by the Druids;

she delayed supporting him in battle, so that he would face a humili-
ating defeat, and she would then gain glory by winning the day. Unfortunately, she mistimed her spiteful gesture, allowing the Romans
to win. Glover's audience is offered no reason to disagree with
Dumnorix's bitter observation: "Too late I find a woman curs'd with
pow'r / To blast a nation's welfare" (*Boadicia*, 3.4.12–13).[16] An anonymous critic protests that this portrayal makes her "more like a Bed-
lamite, a Fury, and fitter for the Confinement of a Madhouse, than
to preside over Nations, and direct an Army."[17] However, an even
more rabidly insane Boadicea appeared in the anonymous *Short History of Boadicea* (1754), where, being "of a bloody disposition," she
"way-laid and destroy'd" her allies with her own hands.[18]

But representations of Boadicea in this period were not all unfavorable. In contrast to these incompetent Boadiceas, there appears
a sequence of wise, capable queens. Milton's close contemporary,
Whitelocke, considered her an example of efficient female rule, ac-
quitting herself well "both in counsel and conduct."[19] In 1697,
Charles Hopkins (1664–1700) wrote a tragedy that laid the ground
for Boadicea's reception as a "national heroine" in the eighteenth
century.[20] She is an efficient leader who cares for her army in every
contingency:

> Fly, fly, my Soldiers, with a fresh Recruit,
> Where Britain faints beneath the fierce Dispute.
> Rush with Reserves to every stagg'ring Troop;
> Drive with new Force the broken Squadrons up.
> (*Boadicea Queen of Britain*, 5.2)[21]

She proves herself a better tactician than her commander in chief,
Cassibelan, who loses a battle by disobeying her eminently sensible
orders. Her tragic flaw is not madness or incompetence but racial
prejudice: she refuses Governor Suetonius Paulinus's offer to fight
on her side, because she hates Romans.

By the middle of the eighteenth century, a Boadicea appears
whose administrative talents and experience are so impressive that
it is hard to see how she came to lose: the historian John Campbell
(1708–75), in his brief "History of Boadicia, a British Queen"
(1750), declares that she was an outstandingly intelligent ruler who,
"on Account of her great Wisdom, had been intrusted with a large
Share of the Government, by her Husband in his Life-time."[22] Consequently, Campbell's Paulinus was surprised by the competence of
her troops, and found "all the motions of the British Army confess-
ing rather the Prudence of a consummate Commander, than the

hasty Resentment of an unexperienc'd Woman."[23] Not surprisingly, women found in her a positive role model. Cassandra Cooke, née Leigh, the cousin of Jane Austen's mother, was probably thinking along similar lines to Campbell when she casually referred to Boadicea as a standard for "stability of mind" in her novel *Battleridge* (1799).[24] Another lady writer, Anne Powell, makes it quite clear in her narrative poem *Boadicea* (1821) that her heroine ran her own campaign most effectively:

> Supreme in council was the queen rever'd,
> And slaughter'd Romans in the dust appear'd.[25]

Since there is such a broad spectrum of opinions on Boadicea herself, it is not surprising that the presence of other women in her forces should raise many conflicting possibilities. Tacitus makes Suetonius Paulinus remind his troops that more women than men appear when the British forces are surveyed, and says that, in the final slaughter, they did not even spare women, but it is hard to be sure if any of them were fighting, or if they were all mere spectators (*Annals,* 14.36, 37, 34). Dio puts a statement into her mouth that is highly ambiguous: "As for the rivers, we swim them naked" (62.5).[26] Who, exactly, are "we"? She also claims that the women are as brave as the men (62.6). Yet Dio makes no mention of women fighting in the last battle (62.8).

The first writer to provide Boadicea with female soldiers was the Scottish historian Hector Boece (ca. 1465–1536), who invented a contingent of five thousand ravished ladies.[27] They caught the imagination of some Elizabethans, but were summarily dismissed in the early seventeenth century.[28] There was little trace of them after that. They do appear in a poem by the Reverend Edward Davies (1756–1831), entitled *Aphtharte, the Genius of Britain* (1784), but it is probably significant that it is supposed to be "*Written in the Taste of the Sixteenth Century,*" evoking the era before they were so decisively demobilized. Besides, the performance of Davies's female warriors is, quite literally, pathetic. They are not resilient victims of sexual violence, but beautiful maidens, and the Romans are frightened only because they are so depressingly easy to kill.

> In fair array her virgin bands she drew,
> The Roman eagle trembled at the view:
>
> . . . .
>
> See the red tyrants mourn the deaths they give,
> And stop the brandish'd lance, and bid you live.[29]

Davies does not manage to create a convincingly sixteenth-century atmosphere, but he succeeds in conveying the cloying sentimentality so fashionable in his own age, especially when helpless young women were being described.

There might be more to hope from Boadicea's daughters, who were in her chariot before the final battle, according to Tacitus. At first, their career seems to be a process of progressive disarmament, following the trend set by their mother's female army. In *The Tragedie of Bonduca* (1609–14) by John Fletcher (1579–1625), they are proactive, feisty, and dangerous; they lure Roman officers into a trap and threaten to kill them with their bows and arrows: only the intervention of Caratach, Bonduca's commander in chief, prevents them. These weapons, like the accompanying threat, fail to reappear in even the closest eighteenth-century adaptation of Fletcher's play.[30] Further doubt is cast on their martial accomplishments in a version published in 1696 by George Powell (1658?-1714). On their first entrance, Bonduca's daughters are described as "the partners of her Blood and Spirit," and all three women wear "*an* Amazon *dress*" (*Bonduca*, 1.2).[31] Yet the younger daughter, Bonvica, shows no enthusiasm for warfare. Claudia, the elder, seems a better prospect for female military glory: her fiancé Venutius hails her as the "generous Heir to all / Thy Mother's beauty, and thy Father's Virtue!" and prophesies that her story will inspire virgins to "change all their Womans Fears for Manly Courage" (4.1).[32] Throughout the action of the play, however, Claudia neither fights nor expresses an intention to do so. From now on, she seems to be leaving such matters to Venutius, declaring that,

> Like a true *Britain,* like *Bonduca*'s Daughter,
> I'll dress my Hero, bring his Shining Armour.
>
> (1.1).[33]

Surely Bonduca's daughter could have done more than that! When Venutius returns from battle, Claudia will ask

> A thousand Questions of the War;
> With trembling pleasure I will hear it all,
> Heal every Wound you name with balmy Love,
> Clasp my Victorious Hero in my Arms,
> Praise him in every little tender way.
>
> (1.1)[34]

Claudia's Amazon outfit has degenerated into fancy dress: its only remaining use is to provide a little protection from the advances of

an unwanted lover. Some observers clearly considered that exploit-
ing the sex appeal of the daughters was in fact the most efficient way
to deploy their military potential: Aylett Sammes (ca. 1636–ca. 1679)
points the moral in a little poem, indicating that Boadicea and her
daughters played to the strengths appropriate to their age:

> *She for her Wisdom, followed They for Love;*
> *What Roman force, Such joined powers could quell;*
> *Before so murdering Charmes whole Legions fell.*

(lines 2–4)[35]

By the early nineteenth century, Anne Powell is describing the
daughters' chief function as ministering at their mother's breakfast
table:

> Her lovely daughters grace her either side;
> To hand her early viands was their pride.[36]

This looks like the end of their military ambitions. Yet, as with Boadicea herself, the same period can yield texts with contrary tendencies:
in two publications which represent opposite ends of the publishing
spectrum, we find daughters depicted as warriors worthy to stand
alongside their mother. The anonymous *Heroic Females* (1805–20), a
sensational catch penny publication, offers its readers two sisters
who between them exemplify the best and the worst qualities attributed to Amazons: Gelina was "constantly at the head of the army,
inventing new torments" for enemy prisoners, while Perestina
"blended all the softer feelings and delicacy natural to a woman,
with the heroic ardour and military skill of Boadicea."[37] In the con-
trasting sumptuously scholarly Delphin Tacitus (1821), a note to *Annals* 14.35 claims that the daughters in Boadicea's chariot were not
there merely to inspire the war-host to avenge their injuries: if Boadicea were eliminated from the conflict, they would take over control of the kingdom, the campaign, and their own vengeance
("regno belloque et vindicate superessent").[38] In political and military terms, they could be regarded as efficient colleagues for their
mother.

Religion provided another context for interaction between Boadicea and other female figures, generally to her discredit. According
to Dio, she inaugurated her campaign by delivering a very long
speech, in which she evoked a goddess named Andraste, as one
woman addressing another (62.6). Later, Dio mentions that the Britons subjected their prisoners to hideous tortures, accompanied by

sacrifices and revelry, in all their holy places, and particularly in the grove of Andate, their Goddess of Victory, whom they held in great reverence (62.7). Roman soldiers were impaled, disembowelled, or boiled alive (62.12). A worse fate awaited high-ranking female prisoners: they were impaled, and their breasts cut off and fastened to their mouths as if they were being eaten (62.7). Some historians added still more horrors; according to Paul de Rapin-Thoyras (1661–1725), the mothers endured a special torture: "They hang'd up women with children fasten'd to their breasts, to make them in some measure suffer a double death."[39] Andraste and Andate are generally regarded as variants of the same name.[40] The main issue, however, was not the number of deities involved, but the nature of their worship. For example, Aylett Sammes, who had noted that Boadicea was "highly devoted" to Andate, found the prospect of a powerful woman addressing a goddess on a woman-to-woman basis extremely disconcerting.[41] Boadicea's stress on their common femininity indicated the self-sufficient pride which was the Amazons' primal sin: she "seemed much to triumph in her self, for in her address to that Female Deity, she used these expressions; I being a Woman, adore thee O *ANDATE* a Woman."[42] To Christians in his period, accustomed to an all-male Trinity, the worship of a female being was particularly alienating: this was not an early attempt at seeking out the true God by the light of reason, but superstitious idolatry. Observers today might focus on the conspicuous absences of the solidarity with other women and reverence for motherhood that are commonly supposed to accompany goddess-worship. By the impalements and Amazonian-style amputations inflicted on the female prisoners, Boadicea was not just erasing the signs of tenderness in herself that would have been taken as the normal accompaniment to her own maternal femininity, but desecrating the reproductive and nurturing potential of others.

Similarly, Richard Glover's *Boadicia* powerfully expresses his sense that Boadicia's goddess-worship is a hideous perversion of proper maternal attitudes, and, on a metaphorical level, normal reproductive processes. When she is thinking of a plan to redeem an unpromising military situation by leading a night attack on the Roman camp, she describes it as a child, begotten by the goddess Andate:

> Ev'n now I feel her aid;
> I feel her here; the warlike queen inspires
> My pregnant soul; the mighty plan is forming;
> It grows, it labours in my ardent bosom;
> It springs to life, and calls for instant action;

> Lead on, exert thee, goddess, till the furies,
> Which heretofore have thunder'd at thy heels,
> Start at the new-born horrours of this night.
> (*Boadicia*, 3.4.107–114)[43]

The main elements for an early modern pregnancy and childbirth are present, but in nightmare form: the child has two mothers instead of parents of both sexes; instead of the normally virtuous and supportive midwife and gossips, demons from hell will officiate, and even they will be terrified by the monster that emerges from Boadicia's "ardent bosom," instead of having the chance to coo over a pretty little baby. As might be expected from its inauspicious origins, Boadicia's plan fails: the Romans know she is coming and her army is wiped out. Her assumption that she could sneak up on them without attracting attention was, to use Glover's imagery, a misconception.

When Boadicea collaborates with other women in religion's name, the effect can be equally horrendous. She makes a brief but telling appearance in *Cymbeline* (1792), a posthumously published tragedy by Henry Brooke (1703?–83), set in a period a generation before Boadicea's ill-fated rebellion. As the highly emotional climax approaches, the priestess of Andate, whose sacred duty it is to sacrifice the hero Leonatus, feels unaccountably reluctant to do so. Seeking help from her band of virgin acolytes, she calls on Bonduca, who promptly replies, "We are ready—When you like!" (*Cymbeline,*5.5).[44] In fact, Leonatus is not sacrificed after all, which is just as well, because he turns out to be the son of the priestess, but Bonduca is in no way responsible for his escape.

William Blake (1757–1827) paints an even darker picture, shadowed with grim political and religious implications: he provides symbolic images of Boadicea cooperating with other ancient British princesses in mass destruction, resulting from their involvement in a traditionally cooperative female activity that was even more widely and frequently practiced than the management of childbirth. As one of the twelve daughters of Albion, she embodies the evils of contemporary Britain's imperialism, militarism, and aggressive quest for foreign markets for British textiles:

> The Daughters of Albion girded around their garments of Needlework,
> Stripping Jerusalem's curtains from mild demons of the hills;
> Across Europe & Asia to China & Japan like lightnings
> They go forth & return to Albion on his rocky couch:
> Gwendolen, Ragan, Sabrina, Gonorill, Mehetabel, Cordella,
> Boadicea, Conwenna, Estrild, Gwinefrid, Ignoge, Cambel,

Binding Jerusalem's Children in the dungeons of Babylon;
They play before the Armies, before the hounds of Nimrod.
                    (*Vala, or the Four Zoas* (1797), Night 2, lines 57–64)[45]

Blake acknowledges that sheep are in themselves "mild": "demons" prepares the reader for the worldwide havoc caused by the trade which originates in their fleece. "Jerusalem's curtains" represent "either the veils of false religion and conventional morality, or, more literally, bales of cloth: probably both at once, since Britain's foreign policy was supported by the doctrines of the established church, which in Blake's opinion endorsed cruelties that matched anything practised by ancient Britons."[46] Hostile writers had previously depicted Boadicea as the kind of madwoman one would hesitate to trust with anything sharp: Blake places her in a female group who, given enough wool, can knit their own Armageddon.

Many eighteenth-century authors provided Boadicea with female companions in a different way, by associating her with later women who, for good or ill, shared some of her characteristics. Later British queens offered particularly fruitful points of comparison. Queen Elizabeth I (1533–1603) made an attractive pairing with Boadicea. The early Romantic poet George Richards (1767–1837) creates a particularly intimate fusion, when an ancient British bard foresees that Elizabeth will be her reincarnation:

> Lo! in a train of golden years
> A virgin queen appears,
> Fir'd by the spirit, which of yore
> Bonduca's warrior-body bore:
> Sublime on Albion's whitening cliffs she stands,
> The schemes of unnam'd empires in her hands;
> And bids Britannia's banners wave unfurl'd
> O'er oceans now unknown, and circle this wide world.
>   ("The Battle," lines 215–22)[47]

Another monarch praised for emulating Boadicea's warrior spirit was Queen Anne (1665–1714). John Dunton (1659–1733) declared that when she decided to make war on France "(our Valiant Queen) like another *Boadicea,* frighted her Enemies, and encourag'd her Subjects by her own Example."[48] Perhaps Anne should have been even more like Boadicea: in 1763, an anonymous poet rebuked her for allowing her military and political resolve to falter toward the end of her reign, and thus failing to follow her predecessor's example:

> Can *Boadicia*'s Prowess, which o'ercame
> Victorious Chiefs—who trembl'd at her Name,
> Die in Oblivion?—No, her Fame shall stand
> Instructive Monument—to each servile Land![49]

Yet Boadicea was not a suitable pattern for all queens. Gilbert Burnet (1643–1715) realized this when writing his eulogistic *Essay* on Anne's elder sister, Queen Mary II (1662—94), who had always left military affairs to her husband, William III (1650–1702). Burnet dealt with this situation by playing the well-thumbed gender card; warrior queens may be impressive, but they are not proper ladies: "If She did not affect to be a *Zenobia* or a *Boadicia,* it was not because She wanted their Courage, but because She understood the decencies of her Sex better than they did."[50]

Recruiting female followers for Boadicea was not a politically neutral exercise. Her opposition to Roman invaders resonated with British fears of invasion by foreign Roman Catholic powers. Boadicea was transformed into a symbolic champion of Protestants, and a supporter of the ruling House of Hanover against the Roman Catholic Stuart claimants. The one apparent exception, published in 1722, is *The Plotters; a Satire:* in the previous year Francis Atterbury, Bishop of Rochester (1663–1732), had been arrested on suspicion of conspiring to capture the royal family, depose George I (1660–1727), and put James Francis Edward Stuart (1688–1766) on the throne in his stead. *The Plotters* purports to be a collection of verse letters written by the conspirators, including one from James's wife, Maria Clementina Sobieska (1702–35), to Atterbury's wife, Katherine Osborn (d. 1722). Clementina urges her to help the cause by every means possible:

> On *Boadicea* think! Or on your late
> *Eliza!* and the Shades of Sloath ye'll hate;
>
> . . . .
>
> Scorn to subdue Mens Hearts by idle Charms,
> 'Tis better captivate'em by thine Arms.[51]

But this brief visit to the Jacobite heartland is, of course, highly ironic: the reader is not expected to share Clementina's assumption that Boadicea, or the resolutely Protestant Elizabeth I, would be an appropriate patron for the present enterprise. Furthermore, the picture of a woman inciting another woman to fight is probably not meant to be appealing: Clementina and the Bishop's wife are unruly women, forming a treasonous combination.

Such playful ambiguities were abandoned completely when Clementina's son, Charles Edward Stuart (1720–88), marched from Scotland to England in 1745. William Henry, Rector of Urney (d. 1768), explicitly used Boadicea to recruit female support for the Protestant cause: "It was an heroic Resolution of our *British* Queen *Boadicea,* when entering into Battle with the *Romans,* who had invaded the Liberties of *Britain,* that 'She, for her Part, was resolved to Conquer or Die; but as for the Men, they might, if they pleased, Live and be Slaves,' and I make no doubt, but that there are many *Women,* in the *North of Ireland,* who have the like Spirit and Resolution."[52]

Sexual politics provided further meeting points between Boadicea and eighteenth-century women. She made a particularly effective appearance in the pamphlet *Woman Not Inferior to Man* (1739), by "Sophia, a Person of Quality," whose analysis of patriarchal circular reasoning remains an object lesson in the dissection of intellectually bankrupt ideologies: "Let it be observ'd, what a wretched circle this poor way of reasoning among the Men draws them insensibly into. Why is *learning* useless to us? Because we have no share in public offices. And why have we no share in public offices? Because we have no *learning.*"[53] Sophia argues in favor of changes that would give real power to women—or, at least, to ladies. (Learning and public offices were not normally bestowed on members of the lower classes, whatever their sex.) The main limitation of her approach is the absence of any practicable proposal for bringing it about; this might well have been impossible in her lifetime. But there is nothing dated about her perception of the dangers of masculine chivalry:

> If you are doting enough to hold upon trust what the *Men* themselves say, you are to take it for granted, that *Women* are such senseless mortals by nature, as to be absolutely incapable of taking the least care of themselves. "It is therefore, say they, a cruel tenderness, a false complaisance, to abandon the fair-sex to their own conduct. The more they are made to please and charm, the more it imports them to fly from those dangers, to which they are exposed by being so." A plain proof of their speaking from their hearts, is their imagining us weak enough to be wheedled out of our liberty and property, by such jingling, empty stuff.[54]

Determined to disprove this nonsense, Sophia trawls through ancient and modern history for women who were a match for men in every field of human endeavor, including warfare:

> To pass over the many instances of warlike bravery in our sex, let it suffice to name a *Boadicea,* who made the most glorious stand against the *Romans* in the defence of her country, that ever that great empire was witness to; and if her endeavours did not meet with the success of an

Alexander, a *Cæsar,* or a *Charles* of *Sweden,* in his fortunate days, her courage and conduct were such, as render her worthy to be consider'd equal, if not superior, to them all, in bravery and wisdom; not to mention the nicer justice of her intentions.[55]

Sophia was promptly answered by "A Gentleman," who makes predictably patronizing claims to be inspired by "the very great Tenderness, I have always express'd and really felt for the Fair-Sex."[56] He declares that making themselves "agreeable to us" is "the great Business they were created for," and demands, "How shall they appear any longer agreeable in our Eyes, once they throw off that Modesty and Subjection which alone can give even their native Charms the Force to please us?"[57] He tries to demonstrate his fairness by expressing respect for the celebrated women cited by Sophia, but says they are not patterns whom all women could aspire to imitate: although "the immortal *Boadicea*" was truly courageous, she was "a Miracle, out of the common Course of Nature."[58] These attempts to preserve the status quo by separating Boadicea and other successful women from Sophia's readers are a classic example of the "divide and conquer" strategy. Read against the grain by intelligent and discontented women, they might also reveal the possibility that, if only they dared to emulate such glorious examples, they might change the world.

Sophia had already achieved something very important, and possibly threatening to the patriarchal establishment, by committing her ideas to writing and getting them published. Samuel Johnson was jesting when he described women's writing in terms appropriate to warfare, but there might have been some underlying truth: "the revolution of years has now produced a generation of Amazons of the pen, who with the spirit of their predecessors have set masculine tyranny at defiance, asserted their claim to the regions of sciences, and seem resolved to contest the usurpations of virility."[59]

Was Boadicea herself an Amazon of this type? John Campbell does not suggest that she composed works for publication, but he credits her with the high level of talent and culture that would have enabled a woman to distinguish herself in the best eighteenth-century salons: "Her Education had been excellent, such as gave the highest Polish to natural Abilities uncommonly strong and lively."[60] He bases his assumption on the extensive general knowledge displayed in the speech attributed to her by Dio: he acknowledges that the form may have been invented by the historian, "but as to the Sense, I am persuaded that is the Queen's."[61] Campbell is to be commended for resisting the temptation to make even larger claims. For the previous two centuries, there had been catalogs available listing works by high-ranking Britons, Boadicea among them.[62] Such compilations were assembled on the assumption that every recorded deed, oration, or message must have borne literary fruit, even if it no longer survived. Horace Walpole (1717–97) ended Boadicea's claims to authorship when he omitted her, along with many equally doubtful entries, from his *Catalogue of the Royal and Noble Authors of England, with Lists of their Works* (1758). As he explained, "letters or speeches" did not qualify, because "such pieces show no intention in the writers to have been authors, and would swell this treatise to an immense magnitude."[63] His decision to start at the Norman Conquest gave his collection much greater reliability, as well as saving him from having to deal with "that Virago Boadicia."[64]

Boadicea, the Amazons, and the power of women's writing are brought together most impressively in the career of the Welsh poet Katherine Philips (1631–67), the "Matchless Orinda." She herself expressed a high opinion of Boadicea's words and actions in her poem "On the Welch Language":

> In this once *Boadicia* valour taught,
> And spoke more nobly than her Souldiers fought:
> Tell me what Hero could do more than she,
> Who fell at once for Fame and Liberty?
> Nor could a greater Sacrifice belong,
> Or to her Childrens, or her Countries wrong.
>
> (lines 35–40)[65]

Abraham Cowley (1618–67) claims that Philips has demonstrated greater genius than could be found in any Roman woman. In fact, she seems to have written so well that women, from now on, will be considered better poets than men, much to the delight of the Amazons, whose disembodied spirits have abandoned warfare for literary pursuits:

> *But* Rome *with all her arts could ne're inspire*
> *A Female Breast with such a fire.*
> *The warlike* Amazonian *Train,*
> *Which in* Elysium *now do peaceful reign,*
> *And Wit's wild Empire before Arms prefer,*
> *Find 'twill be settled in their Sex by her.*
> ("To the most excellently accomplish'd, Mrs. *K. P.* upon her Poems," 5.1–6)[66]

Philips's literary conquest finally becomes an acceptable substitute for a successful rebellion:

Even Boadicia's *angry Ghost*
Forgets her own misfortunes and disgrace,
And to her injur'd Daughters now does boast,
That Rome's *o'ercome at last by a Woman of her race.*

(5.11–14)[67]

If writing was not an available option, there was still reading—or just talking. For some women, knowledge about Boadicea, and other historical figures, was in itself a valuable piece of plunder from the overwhelmingly masculine territory of classical learning. Communicating their information to other women offered a welcome relief from the monotonous triviality that beset so much of female existence. Lady Chudleigh (1656–1710), in her essay "Of Knowledge" (1710), inquired, "would it not be more Instructive, as well as more Innocent, to talk of the Victories of an *Alexander,* and of a *Cæsar,* of the Bravery and Courage of a *Boadicia,* or a *Zenobia,* than of the mean, pitiful Conquests of a Coquet, or the Amours of a Fop?"[68] Although it is hard to see how anyone could have disputed the instructiveness of such conversation, Sophia's gentlemanly adversary, and other male supremacists, might have doubted its innocence.

Boadicea's ability to serve equally well as a good or bad influence on eighteenth-century women raises some interesting questions. Do views of her vary according to individual authors' circumstances, character, and preferences? Or are they affected more by historical and literary contexts? Some approaches to an answer can be found in the works of the industrious Samuel Jackson Pratt (1749–1814), who depicts her differently in different genres. In his novel *Family Secrets, Literary and Domestic* (1797) he compares individual female characters to Boadicea when they are behaving badly. A fierce and undisciplined servant prepares for a journey by putting a sword into the carriage, provoking the fear of indiscriminate carnage: "she would slice off an honest gentleman's head as neatly as any of those old tigresses, Boadicea, Zenobia or Joan of Arc."[69] Lady Stuart, trying to get out of a scrape, seized two pistols, and "sallied forth, like another Boadicea, after she had been scourged by the conqueror."[70] Easily disarmed by two unarmed men, she is not only unfeminine but ineffectual. It appears, then, that Pratt considers Boadicea's qualities neither useful nor ornamental for women in contemporary urban Britain, and they might be positively dangerous.

A very different assessment of women who emulate Boadicea appears in Pratt's travel book, *Gleanings through Wales, Holland, and Westphalia* (1800). He mentions that when the forces of Roman Catholic Spain besieged the Protestant city of Leiden in 1574 the women showed exemplary courage:

> It was common to see wives, mothers, daughters, and lovers, rush amidst the thickest dangers of the bloody field, carry off the dead, succour the dying and suck the reeking wounds of an husband, father, lover, or brother. Actions of this kind are mentioned in our own history as great and glorious instances amongst individuals: but in the first approaches to the importance of this little republick, such heroick atchievements were common to the sex, and hundreds of Boadicea's . . . were to be seen acting wonders in the same army.[71]

This exercise of supreme physical courage in time of war, reassuringly packaged within tender devotion to their menfolk, makes these massed Boadiceas thoroughly admirable.

The siege of Haarlem between December 1572 and July 1573 witnessed even more impressive female action, coordinated by a female leader. The Dutch women

> exposed themselves to all the dangers and drudgery of military life, in imitation of a second Boadicea, named Kennava, who led them on. The besiegers were struck with the regular, not riotous, intrepidity of this troop of female warriors. Even they too, as if jealous of the bravery of the men, petitioned that they might be accepted as sacrifices to feed the now almost famished garrison and citizens, many thousands of whom perished for want, notwithstanding these supplies of human flesh.[72]

Kennava (Kenauw Simon Hasselaers [1526–88], more commonly known as Kenau) was a middle-aged widow when she led a force of three hundred women to assist in the city's defense. Haarlem's prolonged resistance contributed to Spain's ultimate withdrawal from the area; Kenau's exploits made her a figurehead of Protestant resistance to Roman Catholicism and of nationalist resistance to the tyranny of foreign invaders, calculated to appeal strongly to the English, whenever they had reason to fear an invasion.[73] Although operating as a self-contained unit, Kenau's troop serve the same religious and political cause as their male comrades. They are not cruel but self-sacrificing: instead of destroying the nutritive potential of other women, they offer their own bodies for male consumption. Pratt had finally endowed Boadicea with a female army who were brave, capable, and untainted by Amazonian sin.

Boadicea's sufferings and exploits, so often endowed with powerful religious and political implications, make her a worthy companion for the other adventurous women in this section of the book. Yet they also touch upon key themes discussed earlier, including motherhood, child care, the high importance placed on female chastity, the education of women, and women's ability to function successfully without male guidance. Above all, Boadicea provides a fascinating example of the ambiguity of female companionship. Her influence, whether seen in terms of her direct impact on female contemporaries, or the effects that knowledge of her story could produce, might be considered benign or dangerous. However much uncertainty might arise about the intellectual, moral, or physical potential of any individual woman, the range of possibilities became much wider when two or more began to work together.

NOTES

1. See Dianne Dugaw, *Warrior Women and Popular Balladry, 1650–1850* (Cambridge: Cambridge University Press, 1989) and Julie Wheelwright, *Amazons and Military Maids: Women who Dressed as Men in the Pursuit of Life, Liberty and Happiness* (London: Pandora, 1989).

2. See Christian Davies, *The Life and Adventures of Christian Davies, the British Amazon*, 2nd ed. (London: R. Montagu, 1741).

3. See *Female Revenge: or, the British Amazon: Exemplified in the Life of Boadicia* (London: M. Cooper, W. Reeve, and C. Sympson, 1753). The most frequent eighteenth-century spelling is "Boadicea": "Boa" is pronounced as in "boa constrictor," the last two syllables are pronounced "sear," and stresses fall on the first and fourth syllables. Other variants will be adopted to suit the text in which they appear.

4. See Josine H. Blok, *The Early Amazons: Modern and Ancient Perspectives on a Persistent Myth* (Leiden: Brill, 1995).

5. Bulstrode Whitelocke, *Whitelockes Notes Uppon the Kings Writt for Choosing Members of Parlement XIII Car II, Being Disquisitions on the Government of England by King Lords and Commons* (London: Andrew Millar, 1766), 1:484.

6. Samuel Johnson, "Dissertation on the Amazons," *Gentleman's Magazine* 11 (April 1741): 203.

7. Samuel Johnson, *The Idler* (London: J. Newbery, 1761), 2:198–99.

8. Ibid., 2:199.

9. Ibid., 2:200.

10. *The Britannic Magazine: or Entertaining Repository of Heroic Adventures. And Memorable Exploits* (London: Printed for the Author, 1794–1807), 1:132–33.

11. Cesare Mussolini, *The School for Marriage* (London: B. Tiffin, 1795), [65].

12. Ibid., [68].

13. Ibid., [75].

14. James Thomson, *Britain: Being the Fourth Part of "Liberty," a Poem* (London: A. Millar, 1736), 37n.

15. John Milton, *The History of Britain, That Part Especially now Call'd England* (London: James Allestry, 1670), 66.

16. Richard Glover, *Boadicia. A Tragedy. As it is Acted at the Theatre-Royal in Drury-Lane* (London: R. and J. Dodsley, M. Cooper, 1753), 31.

17. *Female Revenge*, 19.

18. *A Short History of Boadicea, the British Queen. Being the Story on which the New Tragedy, now in Rehearsal at the Theatre Royal in Drury Lane, is founded—Very Proper to be bound up with the play* (London: W. Reeve, 1754), 19.

19. Whitelocke, *Whitelockes Notes*, 1:478.

20. Mikalachki, *Legacy of Boadicea*, 148.

21. Charles Hopkins, *Boadicea Queen of Britain. A Tragedy, As it is Acted by His Majesty's Servants at the Theatre in Lincolns-Inn-fields* (London: Jacob Tonson, 1697), 47.

22. John Campbell, *Polite Correspondence: or, Rational Amusement; Being a Series of Letters, Philosophical, Poetical, Historical, Critical, Amorous, Moral, and Satyrical* (London: John Atkinson et al., [1750?]), 329.

23. Ibid., 337.

24. Cassandra Cooke, *Battleridge: An Historical Tale, Founded on Facts. By a Lady of Quality* (London: C. Cawthorn et al., 1799), 2:201.

25. Anne Powell, *Clifton, Caractacus, Boadicea, and Other Pieces* (Bristol: Albion, 1821), 96.

26. Dio Cassius, *Dio's Roman History*, ed. E. Capps, T. E. Page, and W. H. D. Rouse, trans. Earnest Cary, on the basis of the version of Herbert Baldwin Foster, Loeb Classical Library (Cambridge, MA: Harvard University Press, 1914–27), 8:91.

27. See Hector Boece, *Scotorum Historiæ a Prima Gentis Origine . . . Libri XIX* (Paris: Jacques de Puys, 1575), 55r.

28. See William Warner, *Albions England* (London: Thomas Cadman, 1586), 74 and Edmund Bolton, *Nero Cæsar, or Monarchie Depraved. An Historicall Worke* (London: Thomas Walkley, 1624), 160.

29. Rev. Edward Davies, *Aphtharte, the Genius of Britain. A Poem, Written in the Taste of the Sixteenth Century* (Bath: C. Dilly, 1784), 14–15.

30. Compare John Fletcher, *The Tragedie of Bonduca*, 59 (separately paginated), in Francis Beaumont and John Fletcher, *Comedies and Tragedies* (London: Humphrey Robinson and Humphrey Moseley, 1647) with John Fletcher, *Bonduca. A Tragedy*, ed. George Colman (London: T. Cadell, 1778), 24–25.

31. John Fletcher, *Bonduca: or, the British Heroine*, ed. George Powell (London: Richard Bentley, 1696), 2.

32. Ibid., 36.

33. Ibid., 6.

34. Ibid., 7.

35. Aylett Sammes, *Britannia Antiqua Illustrata: Or, the Antiquities of Ancient Britain, Derived from the Phoenicians* (London: Printed by Thomas Roycroft, for the Author, 1676), 228.

36. Powell, *Clifton, Caractacus, Boadicea*, 85.

37. *The Heroic Females; Or, an authentic History of the surprising Atchievements, and intrepid Conduct of Boadicea, Queen of Iceni, and her Two Daughters* (London: A. Kemmish, [ca. 1805–20]), 9.

38. Tacitus, *Opera Omnia, Ex Editione Oberliniana cum Notis et Interpretatione in Usum Delphini* (London: A. J. Valpy, 1821), 3:1741.

39. Paul de Rapin-Thoyras, *The History of England*, ed. and trans. John Kelly (London: James Mechell, 1732–37), 1:9.

40. See, for example, William Camden, *Britannia*, ed. and trans. Edmund Gibson (London: A. Swalle and A. and J. Churchill, 1695), col. 366.

41. Sammes, *Britannia Antiqua Illustrata*, 229.

42. Ibid.

43. Glover, *Boadicia*, 34.

44. Henry Brooke, *Poetical Works*, ed. Miss Brooke, 3rd ed. (Dublin: Printed for the Editor, 1792), 3:246.

45. William Blake, *Poetry and Prose*, ed. Geoffrey Keynes (London: Nonesuch Library, 1956), 269.

46. For the former interpretation, see William Blake, *The Prophetic Writings of Wil-*

liam Blake, ed. D. J. Sloss and J. P. R. Wallis (Oxford: Clarendon, 1926), 1:176. For a view that includes a more literal reading of the "curtains," see David V. Erdman, *Blake: Prophet against Empire,* 3rd ed. (New York: Dover, 1977), 332.

47. George Richards, *Songs of the Aboriginal Bards of Britain* (Oxford: J. Cooke et al., 1792), 16.

48. John Dunton (1659–1733), *The History of Living Men* (London: E. Mallet, 1702), 27.

49. A Briton, *A Poetic Chronology. By a Briton* (Coventry: Printed for the author, by T. Luckman, 1763), 11–12.

50. Gilbert Burnet, *An Essay on the Memory of the Late Queen* (London: Ric. Chiswell, 1695), 70.

51. *The Plotters; a Satire. Occasion'd by the Proceedings of the Earl of Or[rer]y; the Lord B[ishop]. of R[ochester]. the Lord N[orth] and G[rey] and Others* (London: [A. Moore, pseud.], 1722), 31.

52. William Henry (Rector of Urney), *A Philippic Oration, against the Pretender's Son, and his Adherents. Addressed to the Protestants of the North of Ireland* (Dublin: Peter Wilson, 1745), 23.

53. Sophia, a Person of Quality, *Woman Not Inferior to Man: or, A short and modest Vindication of the natural Right of the Fair-Sex to a perfect Equality of Power, Dignity, and Esteem, with the Men* (London: John Hawkins, 1739), 27.

54. Ibid., 29.

55. Ibid., 55.

56. A Gentleman, *Man Superior to Woman* (London: T. Cooper, 1739), 1.

57. Ibid., 2.

58. Ibid., 63.

59. *Adventurer* 115 (Tuesday, December 11, 1753), in [John Hawkesworth, Samuel Johnson, Joseph Warton, and others], *The Adventurer* (London: J. Payne, 1753), 2:266–67. For Johnson's authorship of *Adventurer* 115, see Samuel Johnson, *The Idler and The Adventurer,* ed. W. J. Bate, John M. Bullitt, and L. F. Powell (New Haven: Yale University Press, 1963), 324–33.

60. Campbell, *Polite Correspondence,* 329.

61. Ibid., 333.

62. See, e.g., John Bale, *Scriptorum Illustrium Maioris Brytannie quam nunc Angliam & Scotiam Vocant Catalogus* (Basel: Joannem Oporinum [Johann Herbster], 1557–59), 1:20; Boece, *Scotorum,* 53v; John Pits, *De Illustribus Angliæ Scriptoribus* [the running title of *Relationum Historicarum de Rebus Anglicis Tomus Primus*] (Paris: Rolin Theoderic and Sebastian Cramoisy, 1618), 71; Thomas Dempster, *Historia Ecclesiastica Gentis Scotorum* (1627), 2nd ed. (Edinburgh: Bannatyne Club, 1829), 108; Thomas Tanner, *Bibliotheca Britannico-Hibernica: Sive, de Scriptoribus, Qui in Anglia, Scotia, et Hibernia ad Saeculi XVII Initium Floruerunt, Literatum Ordine Juxta Familiarum Nomina Dispositis Commentarius* (London: William Bowyer, Impensis Societatis ad Literas Promovendas Institutae, 1748), 139.

63. Horace Walpole, *Catalogue of the Royal and Noble Authors of England, with Lists of their Works,* 3rd ed. (Dublin: George Faulkner, 1759), 1:ix.

64. Ibid.

65. Katherine Philips, *Poems by the Most Deservedly Admired Mrs. Katherine Philips, the Matchless Orinda* (London: H. Herringman, 1667), 132.

66. Katherine Philips, *Poems by the Incomparable Mrs. K. P.* (London: Richard Marriott, 1664), A5r.

67. Ibid., A5v.

68. Lady Mary Lee Chudleigh, *Essays upon Several Subjects in Prose and Verse* (London: R. Bonwicke, W. Freeman, et al., [1710]), 16.

69. Samuel Jackson Pratt, *Family Secrets, Literary and Domestic* (London: T. N. Longman, 1797), 5:469.

70. Ibid., 4:45.

71. Samuel Jackson Pratt, *Gleanings through Wales, Holland, and Westphalia* (London: T. N. Longman and L. B. Seeley, 1795), 1:342.

72. Ibid., 2:337–38.

73. See Els Kloek, *Kenau: De Heldhaftige Zakenvrouw vit Haarlem* (Hilversum: Uitgeverij Verloren, 2001).

Bibliography

Manuscripts

British Library:

Bentham Papers, vol. 27, accounts, add MSS 33563, fol. 131b.

LETTERS IN ADDITIONAL MANUSCRIPTS.

Add. MS 34048 fols. 61–62, April 6, 1790. Sir William Hamilton to Joseph Banks.

Add. MS 34710, fol. 23, November 17, 1795. Sir William Hamilton to Charles Greville.

Add. MS 34989, fols. 3, 15, 20, September 8, October 20, October 27, 1798. Emma Hamilton to Horatio Nelson.

LETTERS IN THE EGERTON COLLECTION.

Eg. MS 1615, fols. 8, 18–22, 69, 129, June 4, 1795, April 17, 1795, December 3, 1796, [n.d. 1798]. Queen Maria Carolina to Emma Hamilton.

Eg. MS 1616, fol. 38 [1798]. Emma Hamilton to Queen Maria Carolina.

Cornell University Library:

Kroch Rare Books Collection, miscellaneous MSS: 4600 Box 42, M. Lady Barbara Montagu to Samuel Richardson, January 31, 1759.

Gloucestershire Archives (GA):

GA D9282, documents compiled for the Crawley-Boeveys in 1915, including "Mrs. Bovey's Memorandum" dealing with leases, boundary disputes, and Catherine Bovey's accounts.

Note in particular GA Box 22496, D9282, call AC 1982, *Letter Book* # 1433, 42–43. Letter from Catherine Bovey and Mary Pope to Joseph Bate.

The Huntington Library, San Marino, California:

Montagu Collection (MO 5281); Sarah Scott to Elizabeth Montagu, June [20?], 1760.

Mitchell Library (Glasgow):

Cowie Collection MS 215c; May 1842. Letter from Joanna Baillie to Jane Davy.

Archives Nationales, Paris:

Fonds Fourier et Considérant AN10 AS 42 d. 8. Désirée Veret to Victor Considérant, September 7, 1890.

Royal College of Surgeons of England (RCS):

RCS, MS0014/3/22. April 1781. Letter from Agnes Baillie to Matthew Baillie.
RCS, MS0014/3/33. August 1782. Letter from Agnes Baillie to Matthew Baillie.
RCS, MS0014/3/56c. Joanna Baillie's brief autobiography: "Recollections written at the request of Miss Berry." Joanna Baillie's autobiographical papers, 1830.
RCS, MS0014/3/70. ca. 1810. Joanna Baillie to Mary Berry.
RCS, MS0014/12/59. July 8, 1833. Letter from Joanna Baillie to Mary Berry.

Library of the Religious Society of Friends in Britain, London:

Aberdeen Women's Meeting, Epistles.
1675—LSF MS. Portfolio 2/34.
1694—LSF 11a4: Box Meeting MSS/46.
1697—LSF 11a4: Box Meeting MSS/47.
1700—LSF 11a4: Box Meeting MSS/53.

Wellcome Institute for the History of Medicine (WI):

WI MS 5613/68/1–6. Joanna Baillie MS memoirs.
WI MS 5616/64. December 25, 1805. Letter from Joanna Baillie to Mary Berry.

PRINTED SOURCES

Addison, Joseph. *The Spectator.* Edited by D. F. Bond. 5 vols. Oxford: Clarendon, 1965.
Anderson, Karen. *Chain her by one Foot: The Subjection of Women in Seventeenth-Century New France.* London: Routledge, 1991.
Andrew, Donna T., ed. and comp. *London Debating Societies, 1776–1799.* London: London Record Society, 1994.
———. *Philanthropy and Police: London Charity in the Eighteenth Century.* Princeton: Princeton University Press, 1989.
———. "Popular Culture and Public Debate: London 1780." *Historical Journal* 39, no. 2 (1996): 405–23.
Anon. *Female Revenge: or, the British Amazon: Exemplified in the Life of Boadicia.* London: M. Cooper, W. Reeve, and C. Sympson, 1753.

————. *The Heroic Females; Or, an authentic History of the surprising Atchievements, and intrepid Conduct of Boadicea, Queen of Iceni, and her Two Daughters.* London: A. Kemmish, [ca. 1805–20].

————. "The History of the Amazons." In *The Britannic Magazine: or Entertaining Repository of Heroic Adventures. And Memorable Exploits,* 1:129–35. 12 vols. London: Printed for the Author, 1794–1807.

————. *Memoirs of Lady Hamilton.* London: Henry Colburn, 1815.

————. *The Plotters; a Satire. Occasion'd by the Proceedings of the Earl of Or[rer]y; the Lord B[ishop]. of R[ochester]. the Lord N[orth] and G[rey] and Others.* London: [A. Moore, pseud.], 1722.

————. *A Short History of Boadicea, the British Queen. Being the Story on which the New Tragedy, now in Rehearsal at the Theatre Royal in Drury Lane, is founded—Very Proper to be bound up with the play.* London: W. Reeve, 1754.

Armstrong, Isobel, and Virginia Blain, eds. *Women's Poetry in the Enlightenment: The Making of a Canon, 1730—1820.* Basingstoke: Macmillan, 1999.

Astell, Mary. *A Serious Proposal to the Ladies, for the Advancement of their True and Great Interest.* London: R. Wilkins, 1694.

Atkyns, Robert. *The Ancient and Present State of Glostershire.* London: Robert Gosling, 1712.

Auerbach, Nina. *Communities of Women: An Idea in Fiction.* Cambridge, MA: Harvard University Press, 1978.

Austen, Jane. *Catharine and Other Writings.* Edited by Margaret Anne Doody and Douglas Murray. Oxford: Oxford University Press, 1993.

————. *Emma.* Edited by Richard Cronin and Dorothy McMillan. Cambridge: Cambridge University Press, 2005.

————. *Jane Austen's Letters.* Edited by Deidre Le Faye. Oxford: Oxford University Press, 1997.

————. *Mansfield Park.* Edited by John Wiltshire. Cambridge: Cambridge University Press, 2005.

————. *Northanger Abbey.* Edited by Claire Grogan. Peterborough, ON: Broadview, 2002.

————. *Persuasion.* Edited by Janet Todd and Antje Blank. Cambridge: Cambridge University Press, 2006.

————. *Pride and Prejudice.* Edited by Pat Rogers. Cambridge: Cambridge University Press, 2006.

————. *Sense and Sensibility.* Edited by Edward Copeland. Cambridge: Cambridge University Press, 2006.

Bacon, Margaret Hope. *Wilt Thou Go on My Errand? Journals of Three 18th Century Quaker Women Ministers.* Wallingford: Pendle Hill, 1994.

Bailey, J. T. Herbert. *Emma, Lady Hamilton: A Biographical Essay with a Catalogue of her Published Portraits.* London: W. G. Menzies, 1905.

Baillie, Joanna. *The Collected Letters of Joanna Baillie.* Edited by Judith Bailey Slagle. 2 vols. Madison, WI: Fairleigh Dickinson University Press, 1999.

————. *Poems; Wherein it is Attempted to Describe Certain Views of Nature and of Rustic Manners, etc.* London: J. Johnson, 1790.

Bale, John. *Scriptorum Illustrium Maioris Brytannie quam nunc Angliam & Scotiam Vocant Catalogus.* 2 vols. Basel: Joannem Oporinum [Johann Herbster], 1557–59.

Ballard, George. *Memoirs of Several Ladies of Great Britain, who have been Celebrated for their Writings or Skill in the Learned Arts and Sciences.* Oxford: Printed for the Author, 1752.

Banks, John. *An Epistle to Friends.* London: T. Sowle, 1693.

Barbour, Hugh. *The Quakers in Puritan England.* New Haven: Yale University Press, 1964.

Barclay, John. "Memoirs of the Rise, Progress, and Persecutions, of the People Called Quakers, in the North of Scotland." In *Diary of Alexander Jaffray,* 225–592. London: Harvey and Darton, 1833.

Barker, Hannah, and Elaine Chalus, eds. *Gender in Eighteenth-Century England: Roles, Representations and Responsibilities.* London: Longman, 1997.

Barnett, Louise. "Swift, Women, and Women Readers: A Feminist Perspective on Swift's Life." In *Representations of Swift,* edited by Brian Connery, 181–94. Newark: University of Delaware Press, 2002.

Barrett, Eaton Stannard. *The Heroine: Or, Adventures of a Fair Romance Reader.* 3 vols. London: Henry Colburn, 1813.

Batchelor, Jennie. "'Industry in Distress': Reconfiguring Femininity and Labour in the Magdalen House." *Eighteenth-Century Life* 28, no. 1 (2004): 1–20.

———. "Woman's Work: Labour, Gender and Authorship in the novels of Sarah Scott." In Batchelor and Kaplan, *British Women's Writing,* 19–33.

Batchelor, Jennie, and Megan Hiatt, eds. *The Histories of Some of the Penitents in the Magdalen-House, As Supposed to be Related by Themselves.* London: Pickering and Chatto, 2007.

Batchelor, Jennie, and Cora Kaplan, eds. *British Women's Writing in the Long Eighteenth Century: Authorship, Politics and History.* Basingstoke: Palgrave Macmillan, 2005.

Baudino, Isabelle, Jacques Carré, and Marie-Cécile Révauger, eds. *The Invisible Woman: Aspects of Women's Work in Eighteenth-Century Britain.* Aldershot: Ashgate, 2005.

Bauman, Richard. *Let Your Words Be Few: symbolism of speaking and silence among seventeenth-century Quakers.* London: Quaker Home Service, 1998.

Beaumont, Francis, and John Fletcher. *Comedies and Tragedies.* London: Humphrey Robinson and Humphrey Moseley, 1647.

Bellamy, Joan, Anne Laurence, and Gill Perry, eds. *Women, Scholarship and Criticism: Gender and Knowledge, c. 1790—1900.* Manchester: Manchester University Press, 2000.

Benefiel, Margaret. "'Weaving the Web of Community': Letters and Epistles." In Garman, Applegate, Benefiel, and Meredith, *Hidden in Plain Sight,* 443–52.

Berry, Mary. *A Comparative View Of The Social Life Of England And France, From The Restoration Of Charles The Second, To The French Revolution.* London: Longman, Rees, Orme, Brown, and Green, 1828.

———. *Extracts of the Journals and Correspondence of Miss Berry, from the year 1783 to 1852.* Edited by Lady Theresa Lewis. 3 vols. London: Longmans, Green, 1865.

Besse, Joseph. *A Collection of the Sufferings of the People Called Quakers.* 2 vols. London: Luke Hinde, 1753.

Binhammer, Katherine. "The Whore's Love or the Magdalen's Seduction." *Eighteenth Century Fiction* 20, no. 4 (2008): 507–34.

Bishop, Edward. *Emma, Lady Hamilton.* London: Heron Books, 1969.

Blain, Virginia, Patricia Clements, and Isobel Grundy, eds. *The Feminist Companion to Literature in English: Women Writers from the Middle Ages to the Present.* London: B. T. Batsford, 1990.

Blake, William. *Poetry and Prose.* Edited by Geoffrey Keynes. London: Nonesuch Library, 1956.

———. *The Prophetic Writings of William Blake.* Edited by D. J. Sloss and J. P. R. Wallis. 2 vols. Oxford: Clarendon, 1926.

Blok, Josine H. *The Early Amazons: Modern and Ancient Perspectives on a Persistent Myth.* Leiden: Brill, 1995.

Bloom, Donald A. "Dwindling into Wifehood: the Romantic Power of the Witty Heroine in Shakespeare, Dryden, Congreve, and Austen." In *Look Who's Laughing: Gender and Comedy,* edited by Gail Finney, 53–79. Langhorne, PA: Gordon and Breach, 1994.

Boece, Hector. *Scotorum Historiæ a Prima Gentis Origine . . . Libri XIX.* Paris: Jacques de Puys, 1575.

Bolton, Edmund. *Nero Cæsar, or Monarchie Depraved. An Historicall Worke.* London: Thomas Walkley, 1624.

Botting, Fred. *Gothic.* Routledge: London, 1996.

Braithwaite, William. *The Beginnings of Quakerism.* Cambridge: Cambridge University Press, 1955.

British Co-operator, nos. 1 and 2. May and June 1830.

"Briton, A." *A Poetic Chronology. By a Briton.* Coventry: Printed for the author, by T. Luckman, 1763.

Brooke, Henry. *Poetical Works.* 3rd ed. Edited by Miss Brooke. 4 vols. Dublin: Printed for the Editor, 1792.

Bruneau, Marie-Florine. *Women Mystics Confront the Modern World.* Albany: State University of New York Press, 1998.

Brunton, Mary. *Discipline: A Novel.* 3 vols. Edinburgh: Manners and Miller, 1814.

———. *Self-Control: A Novel.* 2 vols. Edinburgh: Manners and Miller, 1811.

Bulwer Lytton, Edward. *Pelham.* Edited by Jerome J. McGann. Lincoln: University of Nebraska Press, 1972.

———. *Poems and Ballads.* 2 vols. London: William Blackwood and Sons, 1844.

Bulwer Lytton, Rosina. *Behind the Scenes: A Novel.* 3 vols. London: Skeet, 1854.

———. *A Blighted Life.* Edited by Marie Mulvey-Roberts. Bristol: Thoemmes, 1994.

———. *Cheveley; or, the man of honour* (1839). Edited by Marie Mulvey-Roberts. General editor Harriet Devine Jump. Vol. 5, *The Silver Fork Novels, 1826—1841.* London: Pickering and Chatto, 2005.

———. *The Collected Letters of Rosina Bulwer Lytton.* Edited by Marie Mulvey-Roberts, with the assistance of Steve Carpenter. Vol. 3. London: Pickering and Chatto, 2008.

———. *Memoirs of a Muscovite.* 3 vols. London: Newby, 1844.

———. *Miriam Sedley.* 2 vols. London: Newby, 1851.

———. *The School for Husbands; or Molière's Life and Times.* 3 vols. London: Skeet, 1852.

Burke, John. *A Genealogical and Heraldic History of the Commoners of Great Britain and Ireland, Enjoying Territorial Possessions or High Official Rank: But Uninvested with Heritable Honours.* 4 vols. London: Henry Colburn, 1835–38.

Burnet, George B., and William H. Marwick. *The Story of Quakerism in Scotland, 1650–1950.* 1952. Reprint, Cambridge: Cambridge University Press, 2007.

Burnet, Gilbert. *An Essay on the Memory of the Late Queen.* London: Ric. Chiswell, 1695.

Burney, Fanny. *Evelina, or, a Young Lady's Entrance into the World. In a Series of Letters.* 2nd ed. 3 vols. London: T. Lowndes, 1779.

Burney, Sarah H. *Clarentine. A Novel.* 3 vols. London: G. G. and J. Robinson, 1796.

Burroughs, Catherine B. *Closet Stages: Joanna Baillie and the Theater Theory of British Romantic Women Writers.* Philadelphia: University of Pennsylvania Press, 1997.

Burton, Paul. *A Social History of Quakers in Scotland, 1800–2000.* Lampeter: Edwin Mellen, 2007.

Camden, William. *Britannia.* Translated and edited by Edmund Gibson. London: A. Swalle and A. and J. Churchill, 1695.

Campbell, John. *Polite Correspondence: or, Rational Amusement; Being a Series of Letters, Philosophical, Poetical, Historical, Critical, Amorous, Moral, and Satyrical.* London: John Atkinson et al., [1750?].

Carter, Elizabeth. *Letters from Mrs. Elizabeth Carter to Mrs. Elizabeth Montagu, between the Years 1755 and 1800.* Edited by Montagu Pennington. 3 vols. London: F. C. and J. Rivington, 1817.

———. *A Series of Letters between Mrs. Elizabeth Carter and Miss Catherine Talbot, from the Year 1741 to 1770. To which are Added, Letters from Mrs. Elizabeth Carter to Mrs. Vesey, between the Years 1763 and 1787.* Edited by Montagu Pennington. 2 vols. London: F. C. and J. Rivington, 1808.

Cassius, Dio. *Dio's Roman History.* Edited by E. Capps, T. E. Page, and W. H. D. Rouse. With an English translation by Earnest Cary, on the basis of the version of Herbert Baldwin Foster. 9 vols. Loeb Classical Library. Cambridge, MA: Harvard University Press, 1914–27.

Chalus, Elaine. "Elite Women, Social Politics and the Political World of late Eighteenth-Century England." *Historical Journal* 43, no. 3 (2000): 669–97.

Chernaik, Judith. "The Two Marys." *Women's Writing* 6, no. 3 (1999): 451–68.

Chudleigh, Lady Mary Lee. *Essays upon Several Subjects in Prose and Verse.* London: R. Bonwicke, W. Freeman, et al., 1710.

Clarke, Norma. *Ambitious Heights. Writing, Friendship, Love: The Jewsbury Sisters, Felicia Hemans and Jane Welsh Carlyle.* London: Routledge, 1990.

———. *Dr Johnson's Women.* London: Hambledon and London, 2000.

Cody, Lisa Forman. *Birthing the Nation: Sex, Science, and the Conception of Eighteenth-Century Britons.* Oxford: Oxford University Press, 2005.

———. "The Politics of Reproduction: From Midwives' Alternative Public Sphere to the Public Spectacle of Man Midwifery." *Eighteenth-Century Studies* 32, no. 4 (1999): 477–95.

Cole, Lucinda. "(Anti)feminist Sympathies: The Politics of Relationship in Smith, Wollstonecraft and More." *ELH* 58, no. 1 (1991): 107–40.

———. "'The Contradictions of Community': Elegy or Manifesto." *Eighteenth Century: Theory and Interpretation* 36, no. 3 (1995): 195–202.

Colley, Linda. *Britons: Forging the Nation, 1707–1837.* London: Vintage, 1996.

Collingridge, Vanessa. *Boudica.* London: Ebury, 2005.

Colman, George, and Bonnell Thornton. *Connoisseur,* no. 49. Thursday, January 2, 1755.

Congreve, William. *The Way of the World.* 2nd ed. London: Jacob Tonson, 1706.

Cooke, Cassandra. *Battleridge: An Historical Tale, Founded on Facts. By a Lady of Quality.* 2 vols. London: C. Cawthorn et al., 1799.

Crainz, Franco. *The Life and Works of Matthew Baillie, MD, FRS, L&E, FRCP, etc. (1761–1823).* Santa Palomba, Italy: PelitiAssociati, 1995.

Crawley-Boevey, Arthur William. *The "Perverse Widow": Being Passages from the Life of Catherina, Wife of William Boevey, Esq., of Flaxley Abbey, in the County of Gloucester. With Genealogical Notes on the Family and Others Connected therewith.* London: Longmans, Green, 1898.

Crisp, Steven. *An Epistle of Tender Counsel and Advice.* London: Benjamin Clarke, 1680.

Crook, John. *An Epistle to Young People Professing the Truth.* Luton: 1686.

Daily News. October 12, 1894.

D'Auvergne, Edmund B. *The Dear Emma.* London: George G. Harrap, 1936.

Davidoff, Leonore. *Worlds Between: Historical Perspectives on Gender and Class.* Cambridge: Polity, 1995.

Davies, Christian. *The Life and Adventures of Christian Davies, the British Amazon.* 2nd ed. London: R. Montagu, 1741.

Davies, Rev. Edward. *Aphtharte, the Genius of Britain. A Poem, Written in the Taste of the Sixteenth Century.* Bath: C. Dilly, 1784.

Davies, Kate. *Catharine Macaulay and Mercy Otis Warren: The Revolutionary Atlantic and the Politics of Gender.* Oxford: Oxford University Press, 2005.

Davis, Natalie Zemon. *Society and Culture in Early Modern France.* Stanford, CA: Stanford University Press, 1975.

———. *Women on the Margins: Three Seventeenth-Century Lives.* Cambridge, MA: Harvard University Press, 1995.

Daybell, James. "Women's Letters of Recommendation and the Rhetoric of Friendship in Sixteenth-century England." In *Rhetoric, Women and Politics in Early Modern England,* edited by Jennifer Richards and Alison Thorne, 172–90. London: Routledge, 2007.

De Certeau, Michel. *The Mystic Fable.* Vol. 1, *The Sixteenth and Seventeenth Centuries.* Translated by Michael B. Smith. Chicago: University of Chicago Press, 1992.

Defoe, Daniel. *Roxana: The Fortunate Mistress.* Edited by John Mullan. Oxford: Oxford University Press, 1996.

———. *A Tour Through the Whole Island of Great Britain.* 2 vols. London: Dent, 1966.

Dempster, Thomas. *Historia Ecclesiastica Gentis Scotorum* (1627). 2nd ed. Edinburgh: Bannatyne Club, 1829.

DesBrisay, Gordon. "Lilias Skene: A Quaker Poet and her 'Cursed Self.'" In *Women and the Feminine in Medieval and Early Modern Scottish Writing,* edited by Sarah M. Dunnigan, C. Marie Harker, and Evelyn S. Newlyn, 162–77. Basingstoke: Palgrave, 2004.

Devey, Louisa. *Life of Rosina, Lady Lytton.* London: Swan Sonnenschein, Lowrey, 1887.

Dewsbury, William. *A general epistle to Friends, from that ancient servant of Christ William Dewsebury.* Warwick, 1686.

Dinan, Susan E. "Spheres of Female Religious Expression in Early Modern France." In *Women and Religion in Old and New Worlds,* edited by Susan E. Dinan and Debra Myers, 71–92. New York: Routledge, 2001.

————. *Women and Poor Relief in Seventeenth-Century France: the Early History of the Daughters of Charity.* Burlington, VT: Ashgate, 2006.

D'Monté, Rebecca, and Nicole Pohl, eds. *Female Communities, 1600—1800: Literary Visions and Cultural Realities.* Basingstoke: Macmillan, 2000.

Dobson, Jessie. *John Hunter.* Edinburgh: Livingstone, 1969.

Dodd, William. *Advice to the Magdalens,* reprinted with an *Account of the Rise, Progress, and Present State of the Magdalen Charity.* London: W. Faden, 1761.

Dodd, William, and M. S. *The Magdalen, or History of the First Penitent Received into that Charitable Asylum; in a Series of Letters to a Lady. With Anecdotes of Other Penitents, by the Late Rev. William Dodd.* London: W. Lane, [1783].

Downing, Christine. *The Goddess: Mythological Images of the Feminine.* New York: Cross-road, 1988.

Dugaw, Dianne. *Warrior Women and Popular Balladry, 1650–1850.* Cambridge: Cambridge University Press, 1989.

Dunn, Judy, and Carol Kendrick. *Siblings: Love, Envy, and Understanding.* Cambridge, MA: Harvard University Press, 1982.

Dunn, Judy, and Robert Plomin. *Separate Lives: Why Siblings Are So Different.* New York: Basic Books Division of Harper Collins, 1990.

Dunton, John. *The History of Living Men.* London: E. Mallet, 1702.

Edinburgh Magazine and Literary Miscellany: A New Series of "The Scots Magazine" 2 (March 1818).

Edwards, Irene L. "The Women Friends of London: The Two-Weeks and Box Meetings." *Journal of the Friends' Historical Society* 47, no. 1 (1955): 3–21.

Eger, Elizabeth, Charlotte Grant, Clíona Ó Gallchoir, and Penny Warburton, eds. *Women, Writing and the Public Sphere, 1700–1830.* Cambridge: Cambridge University Press, 2001.

Elfenbein, Andrew. "Lesbian Aestheticism on the Eighteenth-Century Stage." *Eighteenth-Century Life* 25, no. 1 (2001): 1–16.

Eliot, George. *Adam Bede.* Edited by Mary Waldron. Peterborough, ON: Broadview, 2005.

————. *The Journals of George Eliot.* Edited by Margaret Harris and Judith Johnston. Cambridge: Cambridge University Press, 1998.

Elliott, Dorice Williams. *The Angel out of the House: Philanthropy and Gender in Nine-teenth-Century England.* Charlottesville: University Press of Virginia, 2002.

Ellis, Markman. *The Politics of Sensibility: Race, Gender and Commerce.* Cambridge: Cambridge University Press, 1996.

Erdman, David V. *Blake: Prophet against Empire.* 3rd ed. New York: Dover, 1977.

Escott, Angela. "*The School of Eloquence* and 'Roasted Square Caps': oratory and pedantry as fair theatrical game?" *Women's Writing* 8, no. 1 (2001): 59–79.

Ezell, Margaret J. M. *Social Authorship and the Advent of Print.* Baltimore: Johns Hopkins University Press, 1999.

————. *Writing Women's Literary History.* Baltimore: Johns Hopkins University Press, 1993.

Faderman, Lilian. *Surpassing the Love of Men: Romantic Friendship and Love between Women from the Renaissance to the Present.* London: Junction Books, 1982.

Field, Ophelia. *The Favourite: Sarah, Duchess of Marlborough.* London: Hodder and Stoughton, 2002.

Fielding, Sarah. *The Adventures of David Simple; and The Adventures of David Simple, Volume the Last.* Edited by Linda Bree. London: Penguin, 2002.

———. *The Governess; or the Little Female Academy.* Edited by Candace Ward. Peterborough, ON: Broadview, ca. 2005.

Fletcher, John. *Bonduca. A Tragedy.* Edited by George Colman. London: T. Cadell, 1778.

———. *Bonduca: or, the British Heroine.* Edited by George Powell. London: Richard Bentley, 1696.

Florio, John. *Florios Second Frutes.* London: Thomas Woodcock, 1591.

Foreman, Amanda. *Georgiana, Duchess of Devonshire.* London: Harper Collins, 1998.

Fothergill, Brian. *Sir William Hamilton: Envoy Extraordinary.* London: Faber and Faber, 1969.

Foxton, Rosemary. *"Hear the Word of the Lord": A Critical and Bibliographical Study of Quaker Women's Writing, 1650–1700.* Melbourne: Bibliographical Society of Australia and New Zealand, 1994.

Frankau, Julia [Frank Danby, pseud.]. *Nelson's Legacy: Lady Hamilton. Her Story and Tragedy.* London: Cassell, 1915.

Fraser, Antonia. *The Warrior Queens: Boadicea's Chariot.* London: Phoenix, 2002.

Frazer, Flora. *Beloved Emma.* London: Weidenfeld and Nicolson, 1986.

Freeman, Lisa A. "'A Dialogue': Elizabeth Carter's Passion for the Female Mind." In Armstrong and Blain, *Women's Poetry in the Enlightenment,* 50–63.

Frye, Susan, and Karen Robertson, eds. *Maids and Mistresses, Cousins and Queens: Women's Alliances in Early Modern England.* Oxford: Oxford University Press, 1999.

Gadeken, Sara. "'A Method of Being Perfectly Happy': Technologies of Self in the Eighteenth-Century Female Community." *Eighteenth-Century Novel* 1 (2001): 217–35.

Garman, Mary, Judith Applegate, Margaret Benefiel, and Dortha Meredith, eds. *Hidden in Plain Sight: Quaker Women's Writings, 1650–1700.* Wallingford: Pendle Hill, 1996.

Gaustad, Edwin S. "George Berkeley and the New World Community." *Church History* 48, no. 1 (1979): 5–7.

"Gentleman, A." *Man Superior to Woman.* London: T. Cooper, 1739.

Gerrard, Christine. *The Patriot Opposition to Walpole: Politics, Poetry, and National Myth, 1725–1742.* Oxford: Clarendon, 1994.

Gill, Catie. *Women in the Seventeenth-Century Quaker Community; a Literary Study of Political Identities, 1650–1700.* Aldershot: Ashgate, 2005.

Gill, Sean. *Women and the Church of England from the Eighteenth Century to the Present.* London: SPCK, 1994.

Glaser, Brigitte. "Gendered Childhoods: On the Discursive Formulation of Young Females in the Eighteenth Century." In Müller, *Fashioning Childhood in the Eighteenth Century,* 189–98.

Gleadle, Kathryn, and Sarah Richardson, eds. *Women in British Politics, 1760—1860: The Power of the Petticoat.* Basingstoke: Macmillan, 2000.

Glover, Richard. *Boadicia. A Tragedy. As it is Acted at the Theatre-Royal in Drury-Lane.* London: R. and J. Dodsley, M. Cooper, 1753.

Godwin, William. *Memoirs of the Author of the Vindication of the Rights of Woman.* London: J. Johnson, 1798.

Gouges, Olympe de. "Declaration of the Rights of Woman and the Female Citizen." In *Women in Revolutionary Paris, 1789–1795: Selected Documents,* edited and translated by Darline Gay Levy, Harriet Branson Applewhite, and Mary Durham Johnson, 87–96. Urbana: University of Illinois Press, 1979.

Gray, Irvine. "The Making of Westbury Court Gardens." *Garden History Society* 1 (1968): 15–18.

Guest, Harriet. "Bluestocking Feminism." In Pohl and Schellenberg, *Reconsidering the Bluestockings,* 59–80.

———. *Small Change: Women, Learning and Patriotism, 1750–1810.* Chicago: University of Chicago Press, 2000.

Hamilton, Gerald, and Desmond Stewart. *Emma In Blue.* London: Allan Wingate, 1957.

Hanway, Jonas. *A Plan for Establishing a Charity-House, or Charity-Houses for the Reception of Repenting Prostitutes to be Called the Magdalen Charity.* London, 1758.

———. *Thoughts on the Plan for a Magdalen-House for Repentant Prostitutes.* London: James Waugh, 1758.

Hardwick, Mollie. *Emma, Lady Hamilton.* New York: Holt, Rinehart and Winston, 1969.

Harley, David. "Historians as demonologists: the myth of the midwife-witch." *Social History of Medicine* 3 (1990): 1–26.

Harris, Frances. *A Passion for Government: the Life of Sarah Duchess of Marlborough.* Oxford: Oxford University Press, 1991.

Haslett, Moyra. *Pope to Burney, 1714–1779: Scriblerians to Bluestockings.* Basingstoke: Palgrave Macmillan, 2003.

[Hawkesworth, John, Samuel Johnson, Joseph Warton, and others]. *The Adventurer.* 2 vols. London: J. Payne, 1753.

Hawley, Judith, ed. *Elizabeth Carter.* London: Pickering & Chatto, 1999.

Hays, Mary. *Memoirs of Emma Courtney.* 2 vols. London: G. G. and J. Robinson, 1796.

Hayton, David W., Eveline Cruickshanks, and Stuart Handley. *The History of Parliament: The House of Commons, 1690–1715.* 5 vols. Cambridge: Cambridge University Press for the History of Parliament Trust, 2002.

Haywood, Ian. "Thackeray, Mary Berry, and *The Four Georges.*" *Notes and Queries* 30, no. 4 (1983): 299.

Heller, Deborah. "Subjectivity Unbound: Elizabeth Vesey as the Sylph in Bluestocking Correspondence." In Pohl and Schellenberg, *Reconsidering the Bluestockings,* 215–34.

Henry, William (Rector of Urney). *A Philippic Oration, against the Pretender's Son, and his Adherents. Addressed to the Protestants of the North of Ireland.* Dublin: Peter Wilson, 1745.

Hickes, George. *Linguarum Vett. Septentrionalium Thesaurus Grammatico-criticus et Archæologicus.* 2 vols. Oxoniæ: E Theatro Sheldoniano, 1703–5.

Hill, Bridget. *Women, Work and Sexual Politics in Eighteenth-Century England.* London: Routledge, 1993.

Hingley, Richard, and Christina Unwin. *Boudica: Iron Age Warrior Queen.* London: Hambledon and London, 2005.

Hobby, Elaine. *Virtue of Necessity: English Women's Writing, 1649–88.* London: Virago, 1988.

Hopkins, Charles. *Boadicea Queen of Britain. A Tragedy, As it is Acted by His Majesty's Servants at the Theatre in Lincolns-Inn-fields*. London: Jacob Tonson, 1697.

Hudson, Roger, ed. *Nelson and Emma*. London: Folio Society, 1994.

Hufton, Olwen. *The Prospect before Her: A History of Women in Western Europe, 1500–1800*. London: Harper Collins, 1995.

Inchbald, Elizabeth. *A Simple Story*. 3 vols. London: G. G. J. and J. Robinson, 1791.

Jacobus, Mary. "Intimate connections: scandalous memoirs and epistolary indiscretion." In Eger, Grant, Ó Gallchoir, and Warburton, *Women, Writing and the Public Sphere*, 274–89.

Jaffé, Patricia. *Lady Hamilton in Relation to the Art of her Time*. London: Arts Council, 1972.

Jeaffreson, John Cordy. *Lady Hamilton and Lord Nelson: An Historical Biography*. London: Athenaeum, 1897.

Johnson, Samuel. "Dissertation on the Amazons." *Gentleman's Magazine* 11 (April 1741): 202–8.

———. *The Idler*. 2 vols. London: J. Newbery, 1761.

———. *The Idler and The Adventurer*. Edited by W. J. Bate, John M. Bullitt, and L. F. Powell. New Haven: Yale University Press, 1963.

———. *The Rambler*. 6 vols. London: J. Payne and J. Bouquet, 1752.

Jones, Vivien. "Placing Jemima: Women Writers of the 1790s and the Eighteenth-Century Prostitution Narrative." *Women's Writing* 4, no. 2 (1997): 201–20.

———. "Scandalous Femininity: Prostitution and Eighteenth-Century Narrative." In *Shifting the Boundaries: Transformation of the Languages of Public and Private in the Eighteenth Century*, edited by Dario Castiglione and Lesley Sharpe, 54–70. Exeter: University of Exeter Press, 1995.

Juřica, A. R. J. "Flaxley." In *Bledisloe Hundred, St. Briavels Hundred, The Forest of Dean*. Vol. 5, *A History of the County of Gloucestershire*, edited by N. M. Herbert, 138–50. *The Victoria County History of England*. Oxford: Published for the Institute of Historical Research by Oxford University Press, 1996.

Keats, John. *Selected Poetry*. Edited by Elizabeth Cook. Oxford: Oxford University Press, 1994.

Kingsley, Nicholas. *The Country Houses of Gloucestershire*. 2 vols. Vol. 1, Cheltenham: N. Kingsley, 1989; vol. 2, Chichester: Phillimore, 1992.

Kloek, Els. *Kenau: De Heldhaftige Zakenvrouw vit Haarlem*. Hilversum: Uitgeverij Verloren, 2001.

Kobler, J. *The Reluctant Surgeon: A Biography of John Hunter*. New York: Doubleday, 1960.

Koestenbaum, Wayne. *Double Talk: The Erotics of Male Literary Collaboration*. New York: Routledge, 1989.

Landry, Donna. *The Muses of Resistance: Labouring-Class Women's Poetry in Britain, 1739–1798*. Cambridge: Cambridge University Press, 1990.

Lanser, Susan S. "Bluestocking Sapphism and the Economies of Desire." In Pohl and Schellenberg, *Reconsidering the Bluestockings*, 257–75.

Lennox, Charlotte. *The Female Quixote: Or, the Adventures of Arabella*. 2 vols. London: A. Millar, 1752.

Leranbaum, Miriam. "'Mistresses of Orthodoxy': Education in the Lives and Writings of Late Eighteenth-Century Women Writers." *Proceedings of the American Philosophical Society* 121 (1977): 281–301.

Lofts, Nora. *Emma Hamilton*. London: Book Club Associates, 1978.

Long, W. H. *Memoirs of Emma, Lady Hamilton*. London: Gibbings, 1899, reprint of the 1815 edition.

Love, Harold. *Scribal Publication in Seventeenth-Century England*. Oxford: Clarendon, 1993.

Lux-Sterritt, Laurence. *Redefining Female Religious Life. French Ursulines and English Ladies in Seventeenth-Century Catholicism*. Burlington, VT: Ashgate, 2005.

Lynch, Michael, Gordon DesBrisay, and Murray Pittock. "The Faith of the People." In *Aberdeen Before 1800: A New History,* edited by E. Patricia Dennison, David Ditchburn, and Michael Lynch, 289–308. East Linton: Tuckwell, 2002.

Lytton, Earl of (Victor). *Bulwer Lytton*. London: Home and Van Thal, 1948.

Mack, Phyllis. *Visionary Women*. Berkeley: University of California Press, 1992.

Magrath, Jane. " 'Rags of Mortality': Negotiating the Body in the Bluestocking Letters." In Pohl and Schellenberg, *Reconsidering the Bluestockings*, 235–56.

Major, Emma. "The Politics of Sociability: The Public Dimensions of the Bluestocking Millennium." In Pohl and Schellenberg, *Reconsidering the Bluestockings*, 175–92.

Mali, Anya. *Mystic in the New World: Marie d'Incarnation (1599–1672)*. Leiden, Netherlands: E. J. Brill, 1996.

Manley, Delarivier. *The Adventures of Rivella*. Edited by Katherine Zelinsky. Peterborough, ON: Broadview, 2002.

———. *Memoirs of Europe towards the Close of the Eighth Century*. London: John Morphew, 1710.

[Manley, Delarivier]. *A Key to the Third Volume of the Atalantis, Call'd Memoirs of Europe*. [London?, 1712?].

Manley, Delarivier [Madame Catherine La Mothe. Countess d'Aulnoy, pseud.] *Memoirs of the Court of England. In Two Parts. By the Countess of Dunois . . . To which is Added, The Lady's Pacquet of Letters, Taken from her by a French Privateer in her Passage to Holland*. London: B. Bragg, 1707.

Marcus, Sharon. *Between Women: Friendship, Desire, and Marriage in Victorian England*. Princeton: Princeton University Press, 2007.

Markley, Robert. "Sentimentality as Performance: Shaftesbury, Sterne, and the Theatrics of Virtue." In *The New Eighteenth Century,* edited by Felicity Nussbaum and Laura Brown, 210–30. London: Methuen, 1987.

———. *Two-Edg'd Weapons: Style and Ideology in the Comedies of Etherege, Wycherley and Congreve*. Oxford: Clarendon, 1988.

Marsh, A. *The Ten Pleasures of Marriage, Relating all the Delights and Contentments that are Mask'd under the Bands of Matrimony*. London: A. Marsh, 1682.

Marshall, Joyce, ed. *Word from New France: The Selected Letters of Marie de l'Incarnation*. Toronto: Oxford University Press, 1967.

Mather, G. R. *Two Great Scotsmen, The Brothers William and John Hunter*. Glasgow: James Maclehose and Sons, 1893.

McCarthy, Thomas. Introduction to *The Structural Transformation of the Public Sphere: An Inquiry into a Category of Bourgeois Society,* by Jürgen Habermas, xi–xiv. Translated by Thomas Burger with the assistance of Frederick Lawrence. Cambridge: Polity, 1989.

McGuire, Rita. *Marguerite d'Youville: A Pioneer for Our Times*. Ottawa: Novalis, 1982.

Melville, Lewis [pseud.]. *The Berry Papers, Being The Correspondence Hitherto Unpublished of Mary and Agnes Berry (1763–1852)*. London: John Lane, 1914.

Midgley, Clare. *Women Against Slavery: The British Campaigns, 1780—1870*. London: Routledge, 1992.

Mikalachki, Jodi. *The Legacy of Boadicea: Gender and Nation in Early Modern England*. London: Routledge, 1998.

Mill, James. *Essays on Government, Jurisprudence, Liberty of the Press, and Law of Nations*. London: [J. Innes, 1825].

Milton, John. *The History of Britain, That Part Especially now Call'd England*. London: James Allestry, 1670.

Moore, Rosemary. *The Light in their Consciences: the Early Quakers in Britain, 1646–1666*. University Park: Pennsylvania State University Press, 2000.

Moorhouse, E. Hallam. *Nelson's Lady Hamilton*. London, Methuen, 1908.

More, Hannah. *Coelebs in Search of a Wife*. Edited by Mary Waldron. Bristol: Thoemmes, 1995.

Morris, Brian, ed. *William Congreve*. Totowa, NJ: Rowman and Littlefield, 1972.

Morrison, Alfred, ed. *The Collection of Autograph Letters and Historical Documents Formed by Alfred Morrison: The Hamilton and Nelson Papers*. 2 vols. London: Printed for Private Circulation, 1893–94.

Mowl, Timothy. *Historic Gardens of Gloucestershire*. Stroud: Tempus, 2002.

Mowry, Melissa. "Women, Work, Rear-guard Politics and Defoe's *Moll Flanders*." *Eighteenth Century: Theory and Interpretation* 49, no. 2 (2008): 97–116.

Mullan, John. *Sentiment and Sociability: The Language of Feeling in the Eighteenth Century*. Oxford: Clarendon, 1988.

Müller, Anja, ed. *Fashioning Childhood in the Eighteenth Century: Age and Identity*. Aldershot: Ashgate, 2006.

Mulvey-Roberts, Marie, ed. *The Collected Letters of Rosina Bulwer Lytton*. With the assistance of Steve Carpenter. 3 vols. London: Pickering and Chatto, 2008.

———. "The Corpse in the Corpus: Frankenstein, Rewriting Wollstonecraft and the Abject." In *Mary Shelley's Fictions*, edited by Michael Eberle-Sinatra, 197–211. London: Macmillan, 2000.

———, ed. *The Handbook to Gothic Literature*. Basingstoke: Macmillan, 1998.

Murphy, Arthur. *Gray's-Inn Journal*, no. 83. Saturday, May 18, 1754.

Mussolini, Cesare. *The School for Marriage*. London: B. Tiffin, 1795.

Myers, O. M., ed. *The Coverley Papers from the "Spectator."* Oxford: Clarendon, 1940.

Myers, Sylvia Harcstark. *The Bluestocking Circle: Women, Friendship, and the Life of the Mind in Eighteenth-Century England*. Oxford: Clarendon, 1990.

Nelson, Horatio. *The Letters of Lord Nelson to Lady Hamilton. With a Supplement of Interesting Letters by Distinguished Characters*. 2 vols. London: T. Lovewell, 1814.

Nestor, Pauline. *Female Friendships and Communities: Charlotte Brontë, George Eliot, Elizabeth Gaskell*. Oxford: Clarendon, 1985.

Ng, Su Fang. "Marriage and Discipline: the place of women in early Quaker controversies." *Seventeenth Century* 18, no. 1 (2003): 113–40.

Nicholls, H. G. *An Historical and Descriptive Account of the Forest of Dean*. London: John Murray, 1858.

———. *The Personalities of the Forest of Dean: Forming an Appendix to "An Historical and Descriptive Account of the Forest of Dean."* London: John Murray, 1863.

Nickel, Terri. "'Ingenious Torment': Incest, Family, and the Structure of Community in the Work of Sarah Fielding." *Eighteenth-Century Studies* 36, no. 3 (1995): 234–47.

Owen, Aidan Lloyd. *The Famous Druids: A Survey of Three Centuries of English Literature on the Druids.* Oxford: Clarendon, 1997.

Paine, Thomas. *Rights of Man.* London: J. S. Jordan, 1791.

Parfitt, George. "The Case against Congreve." In Morris, *William Congreve,* 21–38.

Parks, Stephen. "George Berkeley, Sir Richard Steele, and *The Ladies Library.*" *Scriblerian* 13, no. 1 (1980): 1–2.

Peace, Mary. "'Epicures in Rural Pleasures': Revolution, Desire and Sentimental Economy in Sarah Scott's *Millenium Hall.*" *Women's Writing* 9, no. 2 (2002): 305–16.

Peachey, G. C. *A Memoir of William and John Hunter.* Plymouth: William Brendon and Son, 1924.

Peakman, Julie. *Emma Hamilton.* London: Haus, 2005.

Pennington, Montagu. *Memoirs of the Life of Mrs. Elizabeth Carter, with a New Edition of her Poems . . . to which are Added, some Miscellaneous Essays in Prose.* 2 vols. London: F. C. and J. Rivington, 1816.

Perry, Ruth. *The Celebrated Mary Astell: An Early English Feminist.* Chicago: University of Chicago Press, 1986.

———. *Novel Relations: The Transformation of Kinship in English Literature and Culture, 1748–1818.* Cambridge: Cambridge University Press, 2004.

Personal Narratives Group, eds. *Interpreting Women's Lives: Feminist Theory and Personal Narratives.* Bloomington: Indiana University Press, 1989.

Peters, Kate. *Print Culture and the Early Quakers.* Cambridge: Cambridge University Press, 2005.

Pettigrew, T. J. *Memoirs of the Life of Vice-Admiral Lord Viscount Nelson.* 2 vols. London: Boone, 1849.

Philips, Katherine. *Poems by the Incomparable Mrs. K. P.* London: Richard Marriott, 1664.

———. *Poems by the Most Deservedly Admired Mrs. Katherine Philips, the Matchless Orinda.* London: H. Herringman, 1667.

Piggott, Stuart. *William Stukeley: An Eighteenth Century Antiquary.* Oxford: Clarendon, 1950.

Pits, John. *De Illustribus Angliæ Scriptoribus* [the running title of *Relationum Historicarum de Rebus Anglicis Tomus Primus*]. Paris: Rolin Theoderic and Sebastian Cramoisy, 1618.

Plumb, J. H. *The First Four Georges.* London: Collins, 1968.

Pocock, Tom. *Nelson's Women.* London: André Deutsch, 1999.

Pohl, Nicole, and Betty A. Schellenberg, eds. *Reconsidering the Bluestockings.* San Marino, CA: Huntington Library, 2003.

Powell, Anne. *Clifton, Caractacus, Boadicea, and Other Pieces.* Bristol: Albion, 1821.

Pratt, Samuel Jackson. *Family Secrets, Literary and Domestic.* 5 vols. London: T. N. Longman, 1797.

———. *Gleanings through Wales, Holland, and Westphalia.* 3 vols. London: T. N. Longman and L. B. Seeley, 1795.

Quintana, Ricardo. *The Mind and Art of Jonathan Swift.* London: Oxford University Press, 1936.

Radcliffe, Ann. *The Mysteries of Udolpho, a Romance: Interspersed with some Pieces of Poetry.* 4 vols. London: G. G. and J. Robinson, 1794.

Rapin-Thoyras, Paul de. *The History of England.* Edited and translated by John Kelly. 3 vols. London: James Mechell, 1732–37.

Rapley, Elizabeth. *The Dévotes: Women and Church in Seventeenth-Century France.* Montreal: McGill-Queen's University Press, 1990.

Rawston, Geoffrey, ed. *Nelson's Letters.* London: J. M. Dent, 1960.

Rediker, Marcus. "Liberty beneath the Jolly Roger: The Lives of Anne Bonny and Mary Read." In *Iron Men, Wooden Women: Gender and Seafaring in the Atlantic World, 1700–1920,* edited by Margaret Creighton and Lisa Norling, 1–33. Baltimore: Johns Hopkins University Press, 1996.

Richards, George. *Songs of the Aboriginal Bards of Britain.* Oxford: J. Cooke et al., 1792.

Richardson, Samuel. *Clarissa. Or, the History of a Young Lady: Comprehending the Most Important Concerns of Private Life.* 7 vols. London: A. Millar, J. and Ja. Rivington, John Osborn, 1748.

———. *Pamela: or, Virtue Rewarded. In a Series of Familiar Letters from a Beautiful Young Damsel to her Parents: and afterwards, in her Exalted Condition, between her, and Persons of Figure and Quality, upon the most Important and Entertaining Subjects in Genteel Life. The Third and Fourth Volumes. Publish'd in Order to Cultivate Principles of Virtue and Religion in the Minds of the Youth of Both Sexes.* 2 vols. London: C. Rivington and J. Osborn, [1741].

———. *Sir Charles Grandison.* Edited by Jocelyn Harris. Oxford: Oxford University Press, 1972.

Rizzo, Betty. *Companions Without Vows: Relationships Among Eighteenth-Century British Women.* Athens: University of Georgia Press, 1994.

———. "Male Oratory and Female Prate: 'Then Hush and Be an Angel Quite.'" *Eighteenth-Century Life* 29, no. 1 (2005): 23–49.

Roberts, Philip. "Mirabell and Restoration Comedy." In Morris, *William Congreve,* 39–53.

Rosenthal, Laura J. *Infamous Commerce: Prostitution in Eighteenth-Century Literature and Culture.* Ithaca: Cornell University Press, 2006.

Russell, Jack. *Nelson and the Hamiltons.* Harmondsworth: Penguin, 1969.

Sabor, Peter. "Fashioning the Child Author: Reading Jane Austen's Juvenilia." In Müller, *Fashioning Childhood in the Eighteenth Century,* 199–209.

Sadleir, Michael. *Bulwer and his Wife.* London: Constable, 1931.

———. *Bulwer and his Wife: A Panorama.* London: Constable, 1933.

Sammes, Aylett. *Britannia Antiqua Illustrata: Or, the Antiquities of Ancient Britain, Derived from the Phoenicians.* London: Printed by Thomas Roycroft, for the Author, 1676.

Sanders, Valerie. *The Brother-Sister Culture in Nineteenth-Century Literature: From Austen to Woolf.* Basingstoke: Palgrave, 2002.

Schlueter, Paul, and June Schlueter. *An Encyclopedia of British Women Writers.* New York: Garland, 1988.

Schwoerer, Lois G. "Women's public political voice in England: 1640–1740." In

Women Writers and the Early Modern British Political Tradition, edited by Hilda L. Smith, 56–74. Cambridge: Cambridge University Press, 1998.

Scott, Sarah. *Millenium Hall.* London, 1762.

Scott, Walter. *Guy Mannering.* Edinburgh: James Ballantyne, 1815.

Secker, Thomas. *Lectures on the Catechism of the Church of England. With a Discourse on Confirmation.* Edited by B. Porteus and C. Stinton. 2 vols. London: J. and F. Rivington, 1769.

Segal, Nancy L. *Entwined Lives: Twins and What They Tell Us About Human Behavior.* New York: Dutton, 1999.

Senhouse, Peter. *The Right Use and Improvement of Sensitive Pleasures, and more particularly of Music: A Sermon Preach'd in the Cathedral Church of Gloucester, at the Anniversary Meeting of the Choirs of Gloucester, Hereford, and Worcester, Sept. 20, 1727.* Gloucester: John Palman, 1728.

Sexton, Anne. *The Selected Poems of Anne Sexton.* Edited by Diane Wood Middlebrook and Diana Hume George. London: Virago, 1991.

Shelley, Mary. *Falkner.* London, 1837.

———. *Frankenstein or The Modern Prometheus.* Oxford: Oxford University Press, 1969.

———. *The Journals of Mary Shelley.* Edited by Paula R. Feldman and Diana Scott-Kilvert. 2 vols. Oxford: Clarendon, 1987.

———. *The Letters of Mary Wollstonecraft Shelley.* Edited by Betty T. Bennett. Vol. 2. Baltimore: Johns Hopkins University Press, 1983.

———. *Lodore.* Edited by Lisa Vargo. Peterborough, ON: Broadview, 1997.

Shelley, P. B. *The Revolt of Islam.* London: C. and J. Ollier, 1817.

Sheridan, Elizabeth. *Betsy Sheridan's Journal: Letters from Sheridan's Sister, 1784–1786 and 1788–1790.* Edited by William LeFanu. Oxford: Oxford University Press, 1986.

Sheridan, Richard Brinsley. *The Rivals, A Comedy. As it is Acted at the Theatre-Royal in Covent Garden.* Dublin: R. Moncrieffe, 1775.

Sherrard, O. A. *A Life of Emma Hamilton.* London: Sidgwick and Jackson, 1927.

Shevelow, Kathryn. *Women and Print Culture: the Construction of Femininity in the Early Periodical.* London: Routledge, 1989.

Sichel, Walter. *Emma Lady Hamilton.* London: Archibald Constable, 1905.

Simonton, Dean Keith. *Origins of Genius: Darwinian Perspectives on Creativity.* Oxford: Oxford University Press, 1999.

Simpson, Colin. *The Life of Lady Hamilton.* London: Bodley Head, 1983.

Simpson, Patricia. *Marguerite Bourgeoys and the Congregation of Notre Dame, 1665–1700.* Montréal: McGill-Queens University Press, 2005.

Slagle, Judith Bailey. *Joanna Baillie: A Literary Life.* Madison, WI: Fairleigh Dickinson University Press, 2002.

Smith, Adam. *The Theory of Moral Sentiments.* Edited by Knud Haakonssen. Cambridge: Cambridge University Press, 2002.

Smith, Charlotte. *Emmeline, the Orphan of the Castle.* 4 vols. London: T. Cadell, 1788.

Smith, Johanna M. "Philanthropic Community in *Millenium Hall* and the York Ladies Committee." *Eighteenth-Century Studies* 36, no. 3 (1995): 266–82.

Smollett, Tobias. *The Adventures of Roderick Random.* 2 vols. London: J. Osborn, 1748.

Sophia, a Person of Quality. *Woman Not Inferior to Man: or, A short and modest Vindica-tion of the natural Right of the Fair-Sex to a perfect Equality of Power, Dignity, and Esteem, with the Men.* London: John Hawkins, 1739.

Staves, Susan. "Church of England Clergy and Women Writers." In Pohl and Schel-lenberg, *Reconsidering the Bluestockings,* 81–103.

Steele, Richard, ed. *The Ladies Library. Written by a Lady. Published by Mr. Steele.* 3 vols. London: W. Mears and J. Brown, 1714.

———, ed. *The Ladies Library. Written by a Lady. Published by Mr. Steele.* 5th ed. 3 vols. London: J. and R. Tonson, 1739.

Surtees, Virginia, ed. *The Grace of Friendship: Horace Walpole and the Misses Berry.* Nor-wich, Great Britain: Michael Russell, 1995.

Swift, Jonathan, and Alexander Pope. *Miscellanies in Prose and Verse.* 2nd ed. 2 vols. Dublin: Sam. Fairbrother, 1728.

Tacitus. *Opera Omnia, Ex Editione Oberliniana cum Notis et Interpretatione in Usum Del-phini.* 8 vols. London: A. J. Valpy, 1821.

Tague, Ingrid H. *Women of Quality: Accepting and Contesting Ideals of Femininity in En-gland, 1690–1760.* Woodbridge: Boydell, 2002.

Tanner, Thomas. *Bibliotheca Britannico-Hibernica: Sive, de Scriptoribus, Qui in Anglia, Scotia, et Hibernia ad Saeculi XVII Initium Floruerunt, Literatum Ordine Juxta Famil-iarum Nomina Dispositis Commentarius.* London: William Bowyer, Impensis Societa-tis ad Literas Promovendas Institutae, 1748.

Taylor, Barbara. *Mary Wollstonecraft and the Feminist Imagination.* Cambridge: Cam-bridge University Press, 2003.

Taylor, Harriet, and John Stuart Mill. *The Enfranchisement of Women* and *The Subjec-tion of Women.* With a new introduction by Kate Soper. London: Virago, 1983.

Thale, Mary. "London Debating Societies in the 1790s." *Historical Journal* 32, no. 4 (1989): 57–86.

———. "Women in London Debating Societies in 1780." *Gender and History* 7, no. 1 (1995): 5–24.

Thomas, Claudia. "'Th'Instructive Moral and Important Thought': Elizabeth Car-ter reads Pope, Johnson and Epictetus." *Age of Johnson* 4 (1991): 137–69.

Thompson, William. *Inquiry into the Principles of the Distribution of Wealth.* London, 1824.

Thompson, William, and Anna Wheeler. *Appeal of One Half the Human Race, Women, against the Other Half, Men, to retain them in political, and thence in civil and domestic, slavery.* Edited by Marie Mulvey-Roberts and Michael Foot. Bristol: Thoemmes, 1994.

Thomson, James. *Britain: Being the Fourth Part of "Liberty," a Poem.* London: A. Millar, 1736.

Tillyard, Stella. *Aristocrats: Caroline, Emily, Louisa, and Sarah Lennox, 1740–1842.* London: Chatto and Windus, 1994.

Times. January 28, 1799.

Todd, Janet. *Mary Wollstonecraft: A Revolutionary Life.* London: Weidenfeld and Nicol-son, 2000.

———. *Women's Friendship in Literature.* New York: Columbia University Press, 1980.

Tompkins, J. M. S. *The Polite Marriage. Also The Didactic Lyre; The Bristol Milkwoman; The Scotch Parents; Clio in Motley, and Mary Hays, Philosophess: Eighteenth-Century Es-says.* Cambridge: Cambridge University Press, 1938.

Tours, Hugh. *Life and Letters of Emma Hamilton.* London: V. Gollancz, 1963.

Towers, Joseph. *Dialogues Concerning the Ladies. To Which is Added, An Essay on the Antient Amazons.* London: T. Cadell, 1785.

Trevett, Christine. *Quaker Women Prophets in England and Wales, 1650–1700.* Lewiston, NY: Edward Mellen, 2000.

———. *Women and Quakerism in the Seventeenth Century.* York: Sessions Book Trust, 1995.

Tristan, Flora. *Flora Tristan's London Journal 1840.* Translated by Dennis Palmer and Giselle Pincetl. Charlestown, MA: Charles River Books, 1980.

Van Sant, Ann. *Eighteenth-Century Sensibility and the Novel: The Senses in Social Context.* Cambridge: Cambridge University Press, 1993.

Vickery, Amanda. *The Gentleman's Daughter; Women's Lives in Georgian England.* New Haven: Yale University Press, 1998.

———, ed. *Women, Privilege and Power: British Politics, 1750 to the Present.* Stanford, CA: Stanford University Press, 2001.

Vrye, Hippolytus de [Hieronymys Sweerts]. *De Tien Vermakelijheden des Huwelykes.* Amsterdam: Joannes Kannewet, [1678?].

Wahl, Elizabeth Susan. *Invisible Relations: Representations of Female Intimacy in the Age of Enlightenment.* Stanford, CA: Stanford University Press, 1999.

Waldron, Mary. "Ann Yearsley and the Clifton Records." Edited by Paul J. Korshin. *Age of Johnson: A Scholarly Annual* 3 (1990): 301–29.

———. "Ann Yearsley: The Bristol Manuscript Revisited." *Women's Writing* 3, no. 1 (1996): 35–45.

———. " 'By No Means Milk and Water Matters': The Contribution to English Poetry of Ann Yearsley, Milkwoman of Clifton, 1753–1806." *Studies on Voltaire and the Eighteenth Century* 304 (1992): 801–4.

———. "A Different Kind of Patronage: Ann Yearsley's Later Friends." Edited by Paul J. Korshin and Jack Lynch. *Age of Johnson: A Scholarly Annual* 13 (2002): 283–335.

———. "The Frailties of Fanny: *Mansfield Park* and the Evangelical Movement." *Eighteenth-Century Fiction* 6, no. 3 (1994): 259–82.

———. *Jane Austen and the Fiction of her Time.* Cambridge: Cambridge University Press, 1999.

———. *Lactilla, Milkwoman of Clifton: The Life and Writings of Ann Yearsley, 1753–1806.* Athens: University of Georgia Press, 1996.

———. "Marriage Prospects: The Austen Treatment." In *Re-Drawing Austen: Picturesque Travels in Austenland,* edited by Beatrice Battaglia and Diego Saglia, 427–35. Naples: Liguori, 2004.

———. "Men of Sense and Silly Wives: The Confusions of Mr. Knightley." *Studies in the Novel* 28, no. 2 (1996): 141–57.

———. "Mentors Old and New: Samuel Johnson and Hannah More." *New Rambler* 1995–1996, issue D, no. 11 (1996): 29–37.

———. " 'This Muse-born Wonder': The Occluded Voice of Ann Yearsley, Milkwoman and Poet of Clifton." In Armstrong and Blain, *Women's Poetry in the Enlightenment,* 113–26.

Walpole, Horace. *Catalogue of the Royal and Noble Authors of England, with Lists of their Works.* 3rd ed. 2 vols. Dublin: George Faulkner, 1759.

————. *Letters of Horace Walpole.* Edited by Mrs. Paget Toynbee. 16 vols. Oxford: Clarendon, 1903–5.

————. *Miscellaneous Antiquities; or, A Collection of Curious Papers: Either republished from Scarce Tracts, or now first printed from Original MSS.* Strawberry Hill: Printed by Thomas Kirgate, 1772.

Warner, Oliver. *Emma Hamilton and Sir William.* London: Chatto and Windus, 1960.

Warner, William. *Albions England.* London: Thomas Cadman, 1586.

Wheeler, Anna. "Letter by Vlasta." In *Hampden in the Nineteenth Century,* by John Minter Morgan, 2:322. 2 vols. London: Edward Moxon, 1834.

————. "Vlasta (Anna Wheeler) to the Editor of *The Crisis,* August 31st 1833." *Crisis* 2, nos. 35 and 36 (1833): 280.

Wheelwright, Julie. *Amazons and Military Maids: Women who Dressed as Men in the Pursuit of Life, Liberty and Happiness.* London: Pandora, 1989.

Whitelocke, Bulstrode. *Whitelockes Notes Uppon the Kings Writt for Choosing Members of Parlement XIII Car II, Being Disquisitions on the Government of England by King Lords and Commons.* 2 vols. London: Andrew Millar, 1766.

Whitmont, Edward C. *The Symbolic Quest: Basic Concepts of Analytical Psychology.* Princeton: Princeton University Press, 1969.

Williams, Carolyn D. "'In Albion's Ancient Days': George Richards (1767–1837) and the Dilemmas of Patriot Gothic." In *The Early Romantics,* edited by Thomas Woodman, 256–72. New York: St. Martin's, 1998.

————. "Poetry, Pudding and Epictetus: the Consistency of Elizabeth Carter." In *Tradition in Transition: Women Writers, Marginal Texts and the Eighteenth-Century Canon,* edited by Alvaro Ribeiro and James G. Basker, 3–24. Oxford: Clarendon, 1996.

————. "*The Way to Things by Words:* John Cleland, the Name of the Father, and Speculative Linguistics." *Year's Work in English Studies* 28 (1998): 250–75.

————. "'This Frantic Woman': Boadicea and English Neoclassical Embarrassment." In *Uses and Abuses of Antiquity,* edited by Maria Wyke and Michael Biddiss, 19–35. Bern: Peter Lang, 1999.

Williams, Kate. *England's Mistress.* London: Hutchinson, 2006.

Wilson, Adrian. *The Making of Man-Midwifery: Childbirth in England, 1660–1770.* London: UCL Press, 1995.

Wollstonecraft, Mary. *Collected Letters of Mary Wollstonecraft.* Edited by Ralph Wardle. London: Cornell University Press, 1979.

————. *The Collected Letters of Mary Wollstonecraft.* Edited by Janet Todd. New York: Columbia University Press, 2003.

————. *An Historical and Moral View of the Origin and Progress of the French Revolution and the Effect it Has Produced in Europe.* London: J. Johnson, 1795.

————. *Maria, or The Wrongs of Woman.* With an introduction by Anne K. Mellor. New York: W. W. Norton, ca. 1994.

————. *Thoughts on the Education of Daughters.* Edited by Janet Todd. Bristol: Thoemmes, 1995.

————. *A Vindication of the Rights of Woman.* London: Penguin, 1992.

————. *The Wrongs of Woman, or Maria; A Fragment.* Vols. 1 and 2, *Posthumous Works of the Author of A Vindication of the Rights of Woman.* Edited by William Godwin. 4 vols. London: J. Johnson, G. G. and J. Robinson, 1798.

Wollstonecraft, Mary, and Mary Shelley. *Mary and Maria* and *Matilda*. Edited by Janet Todd. London: Penguin Classics, 1992.

Woolf, Virginia. *A Room of One's Own*. London: Hogarth, 1929.

Wordsworth, William. *Poetical Works*. Edited by Thomas Hutchinson and revised by Ernest de Selincourt. Oxford: Oxford University Press, 1936.

Wraxall, Sir Nathaniel. *The Historical and the Posthumous Memoirs of Sir Nathaniel William Wraxall, 1772–1784*. Edited by Henry B. Wheatley. 5 vols. London: Bickers and Son, 1884.

York Women's Yearly Meeting. *Epistle from the Womens Yearly Meeting at York, 1688 and An Epistle from Mary Waite*. York, 1688. Reprinted in Garman, Applegate, Benefiel, and Meredith, *Hidden in Plain Sight,* 529–33.

Electronic Sources

Brown, Susan, Patricia Clements, and Isobel Grundy, eds. *Orlando: Women's Writing in the British Isles from the Beginnings to the Present*. Cambridge University Press Online, 2006. http://orlando.cambridge.org/.

Dictionary of Canadian Biography, s.v. "Chomedey de Maisonneuve, Paul de" (by Marie-Claire Daveluy), http://www.biographi.ca/EN/ShowBio.asp?BioId=34251&query=chomedey%20AND%20de%20AND%20Maisonneuve. June 14, 2008.

Oxford Dictionary of National Biography, s.v. "Skene, Lilias (1626/7–1697)" (by Gordon Desbrisay), http://www.oxforddnb.com/view/article/69911. May 2008.

Harris, Judith Rich. "Why Can't Birth Order Account for the Differences Between Siblings?" September 3, 2001, http://xchar.home.att.net/tna/birth-order/sibdiff.htm.

Contributors

JENNIE BATCHELOR is senior lecturer in English and American literature at the University of Kent. She has published various essays on gender and material culture, and is the author of *Dress, Distress and Desire: Clothing and the Female Body in Eighteenth-Century Literature* (2005), and coeditor of and contributor to *British Women's Writing in the Long Eighteenth Century: Authorship, History, Politics* (2005) and *Women and Material Culture, 1660–1830* (2007). She is currently completing a monograph on literary representations of manual and intellectual labor in women's writing between 1750 and 1830.

JOANNA GOLDSWORTHY, writer, historian, and editorial consultant, is the former publishing director of London publishers Victor Gollancz Ltd. She edited *A Certain Age: Reflecting on the Menopause* (1993, 1994); and edited and contributed to *Mothers by Daughters* (1995).

ISOBEL GRUNDY, FRSC, one of the editors of *Orlando: Women's Writing in the British Isles from the Beginnings to the Present* (2006, see http://www.cambridge.org/online/orlandoonline/), received her degrees from Oxford University (St. Anne's College). From Queen Mary College (now Queen Mary, London), where she met Mary Waldron, she moved to the University of Alberta in 1990 as Henry Marshall Tory Professor. She became professor emeritus in 2003. Her *Lady Mary Wortley Montagu* appeared in 1999.

BETTY HAGGLUND is a member of the staff of the Centre for Postgraduate Quaker Studies of the University of Birmingham. She has particular interests in women's writing and in seventeenth- and eighteenth-century Scottish Quakers and is currently editing a collection of poems and theological writings by the seventeenth-century Aberdeen writer Lilias Skene.

JUDITH HAWLEY is a senior lecturer in the department of English, Royal Holloway University of London. She is general editor of the Pickering and Chatto series *Literature and Science, 1660–1832*. She has edited several eighteenth-century texts, including Jane Collier,

The Art of Ingeniously Tormenting and Henry Fielding, *Joseph Andrews and Shamela*. Her edition of works by Elizabeth Carter appeared in the Pickering and Chatto series *Bluestocking Feminisms*. Her research centers on eighteenth-century literary groups and networks such as the Bluestockings and the Scriblerus Club.

TANIS HINCHCLIFFE is reader in architectural history at the University of Westminster. Her areas of research have included English and French domestic architecture, and especially women clients of French architects in the eighteenth century. She is currently engaged in a research project on Canadian convents and their landscapes.

MARIE MULVEY-ROBERTS is a reader in literary studies at the University of the West of England, Bristol. She is the editor of the journal *Women's Writing*, for which she coedited special issues on Mary Wollstonecraft and Mary Shelley with Janet Todd. She has also edited the work of Rosina Bulwer Lytton and her mother Anna Wheeler, and most recently a scholarly edition of *The Collected Letters of Rosina Bulwer Lytton*.

JESSICA MUNNS works on late seventeenth- and early eighteenth-century literature and is editor of the journal *Restoration and Eighteenth-Century Theatre Research*. PENNY RICHARDS, her sister, is an early modern historian who works on later sixteenth-century French history and has published widely in this area. Together they have collaborated on two books and numerous articles. In their Gloucestershire home, they live near Catherine Bovey's Flaxley Abbey and it was this that prompted their initial interest in her life.

JULIE PEAKMAN is biographer of *Emma Hamilton* (2005). She is an honorary fellow at Birkbeck College, London University. Her PhD from the Wellcome Institute was published as *Mighty Lewd Books. The Development of Pornography in Eighteenth-Century England* (2003). She is also author of *Lascivious Bodies. A Sexual History of the Eighteenth Century* (2004), and *Civilising Sex. A World History* (forthcoming 2010).

JUDITH BAILEY SLAGLE is professor and chair of English at East Tennessee State University. She is editor of *The Collected Letters of Joanna Baillie* (FDUP, 1999), author of *Joanna Baillie: A Literary Life* (FDUP, 2002), coeditor of collected essays entitled *Prologues, Epilogues, Curtain-Raisers, and Afterpieces: the Rest of the Eighteenth-Century London*

Stage (with Daniel J. Ennis, UDP, 2007), and author of various book chapters and articles on Joanna Baillie.

CAROLYN D. WILLIAMS, MA BLitt (Oxon), graduated in English at Oxford University, where she completed her thesis on Dr. Arbuthnot and the Scriblerians. A senior lecturer in the School of English and American Literature at the University of Reading, she has written *Pope, Homer and Manliness* (1993) and numerous articles and chapters on gender, life, and literature in the early modern period.

Index

Page numbers in italics denote illustrations